Ordinary
Reflections
from Here, There, and
God's Word

Elouise H Hults

ISBN 978-1-68517-491-0 (paperback)
ISBN 978-1-68517-492-7 (digital)

Christian Faith Publishing
832 Park Avenue
Meadville, PA 16335
www.christianfaithpublishing.com

Printed in the United States of America

Within these pages, you may find a few devotionals that seem to be repeated. That's fine. Scripture has many verses of God's right-on words carried over for the reader's benefit, His specific designed reruns. When read and found to be personalized, God's message will have made its mark.

Note more than one case in point:

In Psalm 42:5 and verse 11, as well as in 43:5, God repeats one of His promises not twice but three times.

Peter's dream and ministry/outreach recorded in Acts 10 were found to be repeated in the following chapter 11.

Also, Psalm 57:5 in the King James Version (KJV) is an exact repeat in verse 11.

We all tend to forget and need gentle reminders. Enjoy each possible recap and receive.

All scripture used at the top of each one of these devotionals, or within the body of a few, is self-paraphrased via the Living Bible and the King James Version. Be blessed.

In summary:

> Repetitive—no
> Similar—maybe
> Glean—for this and future moments
> Use—for daily activities and relationships
> Trust—for eternal values
> Scripture—author's rephrasing

Index of Subjects

---

* Poems: Each of these is also located under another topic.

New Year

The Lord's mercies not used up…but are new at the
beginning of each day (year),great is God's faithfulness.
—Lamentations 3:22–23

What this new year holds are waiting in line for you:

New ideas
Untouched days
Brand-new starts
Unused hours
New approach
Fresh choices
Unknown adventure
Untried schedule
Unfamiliar opportunities
Reinvigorated desire
Second chances
New friends
plus
Read Bible daily
Memorize scripture
Get closer to God
Seek His will

Yes, much is waiting to be learned, seen, known, and take place in
this new year. It or they will bring forth laughter or tears beyond
what can be imagined or understood. Within it all, God remains faithful.

*Dear Lord, thank You for this new year. It is filled with
pristine abilities and wonderful renewals of the many losses.
Whatever it may hold for me, You are there. Amen.*

Daily Living

I will...live a life that declares the truths of the Lord.
—Psalm 118:17

It is not the number of days we live but the type of life we live in our days that wear a worthwhile value. We have been given many days. But a lot of them are now gone, far past in our yesterday, never to be retrieved.

Yet we have this day to live and be a true and faithful Christian witness of our Lord.

This moment is a giant opportunity to live for the whatever, wherever, and whoever we encounter.

Our actions or words of response should pour out kindness, warmth, and a smile with approving gestures. That impression will never again be ours. In this now, we can somehow make a difference for eternity in others, if we reflect the Jesus that lives in us.

We must never overlook today. It is allotted to us, never to be repeated. Check back on our previous days. How have they been lived? How were they expressed to people we met by chance? Schedule or an appointment? Do those memories please us?

Don't just reach out for the preplanned hope-filled biggie witness to be done at some grand time or location. It's in this today, right where we are, that makes a difference in the lives of others. People are there watching us live our lives. May Christ be able to use us at such times.

Dear Lord, starting this day, I want to live for
You here, there, and everywhere. Amen.

Faithfulness

A faithful person...did the promise.
—Proverbs 14:5; 2 Chronicles 34:12

No one appreciates people who walk away from the need we assumed they would care about. After all, they had expressed a concern.

What we presumed they would do and what actually happened didn't equal. *Faithful* would not describe them. Instead, they brought disappointment, displayed unkind reaction, or showed preference to be elsewhere. These ones didn't respond as expected.

May whatever in them failed to be a Christlike representation be not spoken of us. Do we or have we overlooked, forgotten, or substituted our planned in response for another interest?

God heard what we first said we would do and saw what we actually did.

He wants faithfulness. If we say it, we do it. If we promise, we come through. If we don't want to, we say, "No, thank you." But be honest in conversation, behavior, and time.

God wants a faithful witness responsible in agreement and work as unto Him. Whether it's that family member, some friend, those acquaintances, or now which neighbor would that be or an unkempt stranger, we are to be helpful. If the deed is minor in size and price or time-consuming and expensive, we remain faithful.

God is aware of our attitudes before they're expressed. Were they done in genuine Christian love? What rate of faithfulness would the scale of our doing expose? God will repay us the same amount we displayed to others.

Dear Lord, I want to come through on everything I said
I will do. I want to be known as faithful. Amen.

Undo, Redo, to Do

There is an arrangement, I believe, would work better for me.
—Proverbs 14:12 and 16:25

My husband and I have a Lhasa Apso we named Cuddles. This medium-sized dog has been heavily spoiled. He loves to be wherever we are. To please this little boy, we've provided a number of pillows for his comfort.

Yes, he likes to sit on the furniture but does enjoy his pillows. He will cozy down into the shape of a donut or stretch himself out on his personal pillows.

Then this independent Cuddles bounces up and turns around with an abrupt intent to undo the pillow's comfort. Pawing with all earnestness, he attempts to redo the pillow's fluffiness.

But this stubborn pillow won't change its shape no matter how hard the dog works at it. The pillow is designed into its permanency. In time, Cuddles gives up and settles into what was already there.

We, as well, strive to undo and redo what the Lord has given. After our educated, qualified, and dignified efforts are applied, we learn God's original plans are best fitting for us.

No matter how sincere the efforts, God has a better idea. We need to accept His will and settle into His provision. It out-cushions any other self-arrangement we attempt to do, no matter how determined we try.

*Dear Lord, I must undo my thoughts to redo my ideas
and to do it Your way, the best way. Amen.*

Don't Look Back

Do not turn around.

—Genesis 19:17

The squirrel approached the middle of the road. We were driving and saw the animal, and we slowed for it. But the squirrel changed its mind, looked back, turned around, and aimed for the area just left. He didn't make it.

Mr. Bird hit our windshield. This beautiful but now dead bird changed his mind. He might have mistook the correct direction and used his own idea of what's "best for me" and lost.

Then there was the black mole in a road ditch. This know-it-all rodent yielded to temptation. He came upon an empty bottle. It smelled good. So the mole entered the bottle to taste what he thought he smelled. But he got all bottled up.

Mr. Mole didn't continue his route. Instead, he turned around and looked back.

That decision proved to be deadly.

The Bible reports in Genesis 19:1–29 of one "don't look back" attitude.

Destruction was coming to Mr. and Mrs. Lot's hometown. God sent an angel to inform the Lot family so they could escape.

Reluctantly, Mrs. Lot left all her stuff at her husband's insistence. But her heart was back there, and she wanted one last look. And it was. Instantly, she became a pillar of salt. She was the loser for looking back.

When God says go, we go. When He says no, we stop. Obedience brings life.

Looking back brings regret.

Dear Lord, I can't afford to ignore Your leading or my desire to retreating. Your will brings best. My will brings loss. Amen.

If It Was Different, We Wouldn't Be

In Your book I was written…before I was.

—Psalm 139:16

We have parents. They're here because of their parents, and the same goes from grandparents to the great-grandparents generations back.

We've had passing thoughts of *I could've married or had that person over there.* That particular one did grab my attention. We had a conversation but didn't connect. I chose the one I've got.

What would my life have been like if I had gone with that other person? He or she might have brought more financial benefits, public notice, better-looking or behaving children, a bigger house in a nicer neighborhood, or maybe not. If we had gotten the one that got away, our lives would be different today.

We are what God ordained us to be.

What about the *if* in our heritage? If those moms and dads had married differently, they would have had other offspring and made us nonexistent.

It took each of them to make the generation that continued on to us, and here we are, because of the mom and dad we have. Any changes along the way, we wouldn't be.

We're meant to be who we are because God chose us to be so. We're His idea and design. He knew best and made us to give Him praise and tell others of His eternal love.

Dear Lord, I'm here because You wanted me to be. I want to live my life telling others about You that loves them, exactly as they are, because You chose for them to be here too. Amen.

Unnoticed

God does not see as man sees; people look at the
physical appearance, but the God sees the heart.
—1 Samuel 16:7

God told Samuel to go to Jesse's house and anoint one of his sons
to replace King Saul. In so doing, Samuel presumed to find a
tall, dark, and handsome individual for Israel's new king. That's the
very description God had chosen in King Saul.

Good looks proved little value in King Saul's short and troublesome reign. Samuel followed God's directive to Jesse. One of his sons
would become king.

Samuel watched Jesse's many sons pass by him. God kept saying, "No, not this one."

There were no more sons in the house.

Then Jesse remembered his youngest son. David was out in the
field doing an unappreciated and uncomplimentary job—taking care
of the sheep.

David was almost forgotten by his own father, but not by his
Heavenly Father. God knew David and where he was. And he was
aware of the ordinariness of his job. David did not pass the physical
appearance King Saul wore, but David was God's choice. David had
not gone unnoticed.

God had His eye on David all the time. God knew David's size,
shape, and hair color, but it was the condition of David's heart that
made the difference—a pure heart.

*Dear Lord, my life is ordinary to people, but not to You. Take me and
use me just as I am, with my clean heart and unnoticed abilities. Amen.*

No Excuse

And he said, Who are You, Lord?

—Acts 9:5

S aul of Tarsus was intelligent, well educated, and professionally certain he knew best.

This scholar had no difficulty impressing and influencing people in his religious culture.

But a problem was growing. It was a new religion, which he was certain was false.

Its believers Antioch labeled Christians (Acts 11:26). Saul meant to stamp them out.

His way, his understanding, his training was the only way. It was his way or no way. And Saul planned to get these Christians out of his way and everyone's way. After all, people were listening to these Christians, being converted, and they, too, were telling others. Saul of Tarsus meant to eliminate them all.

So he traveled here and there, threatening men, women, and even children to imprisonment and slaughter.

But on one of those trips, a blinding light from heaven knocked him off his high horse. Saul fell to the ground.

"Saul, Saul, why are you persecuting Me?" a voice said.

Immediately, Saul knew who was talking to him. In an instant, this Saul of Tarsus realized the error of his anti-Christian actions. No long theological argument was needed. Without question, Saul realized he was talking to Jesus. And those Christians had also met this Jesus. He truly was (is) the only way.

This was no mere inspiration to Saul. He had recognized Jesus and knew He was the promised Messiah. Thus Saul had no excuse for his menacing intentions.

Dear Lord, as he was without excuse, neither am I. I will accept the truth of Jesus just as this Saul of Tarsus did. Amen.

The Sauls

Obey better than sacrifice.

—1 Samuel 15:22

Blinded to sight.

—Acts 9:9, 18

We read of the Old Testament Saul in 1 Kings 9. His biography grew into many chapters. It began with a quiet, unobtrusive, obedient man.

Saul was looking for his father's donkeys, not attention for himself. He found the prophet Samuel. He told Saul where the lost animals were located. After a short time, Samuel anointed Saul to be king. Israel accepted him as king.

In so doing, King Saul's personality changed. He progressed from a humble man to an arrogant leader. His selfish attitude grew until God rejected Saul as Israel's king.

The Saul of the New Testament's biography started in Acts 7:58 and continued through the rest of Acts on through other books.

He was known as Saul of Tarsus. He watched and approved the murder of Stephen. Now this Saul became certain his training qualified him to rule over any Christian. He was boss and forced imprisonment and worse on many of those Christians.

This continued until the prideful Saul of Tarsus was knocked off his high horse by the bright light of Jesus's presence and words.

King Saul began humble and became full of self.

Saul of Tarsus was full of self and became humble.

The Old Testament Saul lifted himself up. God put him down.

The New Testament Saul put himself down. God lifted him up.

One yielded to God's will. The other did not. Which are we today? Which will we be tomorrow?

Dear Lord, two biblical men with identical names walked different paths, one for self and the other for God. May I follow You in obedience and all You would have me do. Amen.

Blessed Sleep

> I cried to the Lord… He heard me… Then I
> could lay down and sleep: when I awoke, the Lord
> sustained me. So I will…lay down…and sleep.
> —Psalm 3:4–5, 4:8

Sleep. Do you sleep well? Are your nights full of restful, peaceful, with no fear sleep?

We all must have sleep. Quick, brief naps have some value, but do they fulfill the body's need for sleep?

Our families, friends, neighborhood, and this world's culture present challenging and difficult issues robbing our sleep. Few of these matters we are able to control.

Those for which we can work through, we need to ask the Lord for clear wisdom, as James 1:5 instructs. He promises to provide needed answers and directions to help. All those problems for which we can do nothing, we trust the Lord to work out as Proverbs 3:5 instructs.

When we have laid all disturbing complications, setbacks, mishaps (worries) at Jesus's feet, we can sleep. But if this doesn't seem to take place, quote the beginning (of this devotional) scriptures as often as needed. We will sleep because God said so.

He said when we cry, call, whisper, or even whimper unto Him, He hears and will supply nourishing sleep. It's His promise. That makes it ours.

Dear Lord, thank You for a blessed sleep
each time I go to bed. Amen.

Yes, Sleep

God gives sleep to His beloved.

—Psalm 127:2

Long days, troublesome issues, and health problems pull hard on our need for sleep.

Some reports state people need at least eight hours of sleep each day. We all want it.

Life has a way of trying to steal sleep. At times, we are all recipients of not getting enough rest.

But that's not God's plan. He promises a number of times in the Bible that sleep is ours for the taking.

If we belong to Him, His beloved, adequate sleep is automatic.

Nothing is withheld from those living in an upright manner. These honorable people will have this vital need met.

A hard day's work requires sleep. Renewed strength is a must to face another day. God said if you labor, you shall receive sweet sleep.

Again, the word *sweet* is added to sleep. This time, it's found in the book of Proverbs. It says you lie down, you shall receive.

God knows how we're put together. He designed and made all of us—men, women, and children, preborn through teens. And He knows we must sleep. It's essential.

When sleep evades us, be reminded of God's many promises. Read and memorize these verses, so when sleep seems far away, recite these truths God gave for sleep. Let nothing keep sleep away.

What God say is ours—is ours!

Dear Lord, even when distractions seem endless, I am most grateful to be able to have good sleep every day. Amen.

(Psalm 4:8, 84:11; Proverbs 3:24; Ecclesiastes 5:12)

Battle to Keep Sleeping

How long do you plan to sleep?

—Proverbs 6:9

Morning came too early. The alarm says it arrived. I don't see it because I choose not to open my eyes.

My bed is warm, cozy, and oh so comfortable. My pillow fits perfect around my sleepy head. Mm, I love where I am lying, so I snuggle deeper into the security of my position.

No daylight is permitted to invade my safe and closed-in slothful world. If I open my eyes, I need to get active, but my contentedness in my comfort zone holds me.

If I open my eyes and see this day's start, I need to get up, get busy, and get involved. I don't want to face that process, not yet. Give me a few more minutes to sleep time away and ignore personal responsibility.

Then daylight presses more firmly on my eyelids. It edges itself around those closed lids. But shadows push up from the bottom of each one. The battle is on.

Shadow to light, light to shadow, the contest persists until my feet find the floor. The fight is now over. Day has begun. Praise God for the rising sun, and I am alive to see today through.

Dear Lord, thank You that I can open my eyes,
use my feet, and work this day's upcoming hours. I
am grateful for the ability to do what has been given me to do. Amen.

Too Much Sleep

Do not sleep…open your eyes and be
satisfied with needs supplied.
—Proverbs 20:13

Sleep. We love it. We spend much time enjoying its pleasure every night. We are flat-out involved with sleep. We can't function without it. To succeed in anything in our daily schedule, plenty of sleep is a must.

Let's get our sleep. But eight or so out of each twenty-four hours is adequate to bring rest for healthy bodies.

Beyond that amount of time allows laziness to slide in between soft sheets and on the self-chosen pillow. Hmm, sleep, bring it on.

Before it's realized, the lackadaisical couch potato has neglected business at hand. The providing and doing for family gets overlooked. Instead, they stay in a distant dream.

Too much sleep steals from one's relationship with the Lord. Just forty and more winks keeps that individual from applying their God-gifted abilities to work for them. Plus, we deny ourselves the privilege to witness while we comfortably stay in our inactivity.

We still have many miles to travel in this life, people to care about, and those who need to know of Jesus and His love for them. Let's count sheep at its appropriate time and length of hours. Extra sleep opens opportunity for the lazy to continue lying down on the job.

Awake. Alert. Don't shirk.

*Dear Lord, I will rise up, be about, occupy,
and do what is mine to do. Amen.*

Stiff-Necked

They are stiff-necked people.

—Deuteronomy 9:13

Many times I've awakened with a stiff neck. A cold might have settled itself in my neck, or I slept wrong. Either choice brought misery.

It was impossible to turn my head left or right or bend it down. Its stiffness objected to movement. My day was spent inconvenienced with just one way to look.

I prayed and applied heat. They helped. But the stiffness stayed until the cold or kink ran its course. Until then, I remained with my stiff neck.

Now to be a stiff-necked person is one refusing to consider another's idea or suggestion. That one's mind is stationary thinking with only one direction—theirs. Those flaunting such an attitude don't accept facts. Their mind, or maybe I should say neck, is made up, set solid in their viewpoint. No changes possible. They've attained a stiff neck.

This unyielding judgment causes discomfort to those others but will eventually hurt the one holding tight their own stiff neck's point of view.

A stiff neck's appearance and perspective brings no credit to the Lord or one's self and certainly blesses no one. A stiff neck brings adjectives that aren't complimentary.

The Lord wants us to listen to Him and obey His direction and not be self-opinionated. Yes, prayer is essential. We pray for us to yield our stiff-necked and stubborn thinking to Him. If we find that's difficult to do, He might need to apply heat to release the strong-willed, inflexible, bullheaded stiff neck.

Dear Lord, I repent of my stiff neck determination
and will do as You so direct.

One Shovelful at a Time

God gave me strength and made my way easier.
—Psalm 18:32

Those living in a higher elevation expect wintertime snow, lots of snow. It looks pretty and stays until spring, unless we need to walk, drive, and get around. Then we must pick up and cast aside snow's quantity of inches.

The job looks huge and waits to see what we will do. That answer starts with us taking a deep breath, dressing appropriately, and stepping out to face the cold outdoors and do the job.

One shovelful at a time begins the needed process. We see all that lie ahead but do get encouraged with the less to be done because of all that is now behind. Snow removal is happening.

We can't walk away from this responsibility. So we think, sing, and pray, taking advantage of the alone time to clear the path, sidewalk, and open the driveway. Finally, that last shovelful gets tossed to the snowbank.

Throughout this task, we are given an opportunity to get some health benefits as we talk to the Lord, speak faith, and whisper a Christian tune.

Eventually, the snow's accumulation got moved. God was honored. He gave the strength to deal with each shovelful with a song in our hearts.

Dear Lord, I'm grateful for strength and the ability to complete the uncomfortable, inconvenient, time-consuming weather-assigned project of shoveling snow. Amen.

Loincloth

Take your loin cloth…and hide it.

—Jeremiah 13:4

Read Jeremiah 13:1–11.

A loincloth, a small article of clothing that is placed close to the body, becomes extremely personal and important to the individual. This loincloth idea also represents that particular thing we insist on holding tight to ourselves. Now take that loincloth thing and bury it, set it out of sight for an extended period.

Allow it to remain untouched. Then days, weeks, months later, search it out. You'll find it doesn't have the once presumed significance. It has become valueless.

Why do we then cling to earthly things? In time, they, too, will become useless.

Even as that loincloth clung to our person, so have our ideas, plans, and need-to-be-noticed snugged close by. They didn't want to be separated from us, but when we let go and choose to honor God and listen to Him, we'll find that loincloth thing is now no good, worthless.

With Jesus on top in our thoughts and efforts, we'll find that those interested and desired things make us most miserable.

Our forced smiles, words, and endeavors don't convince the inner us. We know that loincloth, not laundered or kept clean, holds nothing for a healthy Christian.

Let go of the "Gotta have, I know best, it's all for me" and bury them. Trust the Lord. He will clean the heart and set us free from the loincloth.

Dear Lord, I do give You that loincloth thing in my life,
allowing You to fulfill and satisfy me far beyond. Amen.

Knower

They know what is correct, but don't do it.

—Romans 2:15

What is a knower? We all have one. Deep inside each human being is a knower.

Questions are asked about God, religions, morality, etc. Yet the answer resides in the knower. The knower knows the yes and the no of those debated topics.

If the person doesn't want to accept what the knower tells them, they make loud noises, use many words by stepping on other voices, or instigate deception to the point of bringing confusion or even harm.

He or she objects to what their knower knows and has been reminding them what they've already known. Yet this person fights to disregard that know. They hope to undo ramifications of the know because the knower already reminded them, and it was accepted or rejected.

Is God real? What about Jesus? Is He the only way to heaven? Does He have the answer for me personally, my family, our country, or the world?

Did God create the world? Are people equal to animals? What about traditional values? Are they the same today as they were in the yesterdays? The response to these and other questions resonate in the knower.

It was given by God for people to know Him and rely on His voice via one's own conviction, gut feeling, or conscience. Listen to your knower. It knows.

Dear Lord, You've given me a knower to know truth. Help me to listen to my knower and double-check with You and Your Word. Amen.

Nervous

I praise You, God, for in You I will trust and not be afraid
what people, snowfall, or whatever can do to me.
—Psalm 56:4

It had snowed. The roads were slick. Frigid air blew no warmth
to improve the road's surface. But I must travel them. My job
required I be in attendance. No work, no pay. I had to be there.

Winter's seasonal process did what it did well. It snowed. These
flakes fell any time of the day or night in varied amounts. I must deal
with results of the driven snow and the layer it brought.

This morning, I was nervous about taking a specific route
ahead. There was no choice but to drive that very snow-covered and
steep road. This would necessitate applying the brakes many times.
Oh, I was nervous.

I prayed continually about my concern. God said nothing. I
had no choice but to start the dreaded trip.

As I turned onto the road that led to this uncertain hill, a van
in front of me backed out of its driveway. This vehicle proceeded to
make the turn to the questionable incline.

I had to smile. God sent an unknowing leader to show me the
path I must drive was safe. And it was. The road crew had cleared and
cindered that stretch of road very well.

God did answer my prayer. He didn't do it as I had presumed
He would. He did in His perfect time.

*Dear Lord, how grateful I am to know You are already on the
scene and preparing my way as I travel each road. Amen.*

God Sees Me

The eyes of the Lord sees the righteous.

—Psalm 34:15

Eighteen hours without electricity. The late winter's storm had downed wires and branches. This resulted with the loss of all power to my house. There was no heat.

Dressed in layers and wrapped in blankets, I made it through the night. Morning sun was welcome. I was still snuggled in my recliner and had no electricity, and the day's entertainment was via a large window Drapes opened displayed the nearby woods bent with snow and ice.

The upper corner of the window displayed a patch of blue sky. Two pine tree tops danced in its lower corner. The first tree wore the tallest peak. Directly behind it was a shorter one.

Cuddled in my wraps, I watched these trees sway in the wind. No matter which way the front tree moved, the smaller one pushed out a bit farther.

I could see the little one peek at me. It would get blown behind the taller tree and then out to face me. Again and again they danced. For many minutes, I enjoyed this scene play out for my benefit. The message was unmistakable.

This short treetop reminded me that no matter how big the storm seemed to be, God saw me. I was never out of His sight. No pine tree could block God's view of me.

The cold temperature in the house continued another ten and half hours. The tree dance stopped. The message remained. It was crystal clear. God is always watching me.

*Dear Lord, You see and know what's going on with
me. I will trust You with the answers. Amen.*

I Am Not Alone

God sees me.

—Genesis 16:13

I woke up with a smile. My dream was solid nonsense. It was just past 5:00 a.m. There I lay in a well-lit room.

The moon was peeking around the upper corner of the window frame. It was a full moon, whole and beautiful.

My smile grew. It was like God was watching over me. He saw my silly dream and felt I needed to awake and change the dream's pages.

It was like God was visible. I could see Him, as I knew He clearly saw me. That was comforting. I could feel the moon's soft beam on my face with reassurance that I was not alone.

God saw even my wacky dream and might have had a chuckle over it. He was there anyway at that late morning hour. I could see His care. The now bright moon slowly moved its brightness along in full view.

God saw me in my bed. He saw my full bedroom. He also saw what was going on outdoors around my house. He was aware of it all. God was truly watching over me.

There I was in the security of my home, my quiet privacy. I was not forgotten. In fact, I was singled out for such an elegant, divine, and calming scene.

The alarm went off and woke me. The moon was now out of sight, but God was still there and would always be with me.

Dear Lord, no matter where I am, You are and
will be with me eternally. Amen.

God's Ten Laws

The commandments of the Lord are perfect...
sure...right...pure...and faithful.
—Psalm 19:7–8

God, our loving Heavenly Father, gave us ten commandments, as any caring parent provides instructions for their children.

Father God, as with Mom and Dad, wants the best for each child. Parents express their affection with many no-nos. If the youngster is left without rules, a life filled with heartache, pain, and even serious injury is in his or her future.

All boys and girls need boundaries for their own sense of security and acceptance. Most parents love their children. God always loves us. He expressed this love by writing ten directives. If followed, they would keep us safe, healthy, and spiritually stronger. Some of them were "yes-yes," and others were "do-don'ts."

As we children grow up, our parents' laws often become the very rules we, their progeny, will use. These were passed on to us and have now become ours. We obey them because they've been proven to work.

God's laws should, as well, be our laws. He gave them with love. They are designed to instruct us in all things and show us how to live a life free of bondage, baggage, hang-ups, and sorrow.

If we follow God's laws, as a child looks to his or her parent for direction, they will guide and remind us while we work, talk, play, stay, and do. We will also attain a godly and victorious life each day, night, and weekend.

Dear Lord, of all the rules You gave, only a few made it to the top 10 list. I will make them part of my life. Amen.

Give God Worship

He worshiped and…said arise for the Lord hath delivered.
—Judges 7:9, 7:15

G ideon believed he was a nobody and not good enough to do a
successful job. Nevertheless, God chose him to lead the battle
against the Midianites.

Simple instructions were given. Three hundred soldiers were
God's requirement for Gideon to use in the battle. He was willing
but hesitant to go forward. How could he, Gideon, "the least in his
father's house," lead, let alone win in combat against an enemy.

But one night, after plans and arrangements were readied for
the upcoming conflict, Gideon slipped into the Midianite camp.
There he heard one man tell his roommate about a dream he had
just had. It caused both men to be certain Gideon was going to fight
them and win.

When Gideon heard this, all he could do was stand still and
worship God. Triumph was in sight.

He went back to his small army. In obedience, Gideon and
company began their unconventional march. They were armed with
only lamps and trumpets. Onward, they moved toward the opposing
army. As the men got in sight of the Midianite camp, they watched
the panicked and confused enemy destroy each other or just run
away. No one turned on Gideon and his troops.

Gideon had learned to listen and obey God. But it was in his
giving God worship first that brought victory.

*Dear Lord, in all things, may I give you praise before I attempt
to do anything or go anywhere on my own. Amen.*

Whoa, Don't Do It

You shall not make…any…image.

—Exodus 20:4

"Isn't it beautiful? I just love it so much I could worship it." We may not say these very words, but our actions express that thought.

That appealing article could be a figurine, photograph, memento, sculpture, piece of furniture, or maybe a person or pet. And yes, beautiful could be true about them. We buy or do much to enhance their winsomeness, spending time admiring or talking to or about that non-hearing object or an individual.

If this attraction is a person, does he or she care about what you say or do or need? Or could our loved animal or object listen with any ability to answer our prayer?

Does the sight or thought of this worshiped one bring a lump to your throat, tears to your eyes, or a warm feeling all over you? Whoa, that sure could send the heart to bending in an idolatry mode.

God is jealous (2 Corinthians 11:2). He cannot and will not take second place to any doodad or being. He wants the top spot in our lives and all we do, see, or desire. He gave the command in Psalm 29:2 that we are to "give the Lord glory due Him and worship Him."

If we have allowed ourselves to put something or someone to worship, we can repent. For God is good and ready to forgive with plenteous mercy to all that call on Him (Psalm 86:5).

Dear Lord, I am sorry for putting that one before You.
Help me never again to worship anything or anyone but You. Amen.

It's a No-No

You shall not speak the name of the Lord your
God with disrespect or to swear falsely.
—Exodus 20:7

"What did you say? Children are told not to talk that way."
Too many people use God's name to curse things and
other people and then vow to use God's name to seal pledges or speak
forth selfish words of pride. All these are vain and forbidden by God.
He says they are all no-nos. It's God's command that we are never to
speak in such a manner.

Matthew 5:33–37 says not to swear by heaven or earth or
Jerusalem or by your own head. Instead, simply say a yes or a no. All
profanity and expletives are banned.

An uncontrolled tongue only causes destruction (Proverbs
13:3), produces a fire (James 3:5–6), and reveals the truth of our
hearts (Matthew 12:34).

Whatever is inappropriate to speak in public or even private,
cancel immediately while these remarks are still in the thought-mak-
ing process. Do not allow ungodly responses to pour forth and spill
out the mouth.

God's name is to be honored, not used for any type of vulgarity.
Let us check out our language habit. Does it reflect God? Today, let's
make it so.

*Lord, please forgive me for allowing verbal action to come
from my lips that breaks this commandment. Help me to
speak forth good for Your glory each day through. Amen.*

Rest and Worship

Six days God used for His creating work. He rested on
the seventh—called the Sabbath. (So must we.)
—Exodus 20:11

The Sabbath was designed for us to have a day of rest in which we would worship God. For six days, our jobs, family, and lifestyle beckon our time. We fill our days with activities.

Each schedule gets brimmed up often weeks in advance. The list of things to be done packs our hours. There's no time for church. Our lives are just so busy with more to do than time to be done.

God said that's not fair. People need rest. So He placed the Sabbath commandment as number four in the top ten. This makes God's rest and worship law vitally important.

He knows people. They need rest. A twenty-four-seven lifestyle will not cut it. Human beings will eventually fall from the heavy loads we place on ourselves. We must stop at some point and rest. God set up the Sabbath for that very purpose.

While we are resting, take time to worship God. He gave us all things—people, jobs, and stuff. Most of all, He gave us Jesus, the savior of our eternal souls.

God has done it all. He tells us to stop and spend a little time with Him. It's no biggie.

Just love the God who loves you. That's His desire for all men, women, teens, and youngsters.

Lord, help me to keep the Sabbath as top priority in my weekly schedule. I need to rest and worship regularly. Amen.

Honor Parents

Honor your mom and dad: so you may live
a long life that God will give you.
—Exodus 20:12

We all have parents. In your upbringing, were they involved or distracted? Did they care or ignore? Did they truly love or just tolerate us?

Whatever they might have been or are, God says, "Honor your father and mother." He allows no exception. God knows people are imperfect, whether they were our parents or we are the parent. The process has not changed:

Parents: mom and dad.

Offspring: sons and daughters.

Birth happens. Years pass. Peer involvement.

Children grow up. Struggles arrive. Honor in question.

Parenting is a long stretch filled with joy and sadness between adult and child. Too much that took place in those formative years influences our grown-up attitude. And even if our parents might not have wanted us, God's rule to honor our parents stays.

However, God does add a postscript to the fifth command. He says we get to have a long life if we honor our parents. And may I add that we get to sleep better and wear a healthier frame when we honor those who gave us life. Plus, our integrity remains intact.

Dear Lord, help me love Mom and Dad regardless of whatever might have been or still remain in our relationship. May they be as special to me as they are to You. Amen.

You Will Not Kill
Exodus 20:13

The Lord God made man…and breathed life into him.
—Genesis 2:7

God formed man with a wonderful design. It was a perfect plan. Only God could have done it.

Upon completion of His work of art, God proceeded to breathe life into the nose of the man He just put together. That man became alive, breathing the air God gave him.

The world has billions of us people. We are preborn, elderly, physically, mentally challenged, and maybe normal. Some of us are considered inconvenient and should be eliminated.

The process of doing this does not include the word *kill*. Other titles are used to hide the murderous action legally done to those believed are unwanted.

Hired personnel make the final decision if some people get to live or die. These so-called professionals are paid well to do the job. Thus people get thrown away.

What a scary thought that there are individuals who have no fear in taking God's given breath of life from someone else. They are willing, for a price, to kill them.

God said, "You will not kill." Period. Not further discussion. We are His idea. We are all special. God created us in His image. He still wants us. Our uniqueness continues. His love for us remains. His blessings are available to all ages and abilities of every offspring.

Dear Lord, help me help others remember we are all here because of the breath of life You've placed in our bodies. Amen.

Willing Participants

You shall not commit adultery.

—Exodus 20:14

He looks at her. She sees him. He gives her a smile. She blushes. He walks toward her.

She meets him. They laugh together, and they make their way to a restaurant. Here, this mister and missus. begin to grow a relationship. But this mister and missus are not to each other. Their spouses are forgotten, as these two lust one for the other.

It's probable to this desired individual you're not the first licentiousness affair. All previous illicit flings have left germs and maybe diseases in this person's body. And now you're the recipient of all that bacteria.

Then a pregnancy happens. This complicates the infidelity. Their innocent and unplanned baby carries the result of parental actions.

Anger, unsettledness, ignored spouses, child support, and so many other problems become giants when two decide to commit adultery.

God knows people. He designed them and understands their makeup. Each person becomes broken when having yielded to adultery. God's fifth commandment is for our physical, mental, financial, and spiritual health.

Today's culture allows for extramarital behaviors. Eventually, heartaches follow such unfaithfulness. Society offers little help. All willing participants are stuck in the results of their sin. Once inside the pain that follows, only God has the balm to heal (Jeremiah 46:11).

Upon repentance of adulterous behavior, God forgives (Psalm 103:3). The road back to purity can be long and difficult, but it's doable. God is available and will walk with us each moment and step of the way.

Dear Lord, thanks for forgiveness to my yielding to sinful temptations. Help me to remain pure. Amen.

Responsible Attitude

Thou shalt not steal.

—Exodus 20:15

It was just a pack of gum.

My lecture only went over ten minutes.

It's Dad's car. He wouldn't care.

They were paper clips from the office.

I took this pencil from the church because I wanted it.

And on go the excuses for taking what is not ours. None of these thieving seem to be a big deal. Getting away with little amounts of robbing encourages more robberies. This conduct continues until it's out of control. Results bring expensive and lengthy penalties. The final judgment shows what we get for what we have done.

No matter how it's excused or defended, anything or time we take that is not rightfully ours is stealing. God said helping ourselves to what doesn't belong to us is wrong. It's disobedience. It's a sin.

Stealing is not worth the pain it causes. Soon the consequences of inappropriate behavior roll back onto ourselves, as well as family and friends.

God said if it doesn't belong to us, it's not ours to take. If we do it anyway, we have stolen it. We become thieves.

God knows us. If we admit our disobedient action with a repentant heart and turn from ungodly acts, He will forgive us. When asked, God will provide strength to resist future temptations.

*Dear Lord, may my responsible attitude reflect
You in all I say and do. Amen.*

That Person

You shall not lie against your neighbor.

—Exodus 20:16

Who is your neighbor? It is that person? Our neighbor is that person. It is that person, wherever he or she resides or crosses our path or attention, or whatsoever they might do or think is still our neighbor.

We—you and me—are not to retaliate against them regardless of any reason or excuse chosen. Instead, we are to love that person as we love ourselves (Leviticus 19:8). It's for sure we do love us.

We would place no untruths on ourselves, for we would not want the repercussions from that accusation. We protect our person with utmost care.

What about that person? He or she is to receive the same amount of fond regard we give to us.

Falsehood, half-truths, far-fetched white lies, fabrication, distortion, misrepresentation, sham, manipulation, and *exaggeration* are just a few descriptive words use to try and cover up the fact it is a lie. This action by word or behavior is never to be placed against that person.

When we point our finger, three other fingers point back to us. As we point with lies about that individual, how many more can be pointed back to us?

To help us, God explains how we can give ourselves the best protection possible. Do not lie. Period.

Dear Lord, I will remember to keep me and my actions honest and clean against my neighbor, that person, even if he or she does get under my skin. I will not lie. Amen.

No, Me

Do not covet anything that belongs to anyone else.

—Exodus 20:17

Look at her outfit. It would be perfect for my special event. I wish it was mine.

He got that truck! I wanted it. I tried but couldn't get the financing. By rights, that four-by-four full bed, four-door, three-fourth ton pickup should be mine.

You've got to be kidding. That promotion went to my substitute. That's not fair. I worked hard, and besides, I have seniority in this department. That job rightfully belongs to me. I deserve it.

We're all guilty at some point in our daily activities to want what another has received. Such an attitude puts us back to a learning-to-talk toddler stage.

These little ones' first words are often *no* and *me*. This small child never needs to be taught to be selfish. Whatever someone else has, the tot covets for the *me*.

Any objection or explanation produces a loud and sharp no. After continual insistence, the baby realizes the *no* and *me* will not happen.

Placing a grown-up in such a frame of reference is unattractive. But as we look at another haranguing on the *no*, it should not be theirs because it should belong to *me*. It makes it easy to visualize the immaturity in coveting.

The *no* and *me* are not complementary to anyone at any age or position in life.

Instead, we can "seek God first and He'll provide for us" (Matthew 6:33).

Dear Lord, I give You my no *and* me *and replace it with
a blessing on those having what I thought I might like.
I trust You to provide what is best for me. Amen.*

Perfection Lost
Perfection to Gain

By one man sin entered this world…but God
sent Jesus to provide for us eternal life.

—Romans 5:12, 6:23

Adam was the first man, perfect, made by God. God gave Adam a perfect wife. He was pleased. Her name was Eve.

God said no to this perfect couple about a certain fruit tree; no touching it.

Eve chose to disobey. She picked the forbidden fruit and ate it. So did Adam. Why? Was he at her elbow when she took fruit from that tree?

Did Adam not see what he was doing? Did he tell her no, or did he agree and participate in the act?

Then God came calling. Oops. Adam and Eve knew they did wrong. There was no place to hide. They were naked in more ways than absence of clothing.

The naked truth of their act was known. Maybe they had fruit pieces on their faces. God saw.

Immediately on that first bite, perfection left them. They became like us—sinners. Today, with hindsight, we know the foolishness of their behavior and its consequences. Sin is now inherited.

In all our five senses and throughout this planet, sin is obvious. Not one sin is exempt.

God had to send Jesus to become our sacrifice so we could be redeemed from that first original sin. The requirements are to repent our sin and take Jesus as our savior.

Then we will eventually get to enjoy perfection. It won't be here but over there in heaven, forever.

Dear Lord, I've followed the requirements for my salvation. Now I'm redeemed from Adam and Eve's chosen disobedience. Amen.

Shadows

> They brought the sick, on beds and couches to the streets,
> trusting Peter's shadow would pass upon them.
>
> —Acts 5:15

Groundhog Day remains a fun issue on the second day of February. It seems when one specific groundhog steps out of its dwelling and sees its shadow (or not), there shall be six more weeks of winter, or in six weeks, spring will arrive. Either way, it singles in on one small critter's shadow.

This animal's worth is simply because of its normal shadow which gets noticed but once a year. What about this groundhog's other 364 days? Do they have any shadow value?

Long before such a groundhog story became a game, a shadow event was recorded in the Bible. It was a real shadow's miraculous use.

At that particular time, some people received healing by using basic objects, such as hankies and aprons, to provide healing to needy seekers. Then God used the shadow of Peter to cure the sick.

Can you imagine how much of the Lord's Word Peter absorbed, and with faith accepted as truth, for God to use him in such a manner?

Peter remembered Jesus said, "Greater things He did, His people could also do" (John 14:12). Peter believed this fact, so when his shadow passed over an ill or injured person, that one was healed.

Which shadow is preferred, a joke or God's provided reality?

Dear Lord, I believe You will do great things through
me as You did through Peter. Amen.

It's Genetic

As in Adam everyone will die, but in Christ all will live.
—1 Corinthians 15:22

Three days after Christmas, my husband, Lew, had a heart attack. This required a four-stint procedure to stop the attack. It was also learned a triple bypass was essential to prevent more attacks. That was done five weeks later.

Through all of Lew's testing and questions, it was learned that the heart problem he acquired was not caused by his lifestyle. Genetic was the probable reason given to Lew's heart disease. He had done nothing to get it, and it took qualified physicians to make needed repairs.

All people are born with a heart disease called sin. We did nothing to get it, but if it's not dealt with, we'll die.

The great Physician Jesus gave His life to provide healing for this inherited sin. Only when we repent of that sin and accept Jesus to do heart surgery, removing the fatal plaque called sin and becoming our Savior, do we get to live on.

Lew's surgeon did eight and one-fourth hours of pump operation to give Lew more years of this life. If we allow Dr. Jesus to do the needed work in our hearts, that cure will last forever.

Lord, I give my heart to You. Save me from my inherited sin. I want an eternal life in heaven with You. Amen.

Safe in God's Arms

Hold me and I will be safe.

—Psalm 119:117

My husband Lew's triple bypass surgery took over eight hours. The waiting process was one long stretch of time.

I occupied those hours with much prayer, silent singing, reading, and writing, as well as listening and watching my family play games. They kept busy. I was lost in the waiting game.

The doctor finally arrived with the diagnosis of Lew's surgery. Upon completion of his report, I passed out.

I remember little of what took place from there on. My family tried to fill in the blanks. I crumbled and then was wheeled off to the emergency room and put through many tests. I was on a gurney and was pushed here and there. The faces I saw and voices I heard were hurried blurs.

I didn't know what had happened and why I had such a response, but I did know I had no fear. I was safe in God's arms.

I went with the flow—no questions, no fight, not even fright. I understood nothing the medical people were doing. I just knew I was okay because I was secure in my Heavenly Father's arms. He was on the scene.

The end result of the whole episode was me being simply released, and I would be fine.

It's true. Whatever, wherever, or however anything takes place in our lives at any time, we rest, protected and safe in God's arms.

Dear Lord, thanks for holding me safe through
all unexpected turn of events. Amen.

Blahsville

Rejoice today, tomorrow, always (regardless of the weather).
—Philippians 4:4

Christmas has color, laughter, and lights. Gray skies are not noticed. Snow-covered ground is enjoyed. It's seasonably accepted. Christmas is now history. Full winter is upon us. Blahsville moves in encouraging no remembrance of the joyful Christmastime and its reason for the season.

The sky stays gray, the ground grows white, we get chilled, and we get lethargic. Blahsville has arrived. No cheer to hear, no smile to see, no giving God praise or shouting victory. I'm stuck in Blahsville.

Short days, long nights, sunless sky leads to "woe is me." Blahsville rolls around and packs in tight as a snowball. No help, no hope, no cure, 'cause Blahsville's here.

Recliners filled with us, feet raised, hot chocolate in hand, with that negative Blahsville dreams of spring. May it come soon.

We're stuck in Blahsville. There is no break in sight, no way to get free. Has its blah blue got a hold of you and me? Blahsville, shake it off.

The same Jesus of Christmas walks with us in Blahsville. Chin up. Notice. He's there, and we're still in His care all winter long.

Kick Blahsville out the door and rejoice. We are here today. God has something special for us to learn and accomplish within these cold months. Rejoice in the Lord *always*, whether the skies are sunless and gray and the snow is piled high. Again, I repeat, rejoice in the Lord.

Dear Lord, admittedly, winter is not my favorite season. I will trust You to take me through with joy in my heart and praise on my lips. Amen.

Nudge

The nudges of a good man or woman are directed
by the Lord, and He delights in the progress.
—Psalm 37:23

Do you have a nudge to do something? Does that idea continue to roll around regularly in your thoughts? Are you tempted to yield but hesitate?

Okay, now that you've admitted you do have a nudge, do you continue to tell yourself, "It's only a nudge. A nudge is nothing. Besides, this nudge would take me out of my comfort zone."

What is your inner wish? Have you had it since childhood or has it been recent? Will it help others or just advance yourself? How much credit would go to the Lord if you step into this nudge's beginning?

But then how could it? Where could it? Should I even try? Oh my, but that nudge will not go away. The question remains to be this: what will it cost me and others if I give in and move forward?

Many questions flood your mind. No answers will come if you do not trust God to help you try. Nudges come from Him.

If the process or product or outcome lines up with God's Word, believe God has a specific purpose in mind for you by placing that nudge in your spirit.

Talk to Jesus with all those questions. Listen to what He says. Accept, with willingness, God's directions. Then be determined to obey. Don't stay. Get underway today. Start. Don't stop. When God's at the top, all will be okay.

Dear Lord, that nudge You gave me, I claim it as my personal assignment from You. All details and results are Yours. Amen.

God's Call

Eli figured God had called Samuel.

—1 Samuel 3:8

Are you being called? Have you been awakened or unable to sleep because God is calling? Do your waking hours get interrupted by God's call? Have you been struggling with the same message over and over again?

You know what it is, but you don't know where it leads. You're afraid to step out and accept the call. You don't want to abandon your own self-made direction. You want life to be smooth and uncomplicated. So you tell yourself God's call could wreck it all.

Excuses are many. Reasons but a few. Others may have the ability, but God has called you.

The path could be tough or downright rough. Yet it could be simple and easy as a breeze. You'll never know if you don't answer God's call. It's certain either way He'll be with you through it all.

Many blessings just for you are being lost because you're worried about its presumed cost. Whatever they may be, remind yourself that answering the call is worth any loss.

The price for Jesus on the cross was very costly. But He answered His Father's call and spent the price because God knew best.

Raise your voice today, right now, and say, "Speak, Lord. This servant is listening." Then praise God and accept all those things in store because you opened that door of obedience.

Dear Lord, there is now peace in my day and sleep through my night because I answered Your call aright. Amen.

Right in My Corner

He that is faithful in the small is faithful in the tall.
—Luke 16:10

Right in my corner, I stand, sit, run, swim, or lie flat. Nevertheless, it's where I am. The world is big. I am not. The world has much. I have little. The world covers the globe. I reign in my corner.

The world is filled with lots of people. I connect with a few. The world can be impersonal. I must not.

Within my corner are people of all ages. They're average, educated, uneducated, have money, or dead broke. Some are kind or grumpy, shy or friendly, and maybe full of dreams or suffered a nightmare. Too many are hurting.

Here I am in my corner. I wear my own understanding, experiences, talents, and instincts. One of these abilities could be the very support someone lacks and is looking to receive.

My corner carries a possible solution for that one or two. Most people are hoping for someone to notice them. I can do that from my corner. That is why God led me this day to do what I can for those struggling. To be a friend or a mentor, provide a plate of cookies, or give a genuine smile.

Whatever the issue may be, if it's brought to my corner, the Lord has provided me, even in a small way, something to aid in the lives of needy people.

Dear Lord, may I brighten someone's life from my corner. Amen.

Are We Clean?

They have all gone awry and become altogether filthy. None of them do good—not one. We too are dirty and mucky.
—Psalm 14:3; Isaiah 64:6

Winter brings a frigid chill to our geographical location and cold to our unheated bedroom. To overcome the undesired temperature, a portable electric heater was installed.

This small machine works fine until it gets clogged. Then an unnatural odor and odd sounds send a concern for our safety.

Yes, this did happen. My husband promptly took our heater apart and searched for the reason for its malfunction.

Yuck. The heater was found to be filthy to the blade. After a thorough cleaning, our needed heat source worked as it had been designed—to send out warmth.

Are we working as God prepared us? Or are we unable to do good because of our obstructed and unkempt condition? Let us search for the unclean thing(s) that fouls up our God-designed purpose.

Dear Lord, cleanse my heart and life. Make me
clean and usable for Your service. Amen.

Waiting Fiancée

If we hope for what we do not yet see, then patiently we wait for it.
—Romans 8:25

Read Matthew 25:1–13.
It was many years ago. I was that fiancée waiting for my man to arrive for our wedding rehearsal. It was winter. Snow and slippery roads were in charge.

There were no phone calls. No message. He knew the plans. He promised to be there but wasn't.

Waiting for his arrival dragged on. I was concerned. Some of the wedding party grew frustrated to have been inconvenienced.

Waiting is not fun. It's tiresome and sends one to the sofa. Time passes with a nap.

The ten virgins mentioned in Matthew's reference were waiting for their promised fiancé. The oil in five of their waiting lamps lost light. Oil was gone. These virgins asked the other five to borrow. They said no, telling them to go and buy for themselves. The first five went to purchase more oil. While they were gone, the fiancé arrived.

The five who shopped for oil were unable to be part of the wedding. They had not planned well. They assumed they would be fine, but instead, they were unprepared.

My man did arrive. He had a minor car accident. He was fine. We all waited for his appearance, even though it was later than expected.

Plan, prepare, and wait are the instructions left for us as we look for our fiancé, Jesus, to return.

He will come. Let's not get weary, but be ready as we wait for Him.

Dear Lord, yes, You are coming to take Christians home, just as You promised. Please help me to wait with patience. Amen.

Slomy

As for me... I will seek Your face... I'll be satisfied.

—Psalm 17:15

(You)...give grace to the lowly.

—Proverbs 3:34

S lomy. Is that a word? Sounds good to me. There are times I feel slomy.

The ongoing cold season's days make me feel slomy. The outdoors may look snowy, but the indoors is where I'm stuck, imprisoned in these walls.

> Too low a temperature,
> too slippery a walk,
> too negative a thought,
> sets my energy to a stop.

My house closes in. The windowpanes display weather's leftover stains, and the sun's brief appearance shines forth winter's gray. The pressure of employment or lack of a job pushes out a scream. Shopping expenses flatten the wallet. Higher prices for cost of living overwhelm the family's household budget. The needs of the loved ones growing up and growing older sets in a discouragement.

Describing such facts is gloomy. It makes me tired. I feel slomy. I miss bright and warm days filled with tasty iced tea. Yet even then slomy kicks in its feel. I believe there's nothing in the surrounding human's existence that can undo slomy.

I sought and found the solution to be the day I looked on Jesus's face. In so doing, all earth's slomy fades away in the brightness of His grace.

Now the Lord helps me
walk and think and move
with no slomy
'ere the temperature be.

Dear Lord, You understand. You said for me to come to You and You will give me rest, strength, peace, and supply all my needs, no matter how slomy I may feel. Amen.

Abraham Lincoln (Nicknamed Abe)

Humility precedes recognition.
—Proverbs 15:33

Our sixteenth president had a humble beginning. He was born on February 12, 1809, in the backwoods cabin in the state of Kentucky.

In 1816, his father moved the family to Indiana, and in 1830, they moved on to Illinois. When Abe was nine, his mother died. A year or so later, his father remarried.

This stepmother liked Abe and encouraged him in all his interests. He loved to read. There was no television, computer, or even electricity to distract him, so Abe was free to read often by firelight from the fireplace.

Abraham read the Bible and knew it well. He taught himself grammar and math and loved the law. He studied enough to practice it and was able to travel the circuit to help others.

Shortly after Abe became president, the Civil War began. Throughout it, he developed a profound understanding of his need for a personal relationship with God.

He saw himself as a humble servant before God. President Abraham Lincoln knew America's leadership was under his direction. Yet he understood he was ordained by God to be used at the very time he was living, and huge responsibilities were given to him.

Abraham took no credit for himself. He remained humble throughout his life.

Dear Lord, thank You for this fine example of what You did with one individual humbled before You and allowed You to lift him up for Your glory. May I be so humble. Amen.

The Question Is More Than Grammar

For as he or she thinks in their heart so they are.
—Proverbs 23:7

Out of the heart flows the problems of life.
—Proverbs 4:23

So what ya thinkin'? Hopin'? Wantin'? Doin'? What rolls around in your wishes and plans? Actions and reactions spill out those answers, describing what's happenin' in ya.

If one takes notice of their own words and behavior, they'll know what's a-goin' on in their own heart. Maybe it's turmoil, peace, gratitude, or emptiness plus surrounding events, family issues, and selfish desires filling the heart. Whatever they might be display themselves through ya feelin's. Soon the real man or woman gets exposed.

Trying to hide that truth can happen only so long. Then it becomes obvious and publicly known. What is, has been, and should be tattles on what we have seen, heard, or read.

Have we been filling us with Jesus and His Word? If so, His values will come forth from the heart for the seein', knowin', and bein'.

Contents of our hearts hold answers. Our lives and all it entails display the accurate response to such a quiz. Will it be that the world sees Jesus in ye?

Dear Lord, the grammar here may not be good, but my desire is to be filled with You and spill forth Your presence unto others. Now that's good. Amen.

St. Valentine

God showed His love to us…while we were
still sinners, Christ died for us.

—Romans 5:8

Do you have a Valentine? Are you one? What are you expected to
receive on February 14? Flowers, candy, cards with red hearts,
or a romantic evening out?

Have you ever thought of dying for the love of your spouse or
fiancé? St. Valentine, a Roman priest, did just that in the AD 269.

Emperor Claudius made a law that there was to be no marriage.
All men fought better on the battlefield if they didn't have wives to
care about.

Consequently, there was a lot of immorality happening at that
time. The sacred marriage of a young couple was prohibited. Many
of these couples were Christian and wanted to follow God's law of
marriage between one man and one woman. No adultery.

St. Valentine secretly married many of these Christ-honoring
couples. Eventually, he was caught, imprisoned, and tortured for per-
forming such ceremonies.

The blind daughter of a judge was healed via St. Valentine's
prayer. His life was briefly extended. He did die by a three-part exe-
cution—beating, stoning, and decapitation—because he believed in
a Christian marriage.

What part of Valentine's Day do you believe? What is its value,
meaning, and purpose in your celebration today?

Father O'Gara, speaking about St. Valentine, said, "Human
love…blessed by God is but also the shadow of the cross. That's what
Valentine means to me." How about us?

*Dear Lord, Valentine's Day is one brief time to express love between
one committed man and woman. May I never forget. Amen.*

Heart's Contents

From out of our heart's contents our mouth speaks.

—Matthew 12:34

What music do we prefer to hear? What are the lyrics? What games do we play? Are they held in our hands, board games, or taking advantage of others?

What do our eyes see? Could it be people, their appearance, action, or attire? Maybe it's some movie, television program, or some piece of technology which opens privacy for our immediate viewing and some printed material that grasps our attention-evoking emotion?

So how have we responded to these questions? Our answers discover the truth of our hearts. All we've permitted to fill our minds is what we become. Yes, of course, family setting and childhood history is also part of the contents in our hearts. Through it all, what we have and do permit to reside in us is us.

I have observed children's behavior after they've watched a TV program, movie, or heard a story. Their behavior revealed the effects of what went into their minds. It displayed itself through their opinions and imagination. They attempted to try to become what they saw or heard.

Child or grown-up, the results are the same:

Good in, good out.
Bad in, bad out.

Learning the reality of our heart's contents requires honest self-examination. Decide today that only Christ-honoring images, sounds, and attitudes will be allowed in our minds and hearts.

Dear Lord, I realize all I've put in my mind expresses itself through every fiber of my being. May my life reflect You at all times in all circumstances. Amen.

Christian Music

I will sing, I repeat, I will sing praise to the Lord.
—Psalm 27:4

Music—Christian music—can raise a lot of ire with agreeable or disagreeable voices in any type of debate.

God tells us to sing. He gave all of us some ability to sing.

There are Christians the Lord gifted with expertise. That one or group of singers release their melodious tune for the world to hear. But the music's presentation, volume, beat, or timing doesn't agree with everyone.

The vital part of Christian music are the lyrics. Do they reflect our Lord by portraying truthfully who and what He is? How are they spoken? Can they be easily heard and clearly understood by *all* listeners?

Do these words draw the singer, instrumentalist, and the hearer close to Jesus?

Is His anointing available and felt by all?

"Be clothed with modesty, also wear an outfit of praise for the uplifting of heaviness" are parts of scripture found in 1 Peter 5:5 and Isaiah 61:3. Does the song, with its accompanist and vocalist's physical appearances, leave the listener flatlined, dead to the Holy Spirit's working and God's blessing?

We've been given the privilege to sing unto Almighty God. It's His will for us to raise our voices in song before Him with love, joy, and humble worship. May it be done in such a way that will inspire even the worst critic, regardless of our musical skill.

Dear Lord, may I bring glory to You and be of some type of encouragement to others as I sing unto You. Amen.

Tell Them

The Lord gave me His words...that I would
know what to say to...the weary ones.

—Isaiah 50:4

My husband and I enjoyed a meal at a local restaurant via a gift card. Our server walked to our table with tired steps and a face to match.

She spoke with her trained form of greeting. We ordered. She delivered the meal with the same weary appearance.

She checked back on us once. Then the Lord spoke to me: "Ask if she has anything we could pray about for her."

On her next trip to check up on the-customer, I asked her that very question. Instantly, her countenance brightened.

She took time to respond to my question. She had no prayer request. We chatted briefly.

It was a pleasure to witness to this lady. Smiles were exchanged. She became a dear.

When the bill was brought, she had given us a discount. She explained it was another customer's unused portion of their gift card. We had received nice savings.

Then her pleasant face turned radiant when we gave the now generous leftover of our gift card back to her for a tip. We also gave her a tract. Gratefully, she accepted both.

Our original gift card was a gift to us. An unknown person's gift card's leftover was also a gift to us. We had acquired a favor from God.

But it was in our giving back that we received a special "I am glad I listened to God's Word" blessing.

Dear Lord, it was fun as I showed Your love to this work-worn lady. I trust she'll be saved, because I spoke the words You gave me to share. Amen.

Truth Revealed

Nothing is hidden that won't be revealed...what we have
spoken in darkness...will be broadcast upon the housetops.
—Luke 12:2, 3

I live in America's northeast. Here winter takes itself seriously. It
seems each day, some measurement of snow must be shoveled.

Our faithful dog Cuddles accompanies me many times I'm in
the outdoors. Often, at these times, he decides to relieve himself.
Promptly, I cover it with clean white snow.

But when springtime appears, these deposits are exposed. The
unsightly dog's wastes are revealed. No longer could they be hidden.

What we speak, do, see, or allow to take place in ourselves can
be kept secret only so long. Persistent heat eventually displays the
truth. Those facts are soon made known.

A cover-up is not worth any shovelful of some assumed clean
disguise. We must consider all of us. How will we react or feel when
that truth becomes known?

Seek God. Let's be pure before Him. Such a lifestyle brings no
issue or problem when eyes and ears are turned our way.

*Dear Lord, thank You for conviction on me that keeps my life
in order. May I always reflect You in all I am. Amen.*

Just Do It

Do not keep back from those to whom
it's due, when you can give it.

—Proverbs 3:27

We borrow, agreeing to repay or return. Then we become aware of a family that has an urgent situation.

What will we do? We've got it. We can deliver.

In today's culture, it's tempting to withhold and not take back or provide for those in need. People are hurting. Finances are scarce.

"They'll do all right," we tell ourselves. "They won't miss the little I have or even what we owe. After all, we can use it for our own benefit."

Responsible? Oops. Responsible before people? Responsible before God? So will we do or donate what's due?

Will we pay? Will we return? Will we give?

These questions are fair. The answer is up to us.

Which direction will we take? What will we say? Will we repay or dawdle and delay, only to replay what we know in our hearts is not ours to stay?

But we would rather keep it for our own selfish advantage. Certainly, it will merit best if we just keep it and overlook that promise or that person or that family's need. I'm sure God will understand. Won't He?

It's foolish of us to ask such a question when God has already given His instructions:

You got it. They need it. You agreed. Give it.

Dear Lord, it's tough to part with the item, time, or money, but I will do what is right. They'll be appreciative, and I'll be blessed. Amen.

When He Comes

Jesus shall come from Heaven...to take us in the clouds
to meet Him in the air and live with Him forever.
—2 Thessalonians 4:16–17

Jesus will be coming when He comes.
He'll be coming for the Christians when He comes.
He'll be coming in clouds of heaven when He comes
For all the redeemed ones when He comes.

Are we ready to meet Him when He comes?
Are we born again through Jesus when He comes?
So we'll meet Him in the air when He comes?
Have we accepted His salvation when He comes?

Are we living, expecting to see Him when He comes?
Are we planning to meet Him when He comes?
We'll be leaving all behind when He comes.
Nothing goes with us when Jesus comes.

When all the above is covered when He comes.
He'll take us high through the air when He comes.
To ride the fluffy, puffy cloud when He comes.
Transporting us to heaven, to live with Him forever, because our
Jesus Christ did come.

Dear Lord, I repent of my sins. I'm born again.
I am ready as I wait to meet You in the air
when You come for Christians. Amen.

Idol?

Before we became Christians, we were in bondage
to idols...now that we are Christians...why do we
return to them only to again become their slave?

—Galatians 4:8–9

Stay from idols.

—1 John 5:21

What are the idols that fill our time, thoughts, words, expressions, activities, and move our hands and feet? Do we sleep, eat, travel, and socialize with it or them? Do they fill our desires? How about televisions, computers, and other types of technology? Do they consume us?

What about the music we prefer, entertainment we watch, or sport (team) we cheer on that pleases our inmost yearning? Do they occupy much of our attention?

Does that house, second house, cottage, fifth wheeler, basic camper, boat, or that lake property absorb our attention?

It is true. A vehicle is necessary to get us from point A to point B. Does that selection pull our strings to drool for a *gotta have a specific model?* How much of our day is wrapped in the whim of that idol?

With our coveted aspirations, do we consider God? Do we allow Him equal amount of time? Do we obey Him? Are we interested or even curious about Him, His Word/instructions, commandments, His history?

Attractions are always available. Whatever we choose above God becomes an idol. It or they can have eternal consequences. What would that be?

May our worship be the Lord our God and Him only shall we serve (Matt. 4:10).

Dear Lord, I will guard the whole of me in this world from potential idols. I want to be clean with no regrets. Amen.

George Washington

He led the way.

—Psalm 78:53

George Washington was born February 22, 1732, in Wakefield, Virginia. He married Martha. She was a widow with two children, John and Patsy. Both died early in life. John's widow had four children. She felt she couldn't raise all of them alone. George and Martha Washington adopted two.

He was our country's first president and known as father of his country. He was the one and only elected to this office unanimously. He never lived in the White House. At the time of his election, thirteen stars were on our nation's flag. At the completion of his two terms, five more states joined the Union.

President Washington spent one quiet hour each night alone in his library and again before the sunrise, and he stayed there until breakfast.

His adopted daughter Nelly said that her father attended church with great reverence. He lived a Christian life daily. Her father was not one to be seen when he prayed. He was a quiet and thoughtful man that did not speak of himself.

Nelly wrote of her father, on February 26, 1833, that it would be heresy to doubt George Washington's Christianity. His life and writings expressed the fact he was a Christian. He didn't act or pray to be seen by people. He talked to God in secret. He assured me he was a Christian.

Dear Lord, George Washington was a faithful, truthful, unwavering, and humble Christian man. May I be as reputable an influence as was America's first president. Amen.

The Report

Whoever trusts the Lord is happy.
—Proverbs 16:20

We heard the news
It wasn't good
It affects us all
That's understood.

Only You, our Lord
Can take us through
Whate'r they've
Planned to us do.

Still

We rejoice
We believe
We know
You're here.

For what comes our way
It matters not
Your faithfulness stays
Whate'r man's got.

We thank You, Lord
You are the same
We give You praise
Your love remains.

Dear Lord, blessing and honor and glory be Thine, for
You always have our welfare in mind. Amen.

Watch the Tongue

No person can tame the tongue. It is full of poison.

—James 3:8

Can you imagine God saying our tongues are full of poison? It's hard to accept but not too hard to understand. I have been the bull's eye for too many active tongues.

I have heard and seen results of busy tongues. They whisper to one willing listener or to interested people. Do these tongue owners feel they are superior and exempt from the effects of pain, saying words that are often untrue or misrepresented?

Come, let's be enlightened to the harm our tongues cause. May we refuse to receive any unkind or uncomplimentary tidbits, hearsay, or responses about any one for any reason at any time. It's the Christlike way to live, act, and be. Our tongues reflect what type of relationship we have allowed the Lord to become in us. What kind of an example do our tongues say of our Lord? Let's bless the Lord with all those words that fall off our tongues. That is true professionalism. No more poison from our tongues.

Dear Lord, it hurts to be the end result of an unflattering tongue. Help me not to be the speaker with the I-know-best-and-therefore-can-judge tongue. Keep my words sweet at all times. Amen.

A Prayer Taken from Psalm 101

Sanctify yourself to be holy.

—Leviticus 20:7

1. I will sing praise of Your mercy and justice, unto You, my Lord, I will sing.
2. Lord, I want to behave at home, reflecting You in all I do.
3. There is so much evil on the television, computer, in newspapers, and periodicals that I will not permit me to look at such images or hear those sounds.
4. I reject any crude and boastful attitude I too often express by my own willfulness.
5. I will not speak ill of my neighbor or wear a proud and arrogant attitude.
6. I shall keep company and make friends with the faithful of my household or wherever they may be.
7. Those wicked people masquerading as friends and those known to be untrustworthy and liars, I will not permit to live in my house. I will be kind and helpful but not make them friends.
8. For You, dear Lord, will bring the judgment upon the disbeliever in this world.

You alone know and understand the truth of and about each troublemaker and will deal with them Yourself.

Dear Lord, these verses are my commitment to You.
May I always display the Christ that lives in
me and be a witness to others. Amen.

The Cat Knew

Jesus knew their thoughts.

—Matthew 9:4

For a few months, my husband and I kittysat our son's two-year-old cat. She was overall well-behaved.

One morning, I got up without her hearing me. When I came down the stairs, she then became aware I was approaching. I heard her jump off the kitchen table. It was positioned next to the sliding glass doors, providing a full view of the backyard.

She liked looking out the window, though it was to be done from the floor. This morning, she got caught in her disobedience.

Down she jumped and headed in the opposite direction. But I, too, went the same way. Instantly, she saw me and spun around. Her fear-filled getaway slid the hall runner from under her feet, causing her to fly across the bare floor. At an amazing speed, she flew.

She knew she had done wrong and was exiting as fast as her feet allowed. She just wanted to escape but could not hide from me. I knew where she was going, and I spotted her in an instant.

We, as well, try to run and hide, disappear, ignore, or excuse what our knower is telling us. God sees and knows our hearts, motives, and actions. Let's not be like a cat running away. Let's live according to God's eye. His awareness is because He cares and is there for our whatever.

Dear Lord, I can't hide from You. So I yield me
to Thee to be as I know to be. Amen.

Money

I sought God, He heard me, and rescued me from my fears.
—Psalm 34:4

G ot money? Think about money? Money becomes important from a child's early birthday gift. The young child soon learns to like money and wants more.

That money love goes on into where responsibilities and wishes necessitates for plenty of the greenbacks.

Housing, transportation, medical and family needs, kids' college, vacations, self-advancement, job-related incidents, political preferences, plus taxes are just a few required expenses.

Meeting all these needs becomes an uphill task to financially manage. The cost of everything increases the pressure to get a larger income. Then that salary begins to shrink when the prices to buy, provide, and supply grow by a large percent.

Livelihood requires money. It pushes the "gotta have" to as many overtime hours, extra jobs, or whatever it takes to acquire more money.

Then the unexpected, unwanted, and feared happens, and those funds dissolve like gelatin in water or simply dry up. No job with no essentials and no extravagant spending possible.

As that child looks to its parent to give them money, we, too, can look to our Heavenly Father for money to cover expenses. He loves us, His child, and understands the request we present to Him, and He will give appropriately as any parent would for their child.

Dear Lord, You know my financial issues. You see the need. I'm thankful You have the answer designed just for me. Amen.

Sign Off

All who are co-signers for a stranger will be sorry.
—Proverbs 6:1–2

Read verses 3–5 too.

Can you imagine what it's like being responsible for someone's else's debt? That is if the individual is a person barely known, or we are unsure of their ability to pay the bill themselves.

We signed away our freedom for X number of months or years, hoping we are being helpful. We're stuck in the middle of having a big and easygoing heart and a person that took advantage of us for their benefit.

Now that person is relieved of their bill because sucker us signed away. They owe the money, and we hope they will make each month's payment as promised.

They may, but likely as not they will forget because the contract was secured with our signature. We did it. They've got it. We're bound. They're freed.

Today, if it is at all possible, release yourself from that burden and accountability of that bill you preferred not to be financially strapped.

You are liable for yourself and family. That is a necessity you cannot avoid. It awaits your daily and ongoing attention and funds.

You are a very trustworthy and reliable man or woman that genuinely cares for people that are having a hard time. Don't allow guilt to slide you to an "I can't get out of it" and sign for another's debt. Use common sense and God's directive. Unfetter yourself from their financial obligation.

*Dear Lord, help me to be helpful to someone's need
but not beholden to their debt. Amen.*

He Leaped

Through faith in Jesus name.

—Acts 3:16

Read Acts 3:1–11, 14:8.
It was a leap year, or maybe leap day or momentous moment, when the beggar man met the apostle Paul.

What a time that was. The beggar knew his need for money was met by begging. It was this crippled man's daily means to support himself. He went alone time after time. He had no choice. He liked to eat, and that cost money. For that he had to beg. So he did. It was his life.

Then arrived Peter and his friend John. Peter saw Mr. Unable-to-Walk Beggar and his financial need. Peter wanted to do something for the beggar, but he had no money.

Peter stopped in front of this man and said, "Look at us." The beggar did so, expecting to receive some money.

Peter admitted he had no money, but he would give what he did have. "In the name of Jesus, get up and walk," he said.

Then Peter took the beggar's right hand and lifted him up. Immediately, that beggar man's feet and ankles received strength.

Mr. Beggar leaped up and walked. His leap time arrived. He had let go of his comfort zone and familiar routine to lay hold on the new and exciting possibility to leap and walk with his own two feet.

He had gained victory because he had let go and trusted in Jesus's name.

Dear Lord, when I speak or pray in Your name,
You will do wondrous things. Amen.

Should It Be Our Way?

We proved we're right, but what truth does the Lord know?
—Proverbs 16:2

Is God convinced we're right? We've jumped all the hoops and gave of our time. We did all that was required to accomplish our passion. That's okay. Right?

The Lord has been watching us. Maybe it was an unsympathetic and exhausting process for us to achieve, but we connived our way through anyway.

We planned, prepared, made connections, plus withdrew cash to set it up. We assured ourselves the undertaking was best to attain our desire.

But God sees the heart. He knows the very part we have craved, saved, and made to present our coveted image. We allowed that specific situation to produce our purpose for us.

The value was for our recognized benefit and to fulfill our determined aspirations.

Its conclusion was designed to cancel any challenge of the way in which it was done.

Our presentation slipped through just fine.

No problem. We're satisfied. We successfully shut all others out of the opportunity we chose to achieve just for us. We're certain our way was correct. Wasn't it?

God does know the why in which this was pursued. But is God pleased with us, the results of what we accomplished, and the effect on people along the way?

Dear Lord, now I believe I was unchristian in the manner in which I proceeded with my selfishness. I give the whole thing to You. Either I keep it or it's given to someone else. You know best. Your will is perfect. Mine is flawed. Amen.

Take Time with the Lord

O God…early will I seek You.

—Psalm 63:1

It takes but a few minutes to start today
In just the right way.
We read God's Word, and pray.
This will guide as we begin
Our day's agenda to win.

Yesterday is gone. Cannot be undone.
We sit alone with Jesus, God's son.
His mercies are fresh each day,
With newness in every way,
All planned just for me and you
In all we must need to do.

When staying,
And praying
We're lying
Life's weighing
For Jesus freeing
Our needing
Then seeing
The resulting
From His answering.

*Dear Lord, thank You for this morning with its new
opportunities. I trust You with help and answers
for all that lie ahead for me today. Amen.*

ER Crisis

It's God whose hand holds my breath.

—Daniel 5:23

It was in the wee hours of that Sunday morning I went to the emergency room with chest pains. My husband drove me to the hospital. Immediate attention and genuine care began for me. A heart attack was expected to be found. Consequently, a nitroglycerin tablet was offered. I took it and remarked how bad it tasted and was followed with a horizontal graphic with its left to right, black to dark shadow and a brief serious indescribable pain.

Then many people hovered over me. Lots of voices flooded around my head. The doctor's face came close to mine. What was their problem? I didn't know.

From someone, I heard I had a cardiac arrest. My husband explained what happened to me. It was discovered I was allergic to nitroglycerin and nearly died, so CPR was applied.

Now awake and alert, I knew God was on the scene. Whatever the reason for me to almost leave this world was unknown, yet God was in control of me, my today, and that unknown tomorrow.

Whenever that drastic, unplanned something comes into our lives, remember God is aware of each of us and the situation and will not leave us for a moment. He will be at our side and guide us the whole trying event through.

Dear Lord, how safe and secure I feel nestled in Your loving hands, and I know nothing will ever happen to me without Your permission. I give You praise. Amen.

March Forth

They cried out to God in the battle, and He heard
their plea, because they trusted Him.
—1 Chronicles 5:20

In what part of our private, social, community, or national level do we have a battle?

How deep into it do we become? Does it fill our days with concerns that envelop our minutes?

Being torn between this side and that one perplexes us. We prefer one idea or subject over the other, and that choice should go the opposite direction in which it's heading. Yet we feel helpless to do anything about it.

We are outnumbered, outvoiced, out of funds, but we continue to feel impressed to stay in there and hang on. We count ourselves as only one, and so we are.

Doing, saying, and being the best we can by expressing our opinions as a Christian should, we march forth.

Exhausted and tired, we fall into bed defeated from the day's outcome. Then we take time to slip to our knees, lifting up our hands and hearts, and we cry unto the Lord for help. We can't do alone anymore.

God is pleased we prayed. He heard. He's there on the scene to take us through the situation to its conclusion because we put our trust in Him.

God never fails. Whatever the outcome, He's with us in its result. Because we asked, He will respond.

*Dear Lord, please help in this serious battle. I'm
out of answers and energy to go on. Amen.*

Lent (Fasting)

This can come about by prayer and fasting.

—Mark 9:29

The season of Lent encourages all participants to give up something for the forty days preceding Easter. This usually includes food. The purpose is presumed to achieve a spiritual or maybe selfish end.

Lent is not mentioned in the Bible, but fasting is. A fast can be done at any time of the year. It can go for one meal, one day or longer, and may include fasting from something nonedible, but it is time-consuming, such as a sport or television program for a specified length of time.

Whatever the choice, to "leave be" isn't the issue. The need to set aside something for a time bears reason of the fast. Its purpose can be assigned by God's directive or a personal conviction that one feels led to fast.

Salvation, healing, wisdom, clarity of direction, and a revival are valid reasons to say no to that specific article, entertainment, snack, or feast.

While we fast, prayer must be included. Prayers for that request should be frequent.

Celebrating the Resurrection of our Lord, Easter, is wonderful. The week prior was terrible for Him but necessary for us.

He endured the scourging and the cross, as the sacrifice for people, nation, worldwide repentance and the other things our lives entailed today and every day on this planet.

Fasting is tough but has lasting results. It's worth the selfless and determined effort.

Dear Lord, today I will start a fast. Show me what to give up and the length of time to do so. Amen.

The But of Proverbs

A good person receives favor of the Lord, but a
man of evil intent will be condemned.

—Proverbs 12:2

*B*ut is a conjunction. It connects two phrases together. The first
one goes one direction. Its second can be opposite.

Have you noticed the many times within the book of Proverbs'
thirty-one chapters the word *but* is used? Have you observed the light
and dark side of those many verses?

I will, but.

It should, but.

Etcetera goes the continuous comparison of good and evil.

Evil would like to triumph, but God declares its reality.

Evil may have its way, but it will never prevail over good, for
God is good. He alone will conquer, bringing His children, all believers, through this earthly walk into eternal victory.

Evil tries to overtake people, bringing them hurt, even harm. Its
purpose is to wipe out the person's own witness with hope to eliminate that one entirely.

Evil will have moments of success. God has placed in the midst
of evil's efforts a *but.*

But God! He is there on the scene and will see the fall of evil.

We need to read God's clear book of contrasting evil and good.

Evil with its consequences.

Good with its blessings.

They are an unalike parallel clashing against the other.

If you chose evil, *but* is there to reveal its outcome.

However, if your choice is good with God's worthwhile merits and advantage, you will benefit.

Dear Lord, I will read and learn results obtained in choosing good over evil. Thanks for the clarity but *shows. Amen.*

Seeker or Not

I will talk in parables. I will tell you the mysteries
hidden from the beginning of time.

—Matthew 13:35

Read Matthew 13:12–16.

The seeker who has much wants more, desires more, is on the lookout for more. Therefore more will be made available, prescribed, collected, and even experienced by this one.

But that other person who has little chooses to only have his or her little, is contented with that little, and does not look for or want more. They will remain with the little.

However, the seeker that has heard of Jesus, sought Him out, found Him, studied, and learned more and more about Him, thus believing and accepting, will profit, benefit, and shall receive much reward.

This seeker then spends time, energy, and aspires to learn more of who Jesus is, and His message to him or her will achieve much from their effort.

Yet the other person, who has also heard of Jesus and learned little about Him, such small amount he or she had might soon be lost.

You who are reading this devotional is a seeker. Today, take, love, and appreciate the amount you now know of Jesus, and ready yourself with an open heart and hand for more of Him. For you will be filled.

Dear Lord, no longer will I be satisfied with the amount of knowledge I have of You and Your Word. I want more, much more of You. Amen.

Which Way Do We Live?

If you confess Me, I'll confess you. If you deny
Me, I'll deny you before Father God.
—Matthew 10:32–33

Culture puts Christians into a tight box. We're pushed in and, often with the lid applied, required not to talk of God, the Bible, or Jesus Himself. We can be religious, but on our own time and out of the public eye or hearing.

Culture believes it knows best and Christians know least. With culture's secular education, it presumes that it overrides anything we have to say.

As a result, there are locations where Christian words cannot be used, but our living, beliefs, attitudes, family matters, and all preach a huge message to that culture. They cannot walk away or ignore Christian living out of their faith.

Reactions of kindness, gentleness, and honesty toward hostility makes an impact beyond words. When possible, speak with knowledge and conviction. Don't beat around the bush or fudge a response.

Our witness is the best way to confess Christ to others. In so doing, Jesus will let His Father in heaven know of our faithfulness.

But if we cower or hide and don't speak of Jesus's love, even to the point to deny Him, we'll be denied before God.

It's not an attractive prospect to have our denial reported to the Judge of all judges. That could be forever devastating.

Troubles do surround us with difficult choices. Let's make our choice with true confession of Jesus, His love, and redemption for everyone. The opposite is worse than risk.

*Dear Lord, opportunities are always out there. May I be
willing to speak, pray, or just live reflecting You. Amen.*

Daylight Savings Time

Ask of Me and I will lead you to the unsaved.
—Psalm 2:8

One more hour is now ours
As daylight savings time pours

Extra minutes, sixty at that
For us to come or go or stay where we're at.

Responsibility asks us what we'll do
With extra time given for me and you.

It's too early in the year to swim,
Picnic, or run with the wind.

We must do something worthwhile
As we wear our sleepy smile.

Get up, get out
Get all about
Sharing the love of Jesus
Here and there
And everywhere
With this time available to us.

God is watching
He is pleading

People need the Lord
Go and speak His Word

He'll be with us each step we take
And guide us to contacts we'll make

At the end of this daylight savings time day
We'll be glad we obeyed God before we hit the hay.

*Dear Lord, I will take advantage of the time You
provide for me to tell of Your love. May I do it not
just this day but every day left to me. Amen.*

Worship with Praise

I will sing praises to God while I live.

—Psalm 146:2

What is worship like in our church? Is it noisy? Is it quiet or maybe blah? Is it considered a song service? Are hymns and songs used or just choruses in that time slot for musical praise before the Lord?

The book of Psalms is full of scriptures* instructing us to worship. What means of music is used in our church during its worship time?

Many instruments and loud voices can be involved. A zither, tambourines, harps, other stringed instruments, organs, cymbals, and trumpets are mentioned in Psalm.

Gentle to loud sounds pour from such varied instruments. Our places of worship may be filled with one too many of these music-making apparatuses.

Maybe within your group of Christians, no implements of music are available. They still can have a wonderful time of worship because we people are walking instruments. We all have hands, voices, and feet.

Clapping your hands, shouting with a voice of triumph, making a joyful noise to the Lord, and dance are included in worshiping God. What a time of rejoicing it will be when we're worshiping with victory.

Quiet moments are also included as we give God praise. We can bow before the Lord our Maker and then lift our hands in holiness.

---

* Psalm 47:1; 81:1–4; 95:1–2; 134:2; 150.

Alone we pray, praise, and worship. Within the church sanctuary, we join others in a jubilant time. Individual or together, we give God glory and honor.

Whatever we have and wherever we are, we worship God.

Dear Lord, You are the Savior of my soul. I worship You. Amen.

The Lord Does Not Fail

The Lord is in our midst… He faileth not.
—Zephaniah 3:5

You are the Lord. You do not change.
Therefore…(We) are not consumed.
—Malachi 3:6

So much has befallen us. Much more lies ahead that we must face. Our times have become burdensome and our future questionable. No hope. No help. Nothing positive is positioned with honest assistance. We often feel alone and abandoned.

Situations, family, livelihood, health, and even the government seem to come against us. We are at a loss and at times feel lost. It looks as though we are stuck and unable to defend or provide for ourselves and those under our responsibility.

The sky is gray. The day looks bleak. Its ongoing non-supportive, unsympathetic hours roll our way.

We lament. We weep. We moan. "Yet patiently, dear Lord, You watch and wait for us to turn to You and Your Word, as we wallow in our woe-is-me negativity."

Finally, we cry out to You as we grab hold of the Bible. We read and study its pages. They say You are dependable.

Because and only because of Your continuous unswerving and ongoing compassion, we are not consumed by apprehension. You promised that each and every morning, we are given a new and fresh supply of Your mercies (Lam. 3:22–23).

We are most grateful for Your faithfulness. You alone provide strength for this day and reassurance for tomorrow. You will get us through.

Dear Lord, today I let go of my despair and accept Your promise to always be there for me. I trust You. Amen.

Lower Lights

Let your light shine for people to see.

—Matthew 5:16

Lighthouses aren't used anymore because today's technology is on board all sailing vessels. This equipment registers any and all treacherous conditions that may be nearby and warns of any potential deadly destiny. The boat can then be moved out of possible trouble.

Whether its dial displaying instruments or the old-fashioned lower lights method used, a "peril is waiting for you" alarm would be given, so the water craft's current direction would be moved out of the path of certain hazard.

The Holy Spirit convicts people about some risk they are considering or involved in. But if the individual doesn't listen, see, or chooses to ignore His nudge, our Christian witness must be their lower lights of caution.

Those old-time lower lights exposed what the ship's captain could not see. A dire danger lay positioned to damage the ship. Warning was given. The ship was then intentionally turned aside.

May our Christian influence signal that man, woman, teenager, or child away from the danger waiting straight ahead that will wreck their lives, and pray they will listen.

We are here on purpose to be those lower lights, casting that gleam of light for those in a floundering wave.

Dear Lord, there are many around that are in or heading to a serious, injurious, harmful fate. Help me to be their lower lights of warning. Amen.

We Feel Low

He remembered us in our low estate.

—Psalm 136:23

Down in the dumps. Imperfect skill. Low in efficiency. Slow to respond. Have little prospects or are a new employee.

Too many mouths to feed, clothe, and house. Slim resources. Health conditions. No diagnosis known. Family struggles.

So many more low estate circumstances come at us all the time. Life generates stressful occurrences. Maybe not at the same rate, but they're just as overwhelming. It almost secures us in a recliner, refusing to move until something good or better is made known.

We've tried, pushed, pleaded, surrendered, and still walk every day with no improvement or change seen on the horizon. "Come on. I need an answer now, please."

Our life's world can be tough, but we are not forgotten. God sees us as we struggle, fighting to stay afloat. Within these hard times, He has been teaching us many things. We understand more today than a year ago.

Progress seems slow, but God is working on our behalf. He is aware and will take us from this dreaded here to the hopeful there.

It will not take place as presumed, but it will happen. In the meantime, remember God has not forgotten us, not for a moment. We are evermore in His sight.

Dear Lord, incidents pile high, making me feel so low. I will work and wait, knowing You have answers for me one step at a time. Next year, I will see all You have done for me, as I have progressed along this my life's difficult road. Amen.

Stuff

For what will it profit a person, if he or she obtain the whole
world? Jesus said… Take notice, and beware of greed: a
person's life does not consists of stuff which he or she owns.
—Mark 8:36; Luke 12:15

S tuff. We have it. A year ago, my microwave quit working. Did I
need another? Not necessarily. We still eat fine. Would it be mate-
rialistic or for self-convenience for me to purchase a new microwave?
Maybe.

Weather brings tornadoes, hurricanes, fires, earthquakes, and
floods across our planet. No one has a choice when or where these
disasters will occur. They could take place in our own backyard. Then
what happens to our stuff? Yuck.

What value would we have with a houseful of damaged or
destroyed stuff? All that remains would be bills requiring payments
on our broken or lost stuff.

God says life involves more than a desire for stuff. Unwanted
and weather that is out of our control (or an appliance breakdown)
arrives, causing our stuff to become unusable or nonexistent.

Jesus said stuff is fleeting. Let's position stuff in the last spot of
our priorities and place our life's value in Christ. His purpose for us
goes far beyond the value of a microwave.

Dear Lord, keep my eyes and desires on You. At times,
You will let me save some stuff. Regardless of what might
happen, You will provide all I need. Amen.

Somebody

Therefore humble yourself under God.

—1 Peter 5:6

It is a somebody I must be
To become as good as he.
I push, I climb, I design
My determined path to align.

I climb up high then look back to see
But the world was not looking at me.
Their eyes searched for the Somebody
To care about them, soul and body.

Too much is lacking, too many hurting
World's answers are just a-churning.
Their home and family's prosperity
Is losing peace and security.

The Somebody that is sought
Will He be there as they think He ought
To see, to know, care and understand
And always available, right at hand?

Pressure, heartaches bend their knees
Checking out God to help them please.
Tears and pain bring whispers and cries
For that Somebody to dry their eyes.

Now people and I admit it is true
That Somebody I'm not despite what I do
It was only me and my prideful desire
Wanting to be noticed where I'm hired.

But it's Jesus Christ, life's certain reality
Ranks the same through all eternity
Remains candid, straightforward, and true
This One Somebody, now, for me and you.

*Dear Lord, may I keep my eyes on You, the only Somebody,
and trust You to take care of my family's day-to-day
needs. In Your timing, You will exalt me. Amen.*

Tomorrow's Change

You do not know what shall be…tomorrow.
—James 4:14

It was mid-March. Winter had slowed down to a twenty-four-hour sixty-five-degree sun-filled spring day. Shorts, sundresses, and flip-flops appeared. People were out and taking advantage of the beautiful day.

I was one of them, out and about and among these "warm-weather appreciated" shoppers, walkers, and open-air adventurers. All voices celebrated the wonders of the sunny day. Such a delightful slice of spring continued till bedtime.

Then the overnight's few hours brought on a "don't forget me" winter turn. Rain, sleet, its mixture, then on to all snow. A gusty wind filled the area with poor visibility and troublesome road conditions. The air was bitter. Snow's accumulation grew with its fine and large flakes.

What a drastic difference from cold winter to serious spring to an arctic chill in but three days. It produced a confused *Oh my. How does one live?*

Living within the weather change of this object lesson clarifies the scripture about a tomorrow. We believe our life's schedule is settled only to receive an unexpected and swift U-turn.

This can be brought about by a change of heart, change of mind, or change of plans in a brisk and hurried *Oh my.*

Dear Lord, nothing or no one is always dependable. On You alone can I depend. You are faithful to Your Word and Your care for me (and mine). I rely on You to take me (and them) through all of tomorrow's unpredicted and needed adjustments. Amen.

St. Patrick

They will suffer persecution because
of the cross of Jesus Christ.

—Galatians 6:12

He was born in England in the late fourth century. He was not raised religious.

At the age of sixteen, St. Patrick was captured by Irish pirates and sold into slavery. During this time, he became a Christian and was devoted to Christianity. He hoped to be able to lead his people from Druidism to Jesus.

Eventually, St. Patrick was freed from enslavement. After a time, he became a bishop. He was sent out to preach the gospel and was met with hostility from the very Druids he wanted to lead to the Lord.

Nevertheless, he continued spreading the gospel for miles around. Through faithful preaching, writing, and baptizing converts, many of those malicious Druids left their idolatrous worship and accepted Christ as their personal Savior.

Because of all that, St. Patrick had suffered and thus accomplished for the Lord. March 17, a religious holiday, was named after him.

Today, we remember this godly man by wearing green for the Irish and having a meal of cabbage and ham or cabbage and Irish bacon.

St. Patrick loved the Lord, enduring much maltreatment to tell people about the Savior. May we, as well, be bold and determined to tell others of Jesus's love for them through our lives, words, and actions.

Dear Lord, St. Patrick spoke the truth. May I, too,
not be afraid to tell people of You. Amen.

What We Don't Know Can Hurt Us

My people are perishing, because of their lack of knowledge.
—Hosea 4:6

Do we know our state has its own constitution? Do we know it credits God early on in the document? Have we ever read it? Is it being taught in our local, private, or home schools? Do they, as well, know a constitution was written for each specific state?

Daily news and conversation often mention the federal constitution. Have we ever read it? Do we own a copy? These media and people will say this or that is constitutional. Do we know whether that issue or topic is written in our national constitution or not? How informed can we pride ourselves to be in such matters?

And the Bible, have we read it? Do we read it? Or have access to one? Because this devotional is being read, it's assumed we have a Bible. Do we know and understand what it contains?

Much is happening in our world, globally, nationally, and locally. Have we noticed anything in the Bible that would describe the events of today?

Progress that's taking place against the world's traditional and Christian viewpoint is increasing with an amazing speed. Its changes are concerning. We're stuck in a state of confusion.

"What now?" We ask. "Where do things go from here?"

Pray, read, and be informed. Share that information. Trust God. Do not be afraid. The whatever is out there, so is our God, today, tomorrow, and the whenever.

Dear Lord, I don't want to be responsible for having a lack of knowledge. Beginning this day, I'll become informed on all counts. Amen.

Nothing Has Changed

That which has been is now and that
which is to be has already been.

—Ecclesiastes 1:9

Brave crocus blossoms poke their pretty heads above the frozen ground, nodding in the crisp breeze. These faithful flowers have bloomed again. They've done so each spring since they were planted some bulb seasons ago. Nothing has changed. Crocuses do the same year after year. It's their nature.

Our world is not different. New laws, words, and sins appearing on the land are being approved because we have progressed to an enlightenment. Results of these actions produce the same effect as was done in times past, but they use a different name or application.

Planted ideas produce what's contained in them regardless of their title. Results of any new thing brings to the surface reality of history's past attempts or action of the same.

People are people regardless of who they are, where they are, or what century they are in. They remain people, and what they think has not changed, history's past explains. Whatever is assumed will be because of current culture. It is only an assumption.

Planted crocus bulbs of any color will produce the same brilliant shade today as yesterday. If one uses different soil or location, the contents of the bulb is still a crocus.

Dear Lord, help me not to be fooled with any report or designed words to draw me into that which has been fully shown to fail. May I keep my mind on You and history's truth. Amen.

Our Vision

> Though your vision…may tarry, be patient…it will be done.
> —Habakkuk 2:3

It was our vision we had pictured, and we assumed a soon conclusion. Yet it did not come.

We allotted a reasonable amount of time for it to take place, and still there's no answer to our dream.

We talk about it and wait for that goal to materialize. Nothing. No response. No results of our wishes. "Where oh where may you be, my inspiration that stays with me?" we ask aloud.

We talk to God. We believe He gave that desire and saw such promise in us to use the gift well. We pray again.

The mental image we envisioned would do well with this goal God placed in our hearts. Still we understand anything of real value does not come to us in an instant. It takes a fair passage of time and plenty of patience. Unforeseen circumstances often interrupt and extend our waiting period.

We are then reminded of God's Words recorded in Number 23:19. He said, "What I said I will do, I will do." This reassurance encourages our wait because God promised, and He does not lie.

When our God-given vision is realized, it will be above and beyond all we had dreamed. Now that's worth the wait.

Dear Lord, the vision was clear and exciting. Your answer will be so much more. Patiently, I continue to wait. Amen.

Leaven

Get rid of the...leaven.

—1 Corinthians 5:7

R ead all of chapter 7 of 1 Corinthians.
At certain celebrations, the Israelites went into great detail to be sure no leaven was found in their homes. It was necessary to prepare themselves for better things with the Lord.

Leaven, for a Christian, involves more than a slice of bread, sweet roll, or a type of pastry. Do we recognize the leaven we're living, showing, and approving in our households and all that concerns us? Do we understand leaven can be very wrong?

What do we do to remove or make sure there is no leaven in our lives? It can personally puff us up, spicing our lifestyle at home, at work, or at play that's inappropriate or downright sinful for any godly individual.

Being greedy, lustful, hateful, mean, and demanding are some instances of leaven.

Stuff bought, allowed, or experienced to be part of us or in our houses rise to expose their truth.

Leaven is junk. It's all around and readily available for the taking. We say no to some portion of that leaven, but we might still have a bit of it in our hearts.

Temptation can invite leaven. Jesus has provided a way to escape whatever may tantalize us in 1 Corinthians 10:13. We need not yield to or add any leaven to our appetite.

Wearing a clean life leaves one with no regrets. Pure hearts produce pure lives. All will attract the Lord to trust us for Christian use.

Dear Lord, I will remove the leaven I've permitted to be in and around me. Amen.

We Are Known

Jesus knew the thoughts of their hearts.

—Luke 9:47

We don't like our emails being read by unintended people. We don't appreciate our landline, cordless, or cell phone conversations to be monitored. We don't want our privacy infringed. Yet today's culture says that's impossible. All we say, do, and even eat is known by someone.

Department stores' cameras reveal our behavior on their premises. Many metropolitan intersections position cameras to watch our driving. Many people carry some type of handheld technology that will photograph people and even record voices.

To say we are being watched is an understatement. Satellites can locate and pinpoint everyone and everything to the very numbers on vehicle license plates.

The world sees us and hears us. So does God. But the world does not and cannot know our thoughts or intents of our hearts. But God does.

He knows our very heart's desires, mental ambition, and planning. He is aware of our private strategies, written-out and diagramed plans, and even that very behind-the-door discussion of those plans.

Nothing, absolutely nothing, goes past God. He's thoroughly mindful of you and me and all that involves us.

What the world sees and knows about us stays in this world.

What the Lord sees and knows about us will play into our eternal destiny.

It behooves us to encompass the life our Lord approves and is proud of, and He will welcome us into heaven as true and faithful servants.

Dear Lord, the world makes me nervous with all its seeing-me gear. I can trust You to know the truth of my heart. Amen.

God Watched Us Do It

The Lord watches me and you.

—Genesis 31:49

God stands on the mountain to see the world.
He watches all of us in our swirl

Jim and John over there
Charlie and Gary are here
Jill and Jane at the side
Paula and Stella did not hide.

They worked together to make themselves a name
Till something goes wrong and the other is to blame.

What happened to their concept and the committee meeting's plans
All that was said and done and spent
For the whim, wishes, and strategies decided back then?

The rhyme could go on, but it's understood people shy away from accepting responsibility of their part and its results.

God allows us to do our thing. We get educated and believe we've got it all worked out just fine. Until that day we trip and our knowledge falls flat, and it's our fault. Now what?

God sees and waits for our humility and for us to admit the truth about ourselves. No, we did not have it perfect. We are not perfect. We have a flaw.

We blew it. God knew it. We got around to admit it. Now, Lord, You fix it. We'll abide by it. That's it.

Dear Lord, I can't do it all. I don't know all. I don't have it all. You do. Please help me and take me through it all as must be done, and all will be blessed. Amen.

Spring Brings New

Winters' over, flowers appear, birds sing.
—Song of Solomon 2:11–12

The first evidence of spring in its seriousness is the appearance of crocuses, followed by daffodils and tree buds to blossoms. Energy springs into action with longer hours for people to walk and do yard work to house cleaning. Excitement grows, sun warms, life is alive.

Winter's long, gray, and cold days slide into the background allowed to become but a memory.

Memories hold unkind, unwanted, and often uninvited facts from recent years and winters. We were part of or involved with that something we now regret. Yet it stays snow deep in our emotions and regrets. How we wish we hadn't done, said, or been what we did back then.

Jesus's resurrection brings new life to all seekers. His death purchased our salvation with forgiveness. We repent. He forgives. We then must forgive ourselves. Let it go and let spring grow.

Newness begins a springtime of renewal. All that was in our history and unbidden, we shoveled away with leftover snow.

Fresh and bright prospects will start its growing in our forgiven, restored, and newly inspired self. Accepting our pardon livens up and brings forth God's nature with vivid reality of our own spring.

New, renewed for me and you
Alive and fresh in what we do.
Spring is here
Fresh and new
To energize
Our now to do.

Dear Lord, spring is most welcome in my Christian life. May I be more Christlike in all I do, say, and attempt to be. Amen.

Loose Tongue

Thou shall not be a busybody among thy people.

—Leviticus 19:16

"Have you heard what she said about them?"
"Yes, it came from a reliable source."

From there, the gossip continues and grows. It causes hurt feelings and damaged relationships.

Our Lord instructs us to talk to the person where an offense comes and get the air cleared. He says we are to forgive them just as He forgives us. But if we do not forgive, we will not be forgiven.*

We're never encouraged to whisper to a cooperative ear any unresolved or presumed issue. Doing so could very well mar our Christian witness.

Tattlers, whisperers, talebearers, and other uncomplimentary adjectives are used in the Bible to describe the actions of people telling sympathetic listeners unnecessary information, even revealing secrets.†

We cannot always prevent gossip from coming our way, but we can stop it from continuing and say, "No more," and then offer caring words. Proverbs 16:24 says, "Pleasant words are sweet to our soul and healthy to our bones." With them, we cannot fail.

Unkind and maybe untrue words bring injury and separates friends. Wholesome words protect and bring God's blessings to all concerned people involved. Let's be healthy by loving and praying for others and not extend hurt on them. Do not have a loose tongue.

Dear Lord, please guard my heart and my mouth that I will not be a source of gossip toward or about another. Amen.

---

* Matthew 6:14–15.
† 1 Timothy 5:13; 2 Corinthians 12:20; Proverbs 11:13; 20:19.

Church Dispute

When you Christians have a matter of one against
another, don't tell others bring it before the church.
—1 Corinthians 6:1

When I was a preteen, the members of my family's church had a quarrel.

Whatever was the reason, it caused such a falling out that we and many others moved to different locations.

To this day, I don't know what the argument was, but I'm more confused as to why large signs were placed in from of each church building.

The first sign read, "The skunks are moving out."

The second displayed, "The saints are marching in."

I still wonder why that church's squabble was brought to the public. Why was this division allowed for a community scandal?

No witness of Jesus, no testimony of His mercy and love, no possibility for His glory to be seen, known, or wanted by any aware of the church's blowup. It was available for onlookers to desire.

I was young and didn't understand. Today, I'm ashamed of such behavior by any adult. It's certain people don't always agree. We never have. We never will. But as Christians, we're to obey God's specific instructions for church disagreements. Involved grown-ups are to pray first, have a mature discussion, and keep it all between responsible people and walls of the church. Its neighborhood should never be aware of any altercation at the church.

Let's remember that people need the Lord and not gossip of some church squabble.

Dear Lord, forgive us for forgetting You and
putting our rights front and center. Amen.

The Church's Body Parts

The body is one and has many members.

—1 Corinthians 12:12

What would we be like if we didn't have all of us? From the hair on our heads to the skin under our feet, we consist of a completed we.

I can't imagine attempting to be me if I was only one finger, one eye, one foot, all nose, with no mouth, no lungs, and no heart. Nothing would be accomplished if I only had a small part of me. I need all of me.

If my foot said, "I'm no hand. I'm not part of me," or the ear should respond with "I can't see, so exclude me from me" (1 Cor. 12:14–24). Sounds silly to think the head would tell the feet, "I don't need you."

Yet we often do this to our Christian brothers and sisters, the body of Christ. We need all parts to function properly. It's healthy and beneficial to anyone anywhere.

Some Christians are public and comfortably noticed. Others may stay in the background, and then there are those never seen or known. But all are necessary to keep the body moving.

Tall parts, large parts, moving and active parts, beating and breathing parts, and small, short, and tiny like pinkie toe parts are all essential to keep the church vital and available for fellow believers, sinners needing our Savior, and minister to people of all ages and sizes.

No stepping on toes, no punching in the nose, no better than those. We all share smiles or tears of woe.

Dear Lord, may I remember the whole body. I can't survive without each brother and sister. Amen.

Unity

How great and pleasant...for people to work together in unity.
—Psalm 133:1

Read Nehemiah chapter 4.

God spoke to Nehemiah. He was to rebuild Jerusalem's broken walls and burned gates. This huge responsibility and equally large burden pressed Nehemiah to get permission to do the job.

After inspection of the gates and walls, he motivated the Israelites. A crew was rallied to do the construction.

To be sure, their enemies—Ammonites, Arabians, and Ashdodites—began a series of discontent about Nehemiah and God's people's work and brought physical attacks on them.

Nehemiah fought not to get disheartened. He encouraged the Israelites to remember God and to not be afraid of the enemies' threats.

Their opposition got deadly serious. Nehemiah applied a plan. He said, "You working men arm yourself with a weapon in one hand, and a building tool in the other. The rest of you men stand fully armed to fight off all attempts to bring hurt and interference in this process."

The enemy leaders, Sanballat and Tobiah, were angry. The repair was being accomplished, regardless of efforts to stop its progress.

They failed because of unity that held firm during the rebuilding. The Israelites remembered Nehemiah's words: "Do this difficult assignment for your brothers, wives, children and homes. Our Lord is with us."

Success. The Jerusalem walls were repaired and secure gates installed. It happened because of unity among the men. They remembered their God.

Dear Lord, Your people faithfully labored side by side to bring Your will to completion. May I be in unity with others to get Your work done in this here and now. Amen.

Winter to Spring

Winter is over, spring rains gone, flowers blossom, and birds sing.
—Song of Solomon 2:11–12

Winter brings gray skies, with its sleet, hail, flurries, blizzard, hazardous roads, snow-covered vehicles, sidewalks, and dreary conditions or maybe a spot of sun.

Months of the heavy coat and boot wearing days grow long. Their length draws the corners of the mouth down to a frown.

Wintertime often involves more than weather. Negative feelings and situations can pile high in our thoughts, blanketing anything and everyone nearby.

Then enters spring with its thaw. Slowly the snow accumulation dwindles. Bright blossoms raise their color above ground. Birds multiply in number and variety, blending their song into a chorus of cheer.

Winter moved out, and spring came in. Response to our difficult situation melts into a smile.

God is at work. He was there all along. He designed winter to grow our faith and trust. We couldn't see what was happening when snow covered our predicaments. Then God displays His worked-out answers for us. Time is essential to produce spring brightness and warm breezes.

All seasons are necessary to keep our earth operational. The same reigns true in our lives. We learn as we work out and through all weather, especially winter to spring.

Oh, how I love crocuses, tulips, and daffodils. Their bulbs were kept safe all winter until God says, "Time to grow and show He's been in the know, when our answers will flow."

Dear Lord, winter is trying. Spring is supplying encouragement and strength to face another day. Yet You are with me through it all. Amen.

God's Ongoing Care

Faith is filled with hope providing what we have not yet seen.
—Hebrews 11:1

March was young, sun more frequent, springtime hopeful. But the heating oil's gauge said, "Nearly out." Finances were impossible. Yet ole man winter did not quit. Faith forced up. Circumstances grew bleak. Responsibilities continued.

Indoor thermostat reduced to a daytime cool and overnight double chill. Outside gave little adjustment. Small heaters were put to active use. Heavy sweaters and thick socks gave welcome warmth. Mmm. It was good. And the days went on.

Romans 8:24–25 reminded us that trusting God means we can look to Him to provide what we don't have or now are unable to achieve.

We must have faith, trust, and confidence in God. With optimistic conviction, our need will be met. This will take place in God who remains constant, true, and unswerving. He is dependable, reliable, and always faultless.

After all we get to breathe because our breath to breath He alone provides for us. Thus He will for all that concerns us.

So March marched on, and our furnace did its job. No casualty to us. God came through. No, He did not do it in our time or the way we expected but exactly as He knew best. Spring came on full time as God scheduled it.

What God has done for others, He will also do for us too. Never doubt. God has not left us out of His ongoing care.

Dear Lord, You have been there for me and mine this tail end of winter. You cared for us in every moment of this month. Thanks. Amen.

Blossom Where Planted

> I will place you.
>
> —Jeremiah 42:10

Very early spring, in our southern New York area, brings out tiny yellow flowers.

These little blossoms do not grow tall. They are snug close to the ground. Each one stands by itself. Others may be nearby, but they, too, are individually blooming.

The soil around these particular flowers doesn't appear to be very nourishing. It looks dusty, dry, and covered with leftover winter's road-plowing gravel. Not a drop of moisture is to be seen.

These flowers grow well on or near the country road's shoulder, showing no evidence of lack of water. The late March or early April's air may still be chilly and the sun not warm, yet these blossoms show their pretty faces, looking cheerful and determined, regardless of the weather or any number of passing vehicles, animals, or people. These small, unknown wildflowers continue to express the gift God gave them right where they are located. Each splashes their color against the drab and lifelessness around them.

Where are we? What surrounds us? Do we think we look small or improperly positioned? God's assignment for us is to flourish where we are planted. When we do, those around will see Jesus in, through, and because of us. We're not insignificant. We are noticed offering encouragement to more than we know. We may be the very ones that makes a difference in some person's life.

Dear Lord, I'm Your specifically designed flower. I will be what You planned me to be, wherever You plant me. Amen.

Whoa, Are We Fools?

Each who trust in his/her own healthy heart is a fool.
—Proverbs 28:26

B oth my husband and I had separate near fatal issues associated with our hearts.

We considered ourselves healthy with proper diets and plenty of walking.

Fruits, vegetables, fiber, grains, and protein filled our day's menus with tasty meals. Imagine the surprise when the heart attack arrived, plus an unknown yet severe allergy. They got our attention.

We were fools to trust our lives to our own efforts. For God alone knows the length of our lives. They are but a hand breadth to Him. All our physical attempts to be in the best health possible is vanity (Ps. 39:5).

Yes, we are to be good stewards of our bodies, but we do not dwell so heavily into their size, strength, appearance, and all that glorifies them. We might be tempted to worship the "beauty of me."

Sensible and *moderation* are excellent words to describe the attitude we should wear toward our physical appearance and health.

We cannot make ourselves long-lasting, forever living, immortal human beings. We are just people created in God's image to live on this earth and reflect Him in our education, employment, family raising, and day-to-day routine.

It's the Lord we trust from each sunrise to sunset and through the night hours for as long as we're given. When the unexpected comes our way, we simply rely on God and Him alone at that moment to whatever may lead.

Dear Lord. You were there. You are here.
You will be with me then. Amen.

Outward, No; Inward, Yes

The Lord sees not as people do.

—1 Samuel 16:7

God sees the heart. We see the exterior and presume to know the individual as a search goes out to find that candidate for leadership.

This person stands erect, dresses well, has correct credentials, talks the talk, wears an attractive smile, and home life seems to be okay. This one has it all.

But God knows the truth about this selection. He sees what intentions and ambitions lie in the heart. We believe we know best and give reasons, but he or she would not be God's choice.

Ask Jesse. He understood, as he proudly presented his seven handsome sons to the prophet Samuel. He was to anoint one to be king of Israel.

But God said no to each one. Samuel was puzzled. These men looked fine to him. Then he asked Jesse if he had another son.

Reluctantly, he admitted he had David. But he was the youngest with no presumed qualifications for such an astute position as king. He was only a shepherd.

Samuel knew God wanted a man that would know how to care for His sheep, the Israelites. Who better than a shepherd?

David had a heart for God, and God knew it. God chose David. His family couldn't see what God knew about this son and brother.

People around us cannot see or know what God is aware of and what actually resides in us. May it meet with His approval.

Dear Lord, use me as You see my heart. You know me best. Amen.

Seven Deadly Sins/Abominations

> When that person speaks "pretty," don't believe
> them. Seven abominations are in their hearts.
> —Proverbs 26:25

1. A proud look (mirror)
2. A lying tongue (speaking untruths)
3. Hands shed innocent blood (hatred)
4. Devised wicked imaginations (agreed to upset or hurt)
5. Feet that are swift in running to mischief (carrying out those plans)
6. A false witness (lying)
7. Soweth discord amongst brethren (gossip with unkind intent)

> —Proverbs 6:16–19

We may know people unaware that they're involved in some of these abominations. The dictionary describes abomination to be extreme, disgusting, and loathing. They sound rather bad. God's definition is one word: *evil*.

News reports tell story after story of someone(s) that lived out one or more of the list. Its result brought pain. Unplanned victims also became targets.

Unfortunately, we, too, can be guilty of some of these, such as wearing a proud look. This could include our appearance, education, or possessions.

At some point in time, we'll be in a location to overhear something. What do we do with it? Pass it around?

To be sure, we, too, will own any one of these uncomplimentary behaviors. To keep safe from involvement with that evil, we must continue to be reminded of these specific seven "God hates."

The best way to stay clear from these ugly seven is to keep our lives right before the Lord, which is portrayed by a pure heart. Our heart sends its contents to the mind. Here it's worked and expressed through our words and actions. They tattletale the truth.

Dear Lord, I will keep my heart clean and
true so I will reflect You.. Amen.

Cricket

God has put a new song in my mouth…
that many shall…trust in the Lord.
—Psalm 40:3

Spring welcomes the chorus of many crickets. Doors and windows are opened to pull in their tune as we enjoy their song.

It's fresh. It's new. It tells us winter is through. Pleasant sun-filled days, warm nights, and color-filled world puts a song in the air.

The backdrop of season's change is flooded with music of life living all around. Critters sound off their love of life and sing their song of gratefulness. All these amazing God-created creatures are filled with the beauty of spring.

Now a cricket is designed for the great outdoors with its special song, but it's to be sung outdoors. But when the cricket comes indoors, it can't be ignored. It was a cricket, that night, that came into our house and sang all night long and into the next day.

It seemed to sing, "People hear me. I've something to say. It's worth a listen. I'm here because God said so. With my tune I'll sing that you're here too because He wants you to be."

What a message to receive from a tune-filled cricket. We have the song that Jesus does love me.

People need our music. Let's keep singing and bringing the words of Jesus's love song to those indoors or outdoors and not be outdone by single cricket.

Dear Lord, You've placed a song in my heart.
I can sing Your message of love with a tune, words, or
by my living that music of Your love. Amen.

That Cricket Again

That God's love might be shown.

—2 Corinthians 7:12

It was a cricket's song that met us each time we got up during the night. Sleep wasn't disturbed, but later, we heard him nearby.

The radio's alarm told us to get the day underway. Cricket was forgotten until we reached the living room and kitchen areas.

This unseen insect greeted us with his "I'm still here" tune. How or why he wandered indoors will never be known. Maybe he was playing a game with other crickets and got lost.

Had he been indoors long before nighttime locked doors and lights-out trapped him? Only he knew.

My husband and I went on a search to find the cricket by following his song. He kept singing his merry tune, maybe hoping we'd discover and rescue him.

His chirping sounded like he was under the refrigerator. So we pulled out the large appliance. There he was, Mr. Cricket standing alone. He seemed scared. It took two tries to catch the little cricket and safely transport him to the outdoors and hopefully to his home and family.

Many people are also lost. They hide sometimes in plain sight. These apprehensive and lonely people make their sounds, hoping we'll find them. Have they been successful? They won't come to us. We must go to them. We're needed perhaps to rescue someone from an unknown or unsafe situation.

Dear Lord, may I be there to hear and care
and be available for that one. Amen.

NOYB

He that walks past and gets involved in someone
else's business, is like pulling a dog by its ears.
—Proverbs 26:17

I've never pulled my dog's ears. If I did, I know what would result. My dog would yelp. If I continued, he'd turn and bite me. The longer I pulled, the deeper and multiple the bites. My dog, any dog, would not be happy with deliberate yanking of their ears.

It's certain pulling their ears would hurt, and that dog would express objection in its best way possible. They'd snarl a warning then bite an opinion. Then we would hurt.

If we poke our nose into someone else's business, it could bite back on us. Publicly or privately, in some measure, it may expose our intervention into something that doesn't concern us.

Often the Lord is working in those people's lives. God uses such opportunities, as we observed, for teaching and directing these people. When we put ourselves into some other person's business, we can alter and even cancel God's work in their lives.

Our unwanted snooping or butting in is really *none of your* (our) business (NOYB). It is simply God's allowance in their lives, and our interference can slow or stop progress.

It hurts them and us to get involved where we should not be. We yank. They bite. Ouch to us, and they receive hindrance or delayed learning.

Don't pull the dog's ears. Pet its head. And those people, you can pray for them, permitting God to work without our intrusiveness. He'll do just fine. We'll be grateful to have no painful regrets.

Dear Lord, I need to mind my own business and
trust those people in Your care. Amen.

Clean Out, Clean In

He saved us by washing away our sin.

—Titus 3:5

Do you like taking a shower or maybe prefer a bubble bath to complete your self-cleaning process? Either way, we do enjoy how they make us feel. Our skin becomes invigorated, and we are ready to face what lies ahead. A shower or a bath presents the physical outside as fresh as possible.

What about the inside? Jesus has the answer to that question. He alone can make us spotless on the inside. It happens the moment we repent of our sins. He then washes us clean.

The bath or shower with its fragrances may bring smiles, but that procedure lasts only for a few hours. It's but a temporary procedure for a temporary purpose. That's all we can do for ourselves—temporary.

But Jesus gives the permanent answer for a real clean you and me. Our bathroom scrubbing works for today. His continues on into eternity. Only through Him can we have the inside wash that makes an outside difference. All those people we have any type of contact with will notice.

May it be our prayer that the witness we now live allows our sin-removing, inside-washing Jesus to become an eternal difference in each one of them as well.

It is good we can wash the outside, but only Jesus can take care of the inside. We must be spotless in and out so others will know the Jesus we're about.

Dear Lord, may I be so clean and fresh that
it will draw people to You. Amen.

Faith, Mr. Cardinal

Now faith is the reality of things hoped for
and belief of those things not seen.

—Hebrews 11:1

We have a Mr. Cardinal opposing the windows on one side of our house. These include sliding glass doors.

It's been over a week. This bright red bird has been pecking that glass. We assume there's a nest nearby and Mr. Cardinal is protecting Mrs. Cardinal and her eggs or baby chicks.

With a family in his care, Mr. Cardinal is doing what he knows to do to remove a potential adversary. He works hard at doing just that.

He can't see any actual enemy, only the window's reflection of himself. Nevertheless, he hopes his efforts are keeping it away. This doting daddy-bird cardinal believes his offspring will get to grow to maturity safely because he is doing all he can to ensure these prospects.

All his efforts depend on God to bring about Mr. Red Bird's hopes and dreams. He has faith in his Creator to do what the bird believes will be true.

We can't see the reality to our request, but we have faith in God. He knows our desires. All those plans we have given to Him to bring about the answer to our prayers.

When evidence seems to fail, faith remains.

Dear Lord, I can't see the solution. I don't understand how it will come about, but I do have faith in You it will. Amen.

These Three—Eyes, Feet, Fingers

He winks with his eyes, speaks with his
feet, teaches with his fingers.

—Proverbs 6:13

What does the attitude of the eye display? Does its wink say, "I'm just fooling around or pretending"? Does it say, "It's okay"? Or maybe this eye's action attempts to pull a fast one by encouraging someone to join in on such attempts. Could that wink be an inappropriate flirt or say, "Come, we'll have fun"? Could the wink of the eye relay a nonverbal message of prior arrangement? Does the way we dress our eyes support a specific message?

Where do our feet go? What sermon is preached as we walk or by the style of our walk (sway, strut, arrogant)? Who do we encounter en route to that destination?

How are our feet dressed, decorated? With whom do we wish to impress, or is it simply to achieve much attention as we walk? Why?

We're blessed with moveable and flexible fingers. They can write, draw, paint, point, lead, and type on to that social media. Are these fingers being helpful, hurtful, or move for self-interest?

How are they dressed and decorated? What impression do they present?

With our eyes, do we encourage? Do our feet bear a Christian witness, and our fingers benefit or bring people to Jesus?

These three are so significant that a single verse was dedicated to them. Our eyes, feet, and fingers express the heart of their owner. What do ours say?

*Dear Lord, may all of me speak of Thee in such a
manner that will bring people to You. Amen.*

Curse to Christ

Christ has vindicated us.

—Galatians 3:13

In His time Christ died for the sinner.

—Romans 5:6

God created the world, its sun, moon, stars, land, sea, plant life, critters of all types, and one couple He named Adam and Eve. He saw everything He made and said it was good (Gen. 1:31).

Then Mr. Adam and wife got headstrong and chose to disobey God. Their "gotta know" brought us all a curse. Thorns and thistles arrived, animals became carnivorous, storms got serious, shaking earth grew forceful, and humans had problems and health issues. It started from Adam and Eve's rebelliousness.

That curse has continued these many years. We're living out results of their misconduct. Everything is cursed, even making creation groan. There is no one, with any amount of education or ability, that can undo what Adam and Eve did. We're doomed.

God knew, at time's beginning, that we would be stuck in that curse. We needed salvation, so He sent Jesus to rescue us from that curse.

He came as a baby and grew to become our Savior (John 3:15–21). He was crucified and buried. The exciting part is that Jesus arose from the dead. He's alive, available today to redeem us from the effects of the curse that affect us in all areas of our lives, *if* we take Jesus Christ as our personal Savior.

This globe and its stuff are under God's eye, but we are in His care.

Dear Lord, wherever I am, there You are; on this
earth, its sky or sea, You see me. Amen.

Death to Life?

I am life after death, if one believes in Me, though he dies, he lives.
—John 11:25

Jarius was a daddy. He had an ill twelve-year-old daughter. He loved her very much and sought help. She was dying.

So Jarius found Jesus (Mark 5:22–24, 35–43). He left with Jarius. When they arrived at Jarius's house, the girl had died. Jesus spoke to her. She opened her eyes. She was alive and well.

And there was a crying mother walking beside her dead son (Luke 7:11–17). He was being carried to be buried. Jesus stopped the procession and spoke to the son. He became alive. Mom received a healthy son.

We know of Lazarus (John 11:1–44). By the time Jesus got to the sisters, Lazarus had been dead four days. No problem. Jesus spoke life into that corpse. Lazarus was raised from death.

These once dead people walked, talked, ate, and lived carefree. Death had been. From child to adult, each had met death and had no fear.

They understood life was brief and probably laughed, sighed, and spoke of their experience and what it can tell us.

At any age, for any reason or no reason, death arrives. These three were given another chance at life.

Today, we have life. We are alive because God said so. May we live so others will know there is life after death if they believe in Jesus (John 3:3).

Dear Lord, help me to live so others will live after their death. Amen.

God Lets It Happen

The Lord sees the ways of people and considers where they will go.
—Proverbs 5:21

Life presents happenings. We don't like them and are often helpless to change them.

"It happened overnight. It happened yesterday. Didn't you know?" We hear.

"Why did that happen? Did I do something to cause it? How am I to overcome?" we ask ourselves.

Through some happenings, a health issue may be discovered, or we are warned of a potential physical harm.

Happenings can be painful. They may have given us the opportunity to reach, teach, assist, be available for someone, or keep us from that thing that could be dangerous.

Sad and tragic events do take place in our community, state, and country. God is aware and allows these disappointments. Somewhere in bad times, God has a reason.

Twice in our family's cross-country trip, we had car problems. Each time, needed parts and funds were available.

Our family needed to relocate. The eventual location saved us from a disastrous flood.

My husband, Lew, needed a triple bypass. I had a cardiac arrest. We're fine.

Within all happenings, we may find an opening that'll help us help someone check out Jesus or draw closer to Him.

When we look back, we can see God was with us in all those happenings, and the reminder He will so continue.

Dear Lord, happenings are all around. That's a fact. I'm grateful
You see me and will be with me through them all. Amen.

King David's Temptation

Do not yield...to sinful desires.

—Romans 6:13

It was spring. King David was to go to battle. Instead, he stayed home and sent another to do his responsibility (2 Samuel 2:1–4). What was his excuse not to lead his troops to war?

Maybe those winter months gave too much hanging loose at home, and he got too comfortable in his recliner.

Now it was nighttime. King David should have been getting ready for bed, resting after the evening meal, relaxing with a good book, or spending time with one of his children. Many possibilities could've occupied those late hours. But he chose to wander out of his room to gaze at what, the stars? Not this time.

He focused his attention on a woman taking a private bath. Her only covering was either suds from a bubble bath or steam from a hot tub. Whatever it might have been, she was minding her own business. King David was not.

He got tempted and minded her business. He should have been a respectful adult and gone back to his room or at least turned his eyes. But no, he yielded to his impulsive desire.

We all face many alluring temptations. The problem is, do we yield or not? It's in the yielding that is sin.

We can't prevent all that passes our eyes. We can determine our reaction.

Today we must say, "Nay. We'll not sway toward any bay that comes our way. The price is too high to pay."

Dear Lord, with Your help, I'll resist all wrongful
temptations, however they may cross my path. Amen.

Zacchaeus

No one can come to Jesus unless the Father draws him/her.

—John 6:44

Read Luke 19:1–10.

Zacchaeus. You know, that wee little man probably did feel he was a little person, a real nobody.

His employment was to take, even force more than owed, tax money from people. Needless to say, he wasn't well-liked. He was financially prosperous but sad and lonely.

Then one day, he heard about Jesus, and He was coming to Zacchaeus's vicinity. What could he lose if he left people alone for a day and tried to see Jesus? Zacchaeus chose to walk away from haranguing people and check out this Jesus person.

In the search, Zacchaeus kept a low profile. He did his best not to be seen. He wanted to do the seeing.

He gave his best effort to seek out Jesus's whereabouts. Zacchaeus did not draw attention to himself. He didn't display any importance. He humbled himself to the point of climbing a tree to be out of people's sight but keep Jesus in his sight.

If people saw Zacchaeus, they ignored him, until Jesus spoke his name and invited Himself to Zacchaeus's house for lunch. Then he was noticed and embarrassed, but he accepted Jesus's self-invitation.

That was His plan, to connect with the sinner Zacchaeus. He humbled himself further and admitted he was a sinner in need of a Savior.

Because of Zacchaeus's salvation and immediate life change, he gave money back to people four times over.

Dear Lord, there are many people that need salvation. Please draw them to You and transform them into Christian examples for all to see. Amen.

Taxes

Pay to Caesar that which is Caesar's.

—Mark 12:17

Taxes no one likes them
But everyone pays them.
They're everywhere
Assigned here and there.
For payment of these expenses
May simply bug us.
People fuss
That they must
Give away
To those they don't trust.
The paycheck gets cut short
Even as the debit score grows high.
Still taxes must be paid
Or the revenuers will wonder why.

As long as we're part of this world, fees, extra charges, tariffs, tolls, and dues are levied against adults. Nearly everyone objects to this demand placed on employers, employees, homeowners, shoppers, travelers, plus in and for many other areas affecting our lives.

Grievances are written or spoken expressing disapproval of that "not another tax." We feel weary and drained from them all. Yet we know taxes must be received to provide for public life responsibilities.

God said we are to do so. When we pay them, let's wear a smile and give a kind word. Proper and appropriate measures are available to express disapproval of some specific tax.

Taxes are a must. Jesus approves. We are to give to the tax collector what is required of us. Pay taxes. Do so in obedience to God.

Dear Lord, I admit I don't like paying so many costly taxes. But You said I must, and so I will. Amen.

Art of Giving

Don't give grudgingly with feeling of necessity,
because God wants and loves cheerful giving.
—2 Corinthians 9:7

A number of years ago, I was asked to donate food for a wake. I was willing to do so and used my favorite unlabeled dish.

After a few days, I checked onto the whereabouts of my bowl. Needless to say, it was unknown. I had not wished to make it a gift.

Well, before this date, I gave away a $100. I was in church. A serious need was described, and offering was received. I wanted to give, but all I had was the $100. It was to be a gift. But ongoing mental pressure put that single bill in the offering plate. Immediately, I was sorry.

It's been many years since those events happened. I remember them well. Now I consider each to have been an unplanned privilege to give to a real need.

I'm sure the money's been long ago spent. However, the dish may still be in use and has become an important tool.

Today. I don't begrudge the receiver of those items. It's been a God-teaching lesson for me to learn not once but twice the art of giving.

If you want to keep it, don't give it, no matter how valiant the cause.

If you want to give it, just do so.

If your feelings are confused, trust in God's keeping and let it go.

The doing of the giving brings the blessing.

Smile. Give God thanks you had it available to give. He provides the reward.

Dear Lord, I did it. It's done. The results are
up to You. I give You praise. Amen.

Tithes

Bring all the tithes to your home church…
give unto God that which belongs to God.
—Malachi 3:10; Mark 12:17

Are we part of a church? Do we attend a service with a group of people at some location? How is that building able to house worshipers on any regular basis?

Utilities must be kept on, teachers need usable material, furniture is essential, maintenance to keep all things in shape, janitors for cleaning, equipment to provide an operational facility, and pastors and leader's salaries are just a few expenses to keep a church going.

If we expect that other person or people will keep the church afloat, they, too, may expect the same from us. Then the church fails, doors close, its ministry not available, people untouched and souls go unsaved, because we didn't do our job. We assumed someone else would give the money required. The church needs our tithes to function. No income. No out go.

God gave no *if*, *but*, or *they* excuses for our tithing. His Word is clear: "Give tithe to the church." That responsibility God places solely on us—you and me.

After all, we simply give our tithe to God via the local church's offering, and He directs the distribution of our obedience.

We give. God does. We're blessed.

Dear Lord, giving 10 percent of all our gross income is one tough lesson. But doing so provides wonderful satisfaction. Thanks for the opportunity to give so others may live. Amen.

All the Way to Calvary for You and Me

Simon, a Cyrenian, was required to carry Jesus's cross,
as He went to Golgotha, where He was crucified.
—Mark 15:21–24

All the way to Calvary Jesus walked for you and me
He took each throbbing step one at a time
All the way to Calvary, painful was His trip for you and me
His groans were not heard as He moved along that path
It was our sin that took Him there
Walking in agony
His many steps were slow and dragged
As He forced His feet to move.
The heaviness of our illnesses wore upon His bruised back.
He continued on because He loved us so.
Such love could only be shown by the Lamb of Calvary.
So Jesus took that route for you and me.
Help did come and carried His cross.
But only He could carry our sins you see
As He went to Calvary.
Wearing the stripes and pressed-on thorns
He inched along for you and me
That trip to Calvary.
There He suffered so much more then died on that tree
'Cause He loves both you and me.
No other way could there be
To set us free from sin that binds you and me.
Jesus did it willingly
Yielding to death's availability
Which laid Him in that stone-cold tomb.
But death could not keep Him in that grave.
Jesus would not death behave.

Out from there He came triumphantly
Giving you and me victory
Because Jesus went all the way to Calvary.

Dear Lord, thank You so much. You came and
gave Your all for us people. Amen.

Jesus the Victor

The veil in the temple was torn in two
from its top to the bottom.

—Matthew 27:51

Throughout the time of Jesus's ministry, He had the religious leader's opposition. They were jealous of the attention Jesus received. These Pharisees, Sadducees, and Scribes wanted it for themselves. To me, these men were "stuffed shirts" wanting more attention to puff up their chest to a larger size.

Jesus was closely and critically watched. He received many questions in hopes to undo Him and enlarge the questioner's self-opinion.

At that date, God's people had to go through these proud temple leaders to receive anything from God. But only one of these men was permitted to go into the Holy of Holies and sacrifice for the people's sins.

This room was secluded by a thick ceiling-to-floor curtain.

After the chief priest, scribes, and elders of the people succeeded by getting Jesus eliminated via crucifixion, they were free of Him, but for a moment.

When Jesus drew His last breath, God tore that heavy veil from its top to the bottom. The Holy of Holies was opened for all to access.

God wants us to come directly to Him because of Jesus's sacrifice for us. There would be no person of any rank or religion between us and God. For Jesus is now our Mediator.

Jerusalem's religious leaders were probably in the temple at the time God tore the veil. Those Pharisees and company's shirts were immediately deflated.

Dear Lord, all my connects with God goes through
You because of all You did for me. Amen.

Then Came Sunday

They found the stone rolled away, and no body of Jesus.
—Luke 24:2–3

Jesus was laid in a cold and dark tomb. He was dead. No life. No pulse. No brain waves.

No evidence of life anywhere in His body. He was gone, and people put Him out of sight.

Jesus was not preaching or healing anyone. The previous effect He had on the townspeople was history.

No more Jesus. No more crowds. All went back home to their pre-Jesus routine. Life went on for all those hundreds that had been aware of His ministry. That knowledge of Jesus seemed to be all defeated now.

"He saved others but couldn't save Himself," a spectator at Christ's death said.

All that was said and done was now done, over, kaput, no more, no way, no how could there be miracles and messages. Jesus of Nazareth was now dead.

Then came Sunday three days after His crucifixion. The earth shook. The guards were afraid. Angels appeared. They rolled away the tomb's stone.

Earth's dark cavity was empty, empty of a body. Jesus was not there. He was alive and well. He arose from the grave.

Then came Sunday for all the world to see and know that sepulcher was quite empty.

Christ arose, and we have victory. Because the very Jesus that walked those streets back then is the same Jesus here today, Sunday to Sunday.

Dear Lord, thank You for the victory received because of and through Jesus Christ our Lord. Amen (1 Cor. 15:57).

Jesus Is Risen

The angel told the women, don't be afraid: You're looking
for Jesus… Who was crucified: He's risen; He's not here.
—Mark 16:6

It was dark but not late.
Midafternoon brought blackness.
Our Savior hung upon crucifixion's cross.
Beaten and bloody was He stretched upon that old rough tree.
Splinters jabbed His body, adding pain to agony.
Though He hurt, He forgave His jealous enemies.
Provided eternal life to the repentant man hanging on another cross.
He didn't forget His mother. He provided for her a home.
His last breath, He shouted, "It is finished."
In living Jesus gave. In death He gave again.
The best gift given was His own life.
He gave it because He loves people.
It was sad that He died.
Where do we go now? He's gone.
BUT NO, LISTEN!
Feel the earth. It's shaking. It's giving up its tight hold on Jesus.
No grave could keep Him.
Its stone could not hold Him inside.
The sky brightened.
Out Jesus came
VICTORIOUS!
He provided salvation so all could receive.
Our Lord is ALIVE.
He's not dead.
HALLELUJAH!
Christ arose!
Let's be telling others of Jesus's love

For all those he's and she's, boys and girls,
young and old and teenagers too.
Let's do it today and not delay. People
need Jesus what're they may say.
Our lives, our words, our actions witness Jesus where're we stay.

Dear Lord, I'm grateful for the victory I have in my Christian life because of Your death and resurrection. May I tell others what You have done for me. It's available for them as well. Amen.

Life of Jesus

I came…to do My Father's will.

—John 6:38

Jesus began life on this earth as a newborn.
He was Mary and Joseph's unplanned little One
Who soon became one tyke of a toddler,
Toddling to the age of youngster.
Now no longer was He a babe in His mom's arms,
But a school boy on His way to learning.
He did so well in His Hebrew studies
That amazed those sophisticated men at the temple.
Jesus was twelve, quite the young man,
Facing adulthood with its troublesome climax.
At the age of thirty-three, Jesus began that earthly ministry
Teaching people, healing the sick, feeding the hungry
So much more He showed and shared to all who would listen.
He did, He said, He walked and sailed so people need not fail.
They loved Him, honored Him, scattering palm
branches beneath the donkey's feet.
Soon it all turned to a hate-filled display of jealousy.
Jesus was spat upon, scourged, crown of thorns
applied, and a yanked-out beard.
All such hostility was put upon Him.
Yet His demeanor remained calm. He said nothing.
Now forced to carry His own cross, Christ
dragged it to Calvary's Hill.
Here He was thrown upon that cross, nailed to it, left to die.
There He hung wearing the appearance of ground meat.
He forgave His persecutors,
Remembered His mother,
Provided eternal life to a repentant criminal,

137

Got thirsty,
Cried out to His Father God then commended His spirit to Him.
Jesus called in a loud voice, "It is finished!" and died.
He was then placed in a guarded tomb of soldiers and angels.
The latter told visitors three days later, "Jesus
is not there. He is alive." They said.
Indeed He was, tomb empty, death conquered, Jesus victorious.
Seen after by few, then many.
Known today by all who'll accept His sacrifice for their sin.
He's coming again for those who let Jesus come
into repented hearts and yielded lives.
Know Jesus or no Jesus
Today don't delay.
For this very Jesus that started life on this earth as that little boy,
Who walked and talked for them back then and us in this now,
He is the only way, our only way of salvation,
this Jesus the Risen Lord.

Dear Lord, for such love I give You praise.
Thanks for being my Savior. Amen.

Post-Resurrection

Jesus should suffer...rise again...show truth
to all people including the Gentiles.

—Acts 26:23

Jesus told His disciples He would rise again three days after His crucifixion. The first glance into Christ's empty tomb showed no body. Angels at its entrance said Jesus was not dead. He was alive.

This very Jesus joined a couple of travelers on the Emmaus Road. They were discussing recent events. He gave them a history lesson up to and including His resurrection.

Jesus appeared in the midst of His faithful apostles. Thomas was absent, later admitted he wanted to see and touch the wounds in Jesus's hands and side. And he did.

Jesus had a meal with them.

Many other people got to hear Him. They believed because they could see Him. His resurrection was no secret. They knew the truth. Christ is risen indeed.

In this day and age, we get the privilege to believe, even though we have not seen or eaten with Him. The Bible and our own heart's nudging tells us Jesus is alive. Plus His unoccupied tomb is available for our eyes to see and fingers to touch. There is no body inside.

He is alive this moment. Take time to talk with Him. Jesus responds to yielded hearts. His resurrection is backed by history, archeology, Holy Land tourists, and scripture.

The risen Lord is with us now even more than He was back then. Today we are able to have Him all the time, each twenty-four seven.

Dear Lord, in all my right now, You are there.
What a Savior You are. Amen.

Earth Day

In the beginning God made planet earth.

—Genesis 1:1

Earth exists because God chose to create it. Even before the mountains were, with God's wisdom, He formed the earth, and He filled it with His goodness.

Then God said, "Let the earth be glad, fields be joyful…trees of the wood rejoice." For the Lord designed the earth to be populated.

He made people, male and female, and blessed them. God said have children (multiply) the earth and have control over the fish, the birds, and every animal that moves on the soil, in the waters, or flies in the air.

Thus the Lord said, "God shaped the earth and made it. He established it." His creation was not in vain. He planned it to be inhabited by you and me and all those other billions of people across this world, plus all the critters above, below, and living on this land (Gen. 1:26–31; Ps. 33:5b, 90:2, 96:11–12; Prov. 3:19; Isa. 45:18).

Dear Lord, thank You for preparing the earth for all of us residents to live on. May we be most grateful for such love and join with the earth and all that's on it by giving You full and frequent praise (Isa. 6:3).

Do We Stink?

You have sinned, be assured it will be exposed.

—Numbers 32:23

I stink and am corrupt because of my being foolish.

—Psalm 68:5

My dog Cuddles corrupted himself. He followed a skunk. Because of this foolishness, he suffered "wounds." He was stuck with the result of his choice. He stunk.

His physical appearance had not changed. He expected us to treat him the same. We could not. The closer we got to him, the stronger the odor. The facts of his acts were evident. He smelled bad.

We attempt to react the same as Cuddles did. We assume our smile conceals the actual truth about our hiddenness. With our veneer efforts, we hope our secret actions don't show.

And for a period. they may not be exposed. Colognes and perfumes can do a temporary cover-up. Our dress will be acceptable, even complementary. We continue as usual and adjust to our own stench.

We can keep going, as Cuddles tried, and not become too concerned about the results of sin. Or we can allow God to clean us up and make us not just look good but smell good too.

For God does know and sees us exactly as we are, where we have been, and what we plan to do. Eventually, He will bring it to the forefront for all to smell the real us.

Dear Lord, when I have done wrong, please forgive
me for such foolishness. Thanks for making me
fresh, clean, and smell new again. Amen.

How Will My Desires Smell?

Don't think more highly of yourself than you should think.
—Romans 12:3

It was a hot spring day as I walked by the pasture. Many cattle were scattered around in the open field except one. This individual animal lay proud on top a large pile of manure. I chuckled at such a scene.

Upon my return trip, I made a deliberate stop and looked for that cow. Would she still be there? Sure enough, there she lay. I watched her stand up, stretch her legs, and settle back onto this carefully chosen mountain. The cow seemed rather pleased with the location she had selected to settle herself.

Observing this animal caused me to question the value of my own wistful desires.

I asked myself what I was attempting to attain for my life. When I do get to the top of my successful desires, will I be pleased? Will achievement of that ambition smell any better than that cow's mountain?

Dear Lord, steer me to an aspiration for my life, that its conclusion will be filled with the sweet fragrance of Your presence. Amen.

Will We Walk Away from Jesus?

> Will you also leave Me?
>
> —John 6:67

Our world is wandering far away from God's teachings found in the Bible. God-believing, fearing, and honoring people once ruled our society. God was central in anything and everything that filled our homes, schools, behavior, and laws.

So much of that Christian beginning is now only a faint memory. Too much has and is happening to change our lifestyle, viewing, hearing, and thinking. It's the desire of many in this current leadership to override and undo Christian beliefs.

To know and to love God, be a believer in His Son Jesus and His life, death, and resurrection is on some individual's agenda to outlaw. If that should become so, where would be our loyalty?

Jesus had many disciples. They followed Him until some felt it had become uncomfortable, inconvenient, or not politically correct. These so-called disciples became lazy, afraid, relapsed, or maybe backslid on their faith in Christ. Whatever was the excuse, they quit following Him. The road looked tough, and those people became soft.

If we are true to Jesus, regardless of what might be required of us, our priorities will work their way through. Now what will we do when such struggles arrive? Compromise expected? Conviction is questioned? Friends rejected? Job gone?

Will we also leave Jesus because following Him would be too hard?

Dear Lord, there is no other place to go but You. No one but You has the hope and help for this life and the words of eternal life (John 6:68). I will follow You. Amen.

Exercise

Body exercise is good...but spiritual exercise is better.
—1 Timothy 4:7

All my life, I've done many types of exercises. Walking has been a preferred choice.

This exercise works all parts of the body.

Recently, I've taken up to walking stairs. Now this one simple process works the entire physical system as it pumps the heart. Ten sets at a time five times a day fulfills my daily exercise need.

Exercise strengthens me to be a healthy person today as I prepare to meet tomorrow. My body grows up and then older. In this lifelong process, some type of a continuous exercise to be healthy and become stronger is necessary.

What about my spiritual health? How do I exercise this vital part of my Christian life? How much reading and studying the Bible, talking to the Lord, and listening to His response are we doing? Do we fill ourselves with godly lyrics and tunes? How about the TV, movies, and other electronic viewing we place before our eyes? Do they contain a Christian value with no contrary words or actions? Do we feel blessed of the Lord when they are completed?

Our daily exercise must be designed to develop us into a strong and healthy, being spiritually prepared with a growing biblical understanding and a true witness of the Lord.

Dear Lord, for me to obtain proper fitness time and a "want to" is essential. I desire to be the best me I can be as a person and as a Christian witness for Your glory. Amen.

Blue Jay Couple

God made them one.

—Matthew 19:6

High on an apple tree's branch were many blue jays. Centered on it were two singled-out blue jays with eyes only for each other. Distractions surrounding them didn't undo their attention for the other.

The other birds flew away. It was clear this couple wasn't interested in them.

Soon Mr. and Mrs. Blue Jay cheeked the other. Their necks reached out until each cheek or side of their head brushed the side of their partner. Then their bills pecked as in a kiss.

These blue jays found the love of their life and were contented with that choice. The other birds were as blue as this bird's spouse. But they didn't draw affection from Mr. or Mrs. Blue Jay.

Their relationship wasn't going to be tempted, torn apart, or drawn to another bird. The couple would remain faithful. This union was pledged, in a blue jay way, before God. That oath the birds would keep.

We people are attracted to one of the opposite gender. Matrimony takes place, and so does temptation.

Let's not be outdone by a set of blue jays. Let us remain true to our spouse. God saw us then. God sees us now. Let's be faithful to that covenant we made before Him.

Dear Lord, wedding promises are met to go beyond the reception. Marriage brings forth the truth of that commitment. I will remain true to them. Amen.

Vengeance

Vengeance belongs to Me... The Lord shall judge them.
—Deuteronomy 32:35, 36

Now they've done it. I am ticked. What they did was wrong, unfair, and cruel. I plan to get even.

They are always quick to deliver unkind deeds. People get hurt. I guess today was the "chosen for me" day.

Since it is my turn, I will turn things around with a serious payback. It is due!

Enough already of all this nonsense. Time for sweet revenge.

With strategy, time, and location, I will scheme to retaliate against those actions. After all, I must stand up for me.

No one is going to fight for me but me.

> I've taken far too much
> Of such harmful stuff
> I've gotta set things straight
> With a well-deserved bait.

God reminds:

> People reap what they sow.
> It's not up to you to deliver the blow.

I respond:

> Okay. No matter what the story
> God'll provide me grace and glory
> And strength needed today
> That I should forgive them anyway.

Results:

Now no tricks will ever be
Able to overcome me
For God's peace within me grew
And sleep reigns all night through.

Dear Lord, I leave the agitator(s) with You. You will deal with the rabble-rouser(s) in Your way, time, and manner. Amen.

Pray and Pray

The genuine prayer of a righteous man
or woman produces much.

—James 5:16

The effectiveness and passion of praying is to be an ongoing heart's cry for that someone or something.

It calls out to God in loud screams, gentle words, soft whispers, unspoken thoughts, worship songs, or a deep groaning, often with many tears. The thoughts about these people or situations continue as we sort out and try to understand the whys of it all. Could I have done anything to prevent this issue from happening? Or help provide a different direction for a godly outcome? Only God knows.

Here I am in this day, right now, with this sore need pulling at my heart. So I must pray. How could I stop? I cannot. I continue to seek God on behalf of that person or circumstance. I plead for God's mercy for a soon and good solution concerning that person or event. I pray again.

I may never see or know the answer to the problem. But I will continue to pray wholeheartedly until God gives me a release. Then I will trust Him for the best results. God has promised my prayers would provide much in bringing about positive responses.

Dear Lord, help me to pray hard every day as if it could be my loved one or that urgent request's last day. May I not stop praying until You bring reliable answers or a complete peace. Amen.

Pray Always

Do not stop praying.

—1 Thessalonians 5:17

"If I prayed for all requests that come to me, I would never get off my knees. How can one always be praying? We've got to work, eat, play, sleep, and go to church. My knees would hurt, my body will grow hungry, and I will fall asleep if I am always praying."

"How can God expect it to be done? He gave me life, and I've got to live and care for my family. That takes daily hours to accomplish."

"There is barely enough time to pray, saying nothing of always," we say.

Significance of this scripture is a reminder that whoever, wherever, or however we are, we are to abide in an always attitude of prayer. Pray when at that specific meeting, while we are shopping, driving the car, riding the elevator, watching a movie, eating a meal, playing with the kids, or sleeping.

Our minds are never focused exactly all the time. Thoughts do stray. So when that issue or name comes to mind, pray. The location where we would pray or its length is irrelevant. Just pray.

Nighttime can have many minutes of sleeplessness. We toss and turn or get out of bed. Either way, we're awake. When that happens, pray. If a person or situation comes to mind, pray. That could be the reason we're awake—to pray.

Praying always is not difficult. What's difficult is to train ourselves to pray at these openings.

Dear Lord, to be in the attitude to pray always I can do. Amen.

The New Christian

The Lord asked, "Who will go?"

—Isaiah 6:8

Read Luke 8:4–15.

Spring means preparing the soil and planting the seed. Sun and water feed the baby plants. It's vital to remove any weeds while waiting for tender plants to show their start. Crabgrass and other unwanted growth force their way beside the to-be-seen young plant. This insistence hurts the plant's beginning. Weeds damage the new start, altering its growth. Soon the vegetable or flowers budding is overwhelmed.

The new plant must have safe soil to grow to maturity. This will be stopped if choked out by persistent weeds. They're unwelcome to the nurturing of a new plant.

All seeds are designed to push for growth. But obstruction of any size limits their effort. The garden needs regular attention to keep harm at bay. If constancy is not there, the attempt to grow viable produce or blooms will be wasted.

A person that has just accepted Jesus as their personal Savior needs faithful assistance to learn and grow their Christian life. Distractions of the world must be kept away or at least explained as to the harm they can cause.

A new Christian needs to be treated as a young tender plant and have continuous protections in each step of their growth, or they won't fare so well.

Dote on them. Be responsible. Instruct and set right any of these baby Christians' ungodly thinking. Be a guardian of their soul as the truths of Jesus and His Word takes root, sprouts up, and blossoms out an established Christian.

Dear Lord, I'll be there for the young and growing Christian. Amen.

Streaks and Smudges

Wash me thoroughly...clean me from my sin.
—Psalm 51:2

The windows were washed. They looked great, and it's a pleasure not to see weathered and grungy glass.

Then I noticed one newly cleaned window displaying the truth of the cleaner's job. The afternoon sun was doing its routine and showed the truth. That very window appeared to have dirt smeared around, showing "I hope you can't see me" streak and smudges. It needed a repeat try on the glass.

Sinful actions, thoughts, viewings, and relationships in time get exposed. We attempt to wash away such appearances, but alas, the streaks and smudges remain. No one is fooled. Truth persists, clear as ever. Only we think it was washed, cleared away, removed from sight.

In the end, truth is known to tattle what is and may still be there. Our meager efforts were wasted. Trying to wash us clean from all the streaks and smudges of the world only produces grotty splatters. Our ability to do the job does not exist. Only Jesus can wash us clean.

He alone can cleanse us from the inside out. But it must begin with a repentant heart that wants the smudges and streaks of sin removed.

Purity of heart comes through and by our yielding its uncleanness to Jesus. He alone can wash us clean.

Dear Lord, my efforts are in vain to clean me up. Make me as clear as a freshly washed window so the world will see the smudges and streaks are all gone. Amen.

Experiencing God's Presence

Did not our hearts have a remarkable warmth?
—Luke 24:32

In our personal time with the Lord, when worshiping at a service or fellowship with a few believers, an uplifting experience of Jesus's presence may be made known. Many tears, heavy sobs, sighs, smiles, giggles, a deep laugh, or an awe-filled quiet are ways we may express that one-on-one encounter with Him.

To be in the very center of God's anointing causes people not to want to be disturbed or interrupted. The experience is so blessed and humbling that words can't describe the wonderfulness of it all.

We may attempt to share or explain this special time we had with God with little success. People will listen but cannot understand because they may not have had any similar experience. When these folks do receive that opportunity, they'll know from which you testify.

Time will pass, and these moments get pushed to the category of memory. Let that not happen. We do need to continue in our daily responsibilities, but let's not leave this experience behind, walk away from it, shrug it off, or forget that heart-stirring event we enjoyed. The very warmth of His presence was too precious.

It remains a continuous reminder that Jesus is near and with us all the time. He is available now with the same power we experienced back then to lead, guide, and abide with or without any physical warmth we may feel.

Dear Lord, you see my heart and will respond to
my true love for more of You. Amen.

What a God We Have!

All things alive give God praise. You and me praise Him.
—Psalm 150:6

We speak of creation and the God that did it all. It is easy enough to believe God created the heavens and the earth and all that's in it, on it, and above it. But do we realize how this planet can respond?

It not only can but does and will obey God's slightest command. He made the sea divide into two sections for Moses and company (Exod. 14:21), the sun to set still for Joshua (Josh. 10:12), calmed the stormy sea for His fearful disciples (Mark 4:39), multiplied food (Mark 6:41), and turned water into wine (John 2:9). Many more reports of the living world obeying God are recorded in the Bible. No argument comes from His creation.

Check out Psalm 148 for a brief list (verses 7–12) of the world carrying out God's orders. Ocean depths, fire, hail, snow, rain, wind, weather, mountains, trees, wild animals, snakes, birds, even kings, people, their rulers, young men, women, old men, and children. Plant life, critters of all sizes and habitats, the out-of-this-world universe, that which is contained in water, ground, or sky above, and all that we can't see or even know exists obeys God.

What a God we have! Everything, everywhere, whatever it is submits to God's voice. He speaks, and all comply. Now what was our question, doubt, concern anyway? God can do so much more than we ever thought possible (Mark 9:23).

Dear Lord, oh my, what a mighty God You are. I give You praise. Amen.

Disagreement

The Lord will do your fighting…hold your tongue.
—Exodus 14:14

Controversies come because we're all different. We have our individual opinion and way of seeing the subject.

Whatever the topic was discussed, we still understand the picture from our point of view. We saw the action and heard the words and acknowledged the quandary. Still, we believe our viewpoint is accurate and our perspective matters.

But the dispute can turn ugly, remarks become nasty, debate personal, and allowing the obstacle to become a hindrance in our Christian witness.

Even though we believe what we know is to be correct, it may not be as we assume. Many things that are involved and unknown to us play into the controversy.

Our stubbornness stands its ground anyway. Our feet are stuck in concrete. They don't budge. We tell ourselves we know the reason for the conflict and desire to do what we can to bring about the solution. It might bring opposition, division, and antagonism to us and others, but we want to tell what we know anyway.

Then we remember a small part of a classic Christian chorus that goes like "hold your peace and let the Lord fight your battles." Whoa, that is one tough call for us to be quiet and let God bring about the answer to the dilemma.

Dear Lord, I will zip my lip and let You work out the contention. May I not have been a stumbling block to anyone. They need You not my opinion. Amen.

God Supplies

And it will happen, before people ask, I will answer
—Isaiah 65:24

It was my chosen idea. I talked to the Lord about it and received no negative response. So with paper, pencil, and a full cup of tea, I sat at our kitchen table and made plans to prepare my husband's ordination dinner. I set money aside for expected expenses.

About two weeks before the deadline, I received an envelope in the mail. Our name and address were on its front, but no return address.

Its content was a blank sheet of paper. Within its folds were five twenty-dollar bills. There was no note or a scripture verse to explain the reason for this unexpected gift.

Why the money? We had no clue. There was nothing pressing at that time. We were unaware of any reason needing more funds. But we did know this financial gift was from the Lord. He had sent it through an obedient source who had been listening to God's voice. His instruction was to send us cash—now. We gave God thanks and placed the envelope and its contents in a safe place.

A week later, it was time to shop for my project. Sure enough, I didn't have enough money. I was many dollars short.

God knew this predicament well in advance of that shopping date and provided an adequate amount to cover the lack. God did know my short fall before I did. He provided before I knew to ask.

Dear Lord, for supplying all my needs with Your abundance and not my meager portions, I give You thanks. Amen.

Smile or Snarl

The disciples were labeled Christians.

—Acts 11:26

I like dogs, any breed, any size, or any color. They are cute, even if they're physically ugly. All dogs deserve a kind word with a fair recognition.

I enjoy trying to greet any pooch within my general space. Their response can come with a *smile* or *snarl*. With each *smile*, I offer a biscuit, or with a *snarl*, I just move on.

How do we as Christians line up when people come near our space? Do we react with a *smile* or a *snarl*? A smile could make a friend, share a witness of our Lord, or maybe offer a helping hand. Now any *snarl* from us closes all doors for any possibility to mirror Christ in even a minute way.

I do love dogs and enjoy satisfying them with a simple biscuit. Dog *smiles* are fun to receive in their own unique way. Their *snarls* are unpleasant and send me away.

But it is people that are important. Whatever men, women, children, as well teenagers' reactions or appearances may be, they always deserve a genuine Christlike *smile*, not a *snarl*.

Dear Lord, help me to be a true Christian and reflect You with a smile that touches hearts. May I never snarl at anyone. Amen.

Fear Not

I shall not fear what my health or any person can do to me.
—Psalm 56:4

Thunderstorms scare my dog. A trembling Cuddles runs confused, looking for a hiding place. He does not like the boom.

When the rumbling thunder begins, I corral my dog and hold him tight, trying to let him know he's safe in my arms. He does not settle, but I try every time.

Our journey through life has fear-filled moments and days and dread for the future because things do happen for which we have no control.

Within many of those terrifying times, we, too, want to disappear. Jesus knows hard times and uncertainties can envelop us in its immediate or prolonged tentacles. We become panic-stricken. Grown up or not, we get scared.

Many scriptures remind us not to fear, for the Lord is with us. He will never withdraw or abandon us. He is on our side and has promised to give us love, power, and a sound mind.

Whatever or whoever may try to get a strangle hold on our emotions and terrorize us, the Lord our God is with us and will deliver us from all difficulties.

Cuddles does not accept or understand my attempts to hold him secure, as the classic hymn, "Safe in the Arms of Jesus" promises.

Dear Lord, may I relax and trust Your loving arms when those unforeseen, unwanted, and fearful times come my way. Amen.

(Psalm 34:17, 118:6; Isaiah 41:10; 2 Timothy 1:7; Hebrews 13:5)

Happy Momma's Day

She is a happy "momma" with children.
—Psalm 113:9

I was dear in my momma's eyes.
—Proverbs 4:3

"I want my momma" is a most welcomed cry for a little one by any momma. She loves knowing her child wants her. She is the one and only to that child. No one could ever take her place in that heart.

Momma has the tenderness, compassion, and hugging needed by her son and daughter. She has the extra sense to her child's feelings and need of notice. This momma is able to hear the whimper or soft whisper of her child among others. This lady is uniquely designed to be just that—a momma.

Even adults think often to momma. *Mom* or *mother* would be their preferred choice of words in reference to her maternal devotion.

*M*ostly affectionate, gentle, and devoted
*O*bserves and overlooks with protective mercy
*T*enderhearted with overflowing tolerant compassion
*H*elpful with immediate and continued sympathy
*E*njoys embracing with nurturing encouragement
*R*enders reliability with vigilant care and righteous example

Such a description of a momma leaves one to understand why she is/was loved. "I want my momma" is a cherished phrase readily accepted from our precious children of any age.

Dear Lord, at times I use those very words concerning my late mother. Memories of her sweet and faithful care are a treasure. She was a masterpiece. Thank You for giving her to be my momma. Amen.

Bible

The Lord gives him/her heart's desire.

—Psalm 21:2

While lying in the hospital bed, I got bored. I chose to have no television in the room and hadn't been there long enough to acquire things to do or read.

I did have a window to watch the morning light, but no sun peeked through its many clouds to brighten the gray sky.

I talked to the Lord about my loved ones and current events and tried to remember scripture verses and words to hymns and Christian songs and choruses, but I drew a blank. So I asked the nurse if she could look for a Bible for me. She agreed.

It was a while later that she brought one. She said she had looked in all the rooms in this section and then asked around for a Bible. I had envisioned a small print paperback copy to be found, but instead the chapel loaned me a Bible. I could use it until it was again needed.

Holding that precious book, I was humbled. God's loving care was there, knowing my personal choice. This Bible was a hard cover of my favorite KJV Open Bible. What a special gift I was able to use, even temporarily. And I did.

May we always be appreciative of the privilege to own and read a Bible.

Dear Lord, I was blessed having a Bible to read. You even had my personal preference delivered to me. What a doting God You are. Amen.

Weeds

The thorns (weeds) grew up and choked them.

—Matthew 13:7

Prior to planting flowers, weeds must be removed and discarded before any colorful blooms are secured in clean soil.

Weeds grow stubborn roots. They're determined to stay, even when they appear to be discarded. They hide themselves, continuing as before.

We all have some kind of a weed that tantalizes our nature. Here we stand or there we sit, pondering the weed. Then we drive, ride, walk, talk, text, or watch to fulfil the whim of that weed.

It starts small with little notice. The more we play with the idea, the taller it grows. No hesitating, stopping, or turning around on our part allows that weed to grab hold and carry on.

We let stay what we refuse to believe is there. It takes over. If we do nothing about the pesky weed, it'll choke out our Christian values and witness.

We're stuck with the weed and the displeasing thing it has done to us. Too bad, so sad, not glad, not even a tad what we have permitted to happen in our lives and on our pad.

Now is the time to get mad and take off the put on. Admit the weed is there. Then repent, turn aside from the weed that drew our heart from the Lord and His will, and become the Christians we say we are.

Let's be Christlike in and through all life's temptations. Remove those weeds and become a beautiful garden of fragrant blossoms attracting people to Jesus.

Dear Lord, I will recognize and reject any weed that tries to lure me in. Amen.

Race

We are in a race. One receives the prize. Work to win.
—1 Corinthians 9:24

It was my first time to be at a go-cart race. My adult son had made his own blue and white and specifically numbered go-cart and was going to race it.

This May evening, my husband and I sat on the front row of the bleachers and waited. We were interested. All ages from preschool to any-aged adults drove their machines around the oval racetrack.

It was fun to watch the small and low vehicles zip around the prepared route.

Occasionally, one spun out or something fell off, causing all go-carts to slow while the object was removed from the course. This troubled situation got set straight. The race continued.

At the end of each heat, as it was called, a winner was announced. With pride, this driver held the checkered flag as he drove once around the track. Everyone cheered.

We, too, are in a race. God set one before each of us. Our name is signed on, and we work our race moment by moment throughout our Christian lives.

We'll have engine trouble, get hit or pushed, lose or forget something along the way, get injured, offended, or set on the side for a time. It's part of life's race.

Take notice of the many around who are cheering us on, assisting when we can't continue and walking with us through our bruises.

They all give encouragement as we run the race set before us to its checkered flag finish.

Dear Lord, thank You for placing people here to
help me through my life's race. Amen.

Faithful Vehicle

Wait on the Lord as you rest patiently for Him.
—Psalm 37:7

Vehicles? What do they do? Where do they go? How do they react? They come in all shapes, sizes, and ages. They are driven throughout the city, suburb, and countryside. All are dependable and go through all types of weather and road conditions, like mud, water, slush, snow, potholes, or whatever comes along.

As you observe each vehicle, it becomes clear that the machine is under some person's control. Not once does the vehicle map out its own destination or schedule. When it's parked, it waits and waits until it's moved. No question. No complaint.

But when this vehicle has a physical issue, its owner takes it to a professional for treatment.

We Christians are under a loving Master. Our Savior wants us to be open and willing to come, go, or stay as He leads. His desire is for us to be obedient to whatever assignment we receive. And if we should become ill, He provides healing answers.

When God asks, how do we respond? Are we loyal and devoted to our Savior as a vehicle is to its owner? Could we be shown up by a vehicle? Would that vehicle put us to shame?

Dear Lord, forgive me for my impatience and questioning
with a why. I never want to be outdone by some vehicle.
May I always be obedient to Your call. Amen.

Jesus or Work

I know your deeds. They are not hot or cold. You should be one
or the other. Since you are lukewarm... I could spit you out.
                                                    —Revelation 3:15–16

Sunday comes. We go to church with smiles among the people.
Our conversations blend with theirs. The rest of the week, we
work among coworkers. Our talk sounds like theirs.

Church and work are two different worlds in which we must
reside. But are we trying to do our best to be one of them, whichever
location that might be?

Then our job requires compromising behavior. Do we accept
with a "That's business. Deal with it"?

How have we chosen to deal with it? Are we embarrassed or
ashamed to live our churchgoing life at work? Are we afraid what
people would say if we lived our Christian beliefs on the job?

We say we know God. But is he the God of the Bible? Do they
know? How then shall we live? We need to make a choice.

We believe we must live in two separate worlds. But in time,
truth exposes itself. Reality pours out which life is the world of our
choice. Our attempted disconnect is noticed.

We are seen. Is that recognition we want? Do we know what we
want? Do we want to be a Christian or not? The choice is ours.

When the validity of a Christian life is exposed, others will be
found to be around.

Dear Lord, may I be a faithful and true Christian wherever I
am required to be, at home, at church, or at work. Amen.

Traffic Light

Jesus is the way, truth, and life. No one gets to God, except through Jesus. You are to witness of Jesus…to all areas of the earth.
—John 14:6; Acts 1:8

*R*ed light reminds us of the blood Christ shed. His blood said stop to the death results of our sins. The *red* light shines with brilliant memory that Jesus willingly gave His life for all people, young and older, short and tall.

Yellow light—don't hide behind excuses. Don't feel there is no need to admit, confess, then repent of sin and accept the sacrifice of Jesus to remove the black blot of sin from our lives. There is no other way to get to heaven but through Christ.

Don't be *green* with envy of anything or anyone. Instead, be grateful for the newness of life received by the shedding of Jesus's blood at Calvary. Use the *green light* as a *go* into all the world and be a witness to what Jesus has done for everyone at the cross.

As you negotiate each traffic light, reflect on the wonder of Jesus's love. Then pray for those around you at that very intersection, in vehicles, walking, or standing nearby. When you drive away, share a smile.

Dear Lord, thank You for Your love for me. Help me to live and speak of that precious love gift to those around me every time, everywhere. Amen.

Ordinary

Finally Pharaoh did let the people go.
—Exodus 13:17

It was an elderly shepherd that heard God speak His deliberate message: "Go tell Pharaoh to release My people from servitude" (Exod. 3:10).

God's instructions were clear. Pharaoh received many visual aids carrying the serious warnings that God meant business. The message was "Pharaoh, obey God or pay consequences."

Pharaoh was stubborn and suffered big time before he set God's people free. Pharaoh thought he had control of Egypt and all people residing on that land. They knew their existence was only permitted under Pharaoh's rule. He was certain his word was law and he could require his will to be done. Period. And it was for many years.

Until this ordinary man named Moses yielded himself to God's clear, unquestionable directions and spoke His commands did final and permanent results take place. Finally, God's millions of people received the exasperated Pharoah's urgent order to "get out of here, like now!"

Immediately, they took what they had with little preplanned provisions and left. Excitement filled the air, spirits, and voices as each freed Israelite jubilantly danced away from their bondage into God's adequate provision.

It all happened because an eighty-year-old man obeyed God. He uses common people of any age to do His will. Ordinary He loves. Ordinary describes you and me.

*Dear Lord, You will use me, even though I
am just me, available yet common, basic, and
ordinary. Wow. Thanks. I'm ready. Amen.*

God's the Same Today

Drinking water was made sweet. Many quails...covered
the camp...manna covered the ground. Their clothes did
not wear out nor did their feet swell for forty years.
—Exodus 15:24–25, 16:13–15; Deuteronomy 8:4

Bread and meat
Oh so sweet,
As were clothes and healthy feet
God's care was really neat

This describes the finality of the forty years God led His people under Moses's direction.

Upon their abrupt departure from the land of slavery, the Israelites displayed happiness, but all too soon they fussed with complaints. These opposite attitudes filled much of their wilderness travel.

They began the trip with no preparation for its length. Lots of fun, family, and corporate opportunities were experienced. Tough times brought them rough roads filled with too much grumbling.

God gave them manna (angel's food), low flying quails to kill and eat, clothing that didn't wear out, and strong feet to walk the many, often daily, miles, yet their gratitude was seldom expressed.

Those miraculously rescued Israelites balked and murmured at what they got (or had), but God took care of them anyway. They lacked for nothing.

That very same God is here today, on the scene in each of our lives and situations. He knows the issues and complications pressing our beck and call, and we don't have enough supply to meet them all.

God will provide the needed supply this day, in the now, for the moment, as well as those days and years in our future.

Dear Lord, You did for them, You will do for me.
I trust Your provision for all my varied needs,
for which I am most grateful. Amen.

Understanding

The person with heart felt understanding seeks
for more knowledge of the Lord. But fools speak
out what they've heard from other fools.

—Proverbs 15:14

People with understanding of who Jesus is want more of the same. They pull up all possible information about Him. These people don't trust their own ideas. Instead, they check out reliable people, places, opportunities, and scripture to research for correct assistance.

This serious desire for learning checks out truths through all appropriate means by media or printed and digital resources. Hard work and effort become aware of the solid facts of who God is. With that understanding, they can't be swayed.

Now that other individual gets convinced in their know-it-all-ness, he or she does not take time and effort to do the research required to know the validity of presumed information. Instead of a double-check on facts, this person accepts another man or woman's word (because it's politically correct) and their data. Such accepted particulars may be correct or not. Mr., Ms., or Mrs. quote those very words and run with them anyway.

Embarrassment will be in their future when the genuine facts are displayed. It is wiser to know the truth, facts, than someone else's personal opinion. God knows best, when He says to understand full accuracy and know who He is and not rely on another's personal bias.

Dear Lord, I will be informed and understand the truth of who You are. When I do so, any other information will not distract or confuse me. Amen.

Prayers Answered

God is…near to help anyone and everyone in trouble.

—Psalm 46:1

I advertised for housecleaning jobs. Calls came. Jobs were accepted. At job no. 1, I found the layout of the house to be a maze. I was confused. Where was I to start? "Lord, help." He showed me the best routine. I did it His way. It was amazing how smoothly that task flowed.

A part of job no. 2 presented a different problem. The side-by-side refrigerator was to be cleaned, but its location didn't offer enough space to fully open its doors.

Refrigerator parts don't bend or fold. I tried every angle possible. Each was met with failure. I thought I was unable to complete this part of my work assignment. In near tears, I prayed, "Lord, help."

Instantly, I felt His arms around mine. He guided my hands to solve the puzzle of removing and replacing glass shelves and vegetable drawers in the nonflexible refrigerator.

The Lord brought answers to my prayers. I needed jobs. They came. I needed direction. I received. I needed an immediate answer. It arrived. God does care about me. You too. He is available in all we need to do and will take us through.

Dear Lord, You are with me all the way, in every respect, and to the hilt right now. Amen.

Forgotten

They may forget you. I will not.

—Isaiah 49:15

Nothing is quite so sad as to learn of a mom or a mommy-to-be who forgets her child. This child is so overlooked and ignored that serious injury, even death, may come to him or her. The innocent child reaps the uncaring of its mother.

Being forgotten by a father, offspring, or another family member is equally sad.

People of every age want to be remembered. Any day, time, or excuse, one hopes, even craves, not to be overlooked and forgotten. Unfortunately, the young, older, or challenged people are set on the side while life goes on for the someone else. That someone else may never come around to care, as desired by the forgotten person.

Never forget that we are not forgotten. We are never unwanted or alone no matter where we are. God is there. He is wherever we find ourselves. We will not be stuck there in our solitude. We have not been abandoned. God is with us because He said so.

An extra reminder of this fact is found at the conclusion of Hebrews 13:5. Here it is clearly stated, "God won't leave or forget us." The confirmation of such words encourages us in our lowest moments. We do not have to go it on our own. God is at our side.

Call out to Him. He's here, available, right now, for you and me today.

With God, we are not forgotten.

Dear Lord, when loneliness overwhelms me, I will be comforted knowing You are with me. Amen.

Never Forsaken

I will never leave or forsake you.
—Hebrews 13:5

I will always be with you, even to the end of the age.
—Matthew 28:20

Jesus, I need You
To stay
Today
And on the morrow.

I cannot
Handle
This life
With all its sorrows.

Your presence
Be near
And guide
So that I will follow.

Hold me close
When things
Around
Seem all so shallow.

I must remember
You'll not forsake
Nor leave me
In life's shadows.

For You'll be there
Watching, caring
In my questionable
And unknown tomorrows.

Dear Lord, I know I am safe and never forsaken in Your care. Amen.

King Nebuchadnezzar

> But even if God does not, be aware we will not bow.
> —Daniel 3:18

Read Daniel chapters 3–4.
King Nebuchadnezzar, a Babylonian ruler, fought and conquered Jerusalem. Four young men were among the captured (Daniel, Shadrach, Meshach, and Abednego).

Nebuchadnezzar began to have dreams that only imprisoned Daniel could interpret via God's direction.

Mr. Nebuchadnezzar got rather proud to have been God's chosen for these very dreams. Thus this king had an image built to his own glory. He was to be worshiped.

Such arrogance caused the three other seized men to be thrown into a fiery furnace. But Jesus stood in the flames with them, protecting each one. Recognizing Jesus as the Almighty God King, Nebuchadnezzar rescued the men.

God seemed to overlook King Nebuchadnezzar's dumb actions. This self-assured king felt confident he was the best of leaders, boosting his self-esteem.

Still, another dream brought Daniel before the king. This time, the message to Nebuchadnezzar was sobering. He was given one year to humble himself. He failed to do so.

Now this arrogant king spent seven years walking around on all fours that became bird claws. He was in the fields eating grass as an ox and wearing the weather on his back of hair grown to resemble eagle feathers.

King Nebuchadnezzar wasn't extraordinary. His heart was full of pride. God hadn't overlooked him. God warned him. That warning was ignored. Punishment came.

What notice have we received? Let's realize we aren't exclusive. We don't want what our self-caused consequences will bring us.

Dear Lord, I'm not exceptional. I'm repenting of too much of me. Set me free of me. Amen.

Be a Witness

You shall be a witness of Me.

—Acts 1:8

Hey there. Hi there. Ho there. How are you there, walking, talking, singing, and praising God everywhere your feet meet the pavement, sidewalk, floor, or deck as you connect with people along the way with the message of God's blessing He has for them, that He has given to you from your life, to family, to things that work for you from morning to late and hours in between while you express, explain, describe His love for them, too, as He instructed you to do?

Making the point throughout each day.
Making it clear to those along the way.

Telling them Jesus loves them as much as He loves you and is waiting to hear from your listening or passing audience, that they, too, are seeking out Jesus to get hold of the very One that made you as bold as bold could be, with enough boldness to speak of Him to each and all of them.

Dear Lord, the greatest blessing Christians receive is when they share You with people. Then results of that hey, hi, ho *are reaped by them. Today, I, too, will speak about You to everyone possible along my way. Amen.*

Many Voices, One Lord

Go and preach the gospel to everyone.
—Mark 16:13

You will be My witnesses…to all parts of the earth.
—Acts 1:8

The brave, the wimp
The short and the tall
Those powerful and the powerless
The young and the old
The artistic and the scribbler
The slim and the stout
The musical and the monotone
Mr. He and Ms. She
Those who can and those who won't
The well and the sick
Tall people and short ones
The educated and the illiterate
The proud and the humble
Athletic persons, clumsy people
Those who forgive and those who will not forgive
The pampered and the abused
Stylish dresser and the unkempt
The sad and the glad
Strong ones and those who are weak
Busy people, lazy persons
Those who are slaves and those who are free
The childless and the orphan
The good and the bad
Entertainers and the boor
Givers and takers

Angry persons and calm people
Those living well and the homeless
Some voted in and some voted out.

Too few have found God
Too many have not.
We must be a voice to introduce,
Be available to inform
The genuine or the flippant seeker,
As well as the quiet or the obvious one
(and those not interested)
The answer to their quest of
Who is God?
He's simply:
Yahweh, the Great I AM.
He is God.
Let us tell them. The time is now.

*Dear Lord, help me to be a witness to people
wherever I am, go, or do. Amen.*

Mirror Reveals

> Let's check out and admit our ways and return to God.
> —Lamentations 3:40

Come on, it wasn't that bad. I was allowed to be what was needed at that time. There were problems that required solutions, and I stepped up to the plate.

The information was available, and the opportunity was more than inviting. So I pulled them together and got the issues solved. Bravo to me.

Certainly the method and its process had questions. But I believed the end results would be worth the effort regardless of hurting what or whom along the way. I did it all on my own conniving route.

And then I take a look in the mirror. There I see the truthful all of me. My face reveals back to me what I did and how I got it accomplished.

My eyes speak to me. My heart shouts that God knows and saw the whole scheme I authored and produced.

He says to me to review what I had just done. He continued that it was a sin. I must admit that wrongdoing I pretended was okay, repent of my sin, and return to God.

I believe I will. It is too painful to have walked away from God. Now is the time to be obedient.

Dear Lord, here I am confessing that wrongful thing I did.
Forgive me so I can be trusted to do Your will. Amen.

Forgiveness Brings Praise

Let's lift our hands and raise our hearts in
praise to our Heavenly Father.
—Lamentations 3:41

We repented our sins, received forgiveness, and were set free from the burden of sin that weighed on us. No more conniving anywhere to do wrong at any price is now my promise.

The planning, working to produce what has been hiding in my heart, I admitted to God. Overwhelming and bruising with maltreatment, causing aching injury is no fun.

That which brings joy and blessed rejoicing is a pure heart with clean hands and a godly life. Gratefulness automatically lifts my hands to my Lord and my God. I give Him praise.

We are all guilty of or responsible for some unkind blunder, an incorrect or improper action that produced an erroneous decision at some point in our lives. Then we recognize and admit that truth to ourselves and to God. He forgives.

Giving God praise which flows with uplifted hands and thankful hearts is real fun.

Dear Lord, You saw it. You knew it. You forgave. I raise
my hands in heartfelt praise. Amen and amen.

Memorial Observance

You do this to remember me.

—Luke 22:19

The dictionary describes memorial to be something that com-memorates or keeps remembrance alive.

The Bible has one vital observance played out for our visual understanding. Here it's called the Passover.

Communion began the night of our Lord's arrest. He knew He must walk the brutal path to His horrendous death via crucifixion.

It was necessary for His apostles to partake in this memorable observance of bread and wine or grape juice. Jesus led His followers through the Last Supper.

Here unleavened bread and wine had been prepared. The bread was readied to be a reminder of our Lord's body that would be broken (whipped and beaten) for people's healing (1 Pet. 2:24). The disciples ate the bread.

The wine was drunk in memory of the blood Jesus would be shedding for our salvation/forgiveness of sins (Matthew 26:28).

Today, most places of worship serve communion on a regular basis. Often this is scheduled to be once a month.

If it's not possible to be part of a church service with other believers, we can provide a memorial of our Lord's Supper right where we are.

Bread cubes, cracker pieces, or something similar can be used as well as any type of juice or Kool-Aid we have on hand. Wherever we are, we can find something to use in remembrance of our Lord (1 Cor. 11:24).

Dear Lord, at church with others or at home alone,
I will remember what You did for me. This is the
greatest memorial observance ever. Amen.

Memorial Day

You have eyes. Can you not see? Ears you have. Can you
not hear? Do you not remember...what God has done?
—Mark 8:18

On this set aside day, we need to remember. Remember who
we are, how we got here, and the people by their active duty,
injury, or death has provided for our liberty.

They sacrificed time, civilian life, families, and celebrations as
these willing, or in the past drafted, people went off to serve our
country and maybe off to war.

We expect our constitution will be honored, obeyed, and
upheld and our freedoms remain. But alas, if we forget, ignore, or
reject our beginnings, we may live to see an unwelcome change take
place across our beloved country.

To help prevent the undesirable, we must get serious with God
in humility and repentant hearts, seeking His face, praying, and
remembering from whence we have come.

Remember the men, women, families, and loved ones that have
and are giving up everything so we can live freely here in America and
value our God-given liberty.

A memorable tribute can be given alone or with others as we
think about these dear ones. This treasure goes beyond price.

Today, millions will be expressing their appreciation to these
armed forces and their love for our land, home of the free and the
brave. Let's join them with grateful hearts for our past and present
military, giving God thanks for these precious people. They are a
treasure which goes beyond price.

Dear Lord, help me never forget those people who gave
their all for me to enjoy Your blessings. Amen.

The Dash

What you find to do, do it well…for there is no work, understanding, maneuvering or wisdom in the grave.

—Ecclesiastes. 9:10

When we go to a cemetery, do we notice the dash placed on each tombstone? A dash is there regardless of age of the deceased. That person's life is finalized by a dash. There's the birth date and date of the demise. What happened between those dates?

All of us reading this devotional has had a birthday. In God's allowance of time, we'll leave this earth. Then there will be nothing left to us but a dash.

Today we are at the age we are. We can't make changes in our past. It is what it is. It'll reside in that dash. But we can improve on today and those days beyond. We get to consider what message, example, investment, remarks, fun times, and our witnessing will be remembered.

At the conclusion of that dash, no more can be added, and nothing can be changed. It'll represent what we have been. Nothing more, nothing less but the reality of us.

There is still time to make adjustments. Our number is not yet up. We have time to reflect Jesus and what He has done in us, through us, and what we would like others to see of us.

May our dash not be a rash of "I wish I had done different." Today, make plans to have a life with a dash worth remembering.

Dear Lord, in time, death will come to me. May my loved ones and all those other ones have seen Jesus in me. Amen.

The rest of my life begins now
I'll be working it through somehow.

What each day may be
Is yet to be seen.
It could be fun
It could be ill
What'er it is.
Is a mystery still.

Choices I make from now will be
On to some good
Or something sad.

There are my friends
And loving family
Walking with me
To my finale.

Even then life doesn't end
Eternal life will just begin.
Where shall that be
That I'll spend eternity?

The completion of this life
Will have come to an end
From here to then
What will I have been
And done
And said
Or repented
Of my sin?
With repentance comes forgiveness.
This forgiveness brings salvation.

True salvation produces change, a life rearranged.
This explains the rest of my life's story
Will someday be history.
And may that destiny
Encourage others to follow me.

It all begins now
As I witness somehow.

Dear Lord, may it be so. Amen.

Our Readiness

Nothing good will God withhold from those that walk honorably.
—Psalm 84:11

Nothing. Absolutely nothing good is withheld from us if we live an upright Christian life. The Lord won't say no.

My first great-grandchild recently arrived. This little boy named Carter is perfect in our eyes. He's the first child to his parents, first to both sets of grandparents, and first to us in the great department.

Carter is a newborn with the world of years before him. If he was able to understand and decided he wanted a car, insisting to have it now, his family would only smile and set aside the request.

Carter will receive many blessings from all involved. They will consider each desire and set a date when it might be delivered if they believe it would be best for him. But today is not that day.

Carter has to grow to a responsible age to handle such a want. When he gets there, his wish could be granted.

The same goes with us. We ask. We get impatient. We then insist. But the Lord knows if we're ready and if our plea is best for us. When we have allowed Him to make us ready, He will provide the answer.

He is our Father and will keep nothing good from us any more than Carter's parents will from him. God knows best. When He sees our readiness to receive the answer, it will become ours.

Dear Lord, today I begin the willingness to trust You
for the best for me and my request. Amen.

My World

Ye are the light of the world.

—Matthew 5:14

My community is the world where I can make a difference. Compared to others, my world may be small and my influence limited. But it's where I am and what I can do or be or care for those nearby. In that arena, I can make a difference.

This includes family, peers, neighbors, coworkers, and wherever I go, including those I have appointments with and people I see in passing. Today's culture is filled with social media. That puts people in a hurry.

In all these areas, I am to shine forth the truth of the Lord 'cause this is my world.

You can't be here. No other person is able to be my reflection of Jesus in my world but me.

My world should portray such an illumination of Jesus in me, that I would be a beam of light shining Him forth. I may be the only person in which that one will see Him. My actions or words could very well be the turning point for that individual. He or she could then find Jesus Christ, the light of the world, as their Savior.

Yes, the Jesus I reflect in my world is to shine and bring a change in the lives of adults, teens, and children, both near and far.

*Dear Lord, may those in my world be drawn to
You because You shine bright in me. Amen.*

God's Up

People's heart's fail them for fear.

—Luke 21:26

Makes you faint in your minds.

—Hebrews 12:3

Get up
Stand up
Chin up
Look up
God's up

Fix up
What's up
We're up
Give up
God's up

Clean up
Clear up
Set up
Fill up
God's up

Points up
Sums up
Time's up
Rest up
God's up

No matter how it's rhymed, God is up to whatever is or will be coming upon us. He is aware and is there to deal with those things, people, rules, laws of any kind in their least or most. However, they are shaped or formed in any arrangement. God is up.

Dear Lord, everything seems to be in a mess. My efforts only bring a headache. Now, today, I will give them to You and trust You, for You are up to dealing with all of them. Amen.

They Don't Fling It Away

Watch the ant...consider her effort and be wise. They have no leader. Ants gather enough food to have plenty at harvest time.
—Proverbs 6:6–8

Ants. They're pesky insects. They come in various sizes and appear most anyplace. Warm climates invite them to our homes. Any room is open season for them to take up residence.

The cost of the house makes no matter to the ant. Financially well-off people have crumbs and food, as well as those on the lower pay scale.

Location of an available munchie is of no concern to the ant. They take time to find them, because all taste fine and will be carried to their family.

Ants work hard to be sure all those back in their home have what's needed. An ant's family doesn't do without. Their cupboards are full every day from early spring to chilly autumn.

Each ant takes his responsibility seriously. He doesn't expect the other fellow ants to do his job. Never! The ant is on his own, no other ant, of any relationship, is expected to provide for a lazy ant that would rather not be bothered to work.

Ants fulfill much more than their size looks like they could manage, and they still accomplish their job for family's corporate sustenance. They do not fling away each potential for their livelihood.

Ants teach a great lesson. All must be industrious, creative, and get up and out to meet the household's needs.

Where does that put us? Are we doing as much for ours?

Dear Lord, may I not fling away any opportunity
assigned to me to do. Amen.

Overwhelming Waves

The great storm and its waves pounded the ship.
—Mark 4:37

Read Mark 4:35–41.

On this particular day, the sea of Galilee was the backdrop for Jesus's teaching eager listeners. At its conclusion, He and His disciples took a boat to the other side of the sea, maybe to rest.

Jesus did so. He took a nap. While sleeping, this sea got all stormy and spewed up heavy winds and damaging waves.

The disciples panicked. They tried to deal with the water's erupted tempest but failed. Instead, the sea shot higher waves, and the wind turned into a monstrous gale. The apostles were scared and woke up Jesus, rattling off their fear.

Then, probably the still tired Jesus questioned their faith in Him. Nevertheless, He stood and rebuked the storm. Immediately, the sea became calm.

"Whoa!" the men said. "What kind of a Man is this Jesus that even the wind and waves obey Him?"

It was perplexing to those followers as it is to us today in our desperate situations. Jesus remains trustworthy and will deal with all our difficulties and calm the angry waves that endeavor to overwhelm us.

The questions given to those faithful disciples are ours as well. Why are we fearful? Do we not have faith in Jesus to rebuke the storm in our lives with His command of *Peace be still?*

Dear Lord, today I put my full confidence in You to
calm my storm and bring me through my troubles and
problems to an unworried conclusion. Amen.

Notice Others

We'll cut as much wood as you need and deliver it to you.
—2 Chronicles 2:16

That cousin needs the lawn mowed. The heavy snowfall over-whelmed an acquaintance. Someone has been unemployed and needs a few things. Did we notice?

How about that unfriendly neighbor? What need may they have? Do we know or care what's taking place in those around? Are we alert enough to offer assistance regardless of the person's identity?

And then of course we could deliver a plate of fudge brownies and a smile to a lonely resident or make a neighborly phone call to encourage someone's day. Couldn't we?

There are many ways we can share, do, or just be available for that individual, ministry, or home church. Needs abound everywhere.

Some ring loud and clear.
Some are there or near.
Some hide in constant fear.
Some hope that we will hear
their unspoken cry and see their tear.

The range and style of desperation varies as the number of peo-ple involved. Do we have or are we the answer for maybe just one situation? We shouldn't want to miss such a privilege. It's critical, Christlike, and even fun to be charitable. Let's make those necessary, supportive, and accommodating arrangements today, for tomorrow we may be the one with a need.

Dear Lord, I am fine and forget others may not be so blessed. I will pay more attention and do what I can to help where I can. Amen.

Not Inconvenient

Rejoice in the Lord. I'm writing to you, to me it's not inconvenient.
—Philippians 3:1

We rolled down our vehicle's window. Why? It couldn't be to see the outside. The view was the same with the window up or not.

In the winter, cold air blows through. Summer heat attempts to take over the car's cool interior. There are many good reasons to turn the handle or push the button to bring the window down.

This time maybe to talk to or see someone. That person might need help. We are in a hurry to get to our next destination, and this non-favorite acquaintance has an issue. To them, it's urgent. To us, it's an inconvenience.

There they were crumbled in their own self-made situation, and we were sheltered in our newly cleaned and fresh vehicle.

The now opened window threw light on the plight of that confused one falling apart on the other side of our self-interested schedule.

Their disorder reminded us of a plight we once walked. Someone else saw, cared, and helped us get up and step out of that "soon to wreck us" incident. They were there. We are here.

With gratefulness, we put up the window, pulled the vehicle to the side, and did what we could to help. It was now no trouble, only a blessing to have been there for them.

Dear Lord, You showed me to roll down the window
and see and be available for that special assigned-to-me
individual. I'm glad I did. It was good. Amen.

Provided a Home

I am the Lord…is anything too difficult for me?
—Jeremiah 32:27

Our rented house was scheduled for demolition. We had two weeks, even with five children, including infant twins, to move. We had a problem.

We called all places advertised for rent. Many were adequate in size and rooms, but they wouldn't rent to us. We had too many children.

"Huh?" We were perplexed by such a response.

Prompt preparation began for us to move somewhere. We were too busy for tears or fears. We told the Lord our problem. He heard.

A lady at church, learning of our dilemma, offered us the apartment over their residence. There were seven of us for this five-room second-floor dwelling. This was a sacrifice for both families.

The truck was filled with our belongings. We said goodbye to the spacious house and "Thank you, Lord" for a place to live.

Early at this new address, an unusual and unexpected flood came through the area we had left. Not only did God provide us a home, He kept us safe from the raging water that flooded that town.

None of us know what tomorrow holds or advanced warnings of any emergency that may happen. God does. He's aware of what it will be, where it will be, and timing involved.

If we tell and trust Him, He will give us peace of mind as He takes us through it.

Often our problems are tough for us, but never for our God.

Dear Lord, You brought us through then and will each and every time any need arises. We are grateful. Amen.

Evidence

Look at me. You'll know the evidence if I lie.

—Job 6:28

In our state, a 5¢ deposit is given back for each returned empty pop can or water bottle. When my husband and I take frequent walks on our country road, these containers are found.

There are times we see a potential deposit. We assume it's an empty aluminum can, only to find it to be a gum wrapper or discarded paper cup. The evidence proved to be not as expected.

This, too, could be possible when a mechanic, electrician, plumber, or caregiver is hired to do a job, and the completed work proved they were not as advertised.

Of course, there's that high school play. Actors looked beautiful in their performance. But when one gets to see them separate from the stage, evidence gets exposed of the real them.

Unfortunately, this can be true of a Christian. Their lives display whether one is what they say about themselves. A shiny exterior, smooth presentation, pretty face, lots of hype, or saying we are a Christian soon exposes the reality of oneself. Live and walk as we speak and not as we may be presumed to be.

Dear Lord, I want to be a real Christian in my heart.
May my life validate evidence to that fact. Amen.

Young Person, Be Cautious

Rejoice…in your youth…but know…
God will bring you to judgment.
—Ecclesiastes 11:9

Young person, it is great and lots of fun to be young. The energy, ambition, goals, family, and privileges it offers are exciting.

Plans for after high school, college, completing today's work shift, this weekend, vacation, and next summer activities push high on the "I am young and can do it all" scale. And you may be able to do anything, go anywhere, become anyone you set your mind and effort to accomplish.

Youth has a lifetime of adventures rolling out ahead of them. All the freshness and newness of independent adulthood makes the future look rosy.

Career grows more promising, desirous things are acquired, and spouse and children arrive, fulfilling the image once only a dream. Entertainment and self-gratification become high on the agenda.

What more could one want but youth, for it has it all or soon to be achieved? Youth sees but abundance lying ahead for their taking. Yet within living out those twenties, thirties, even forty years, serious mistakes are often made. Then eyes open, alertness transpires, and regrets grow because, young person, you now realize the results of all you have done, said, or been.

You will give account to God for each one of those minutes you've walked, ran, or wallowed through.

Today, change those plans. Live for Jesus and His glory, and the final result will be an active Christian life to present to God for that accounting.

Dear Lord, I do desire all the years I'm given that
I will be livin' them for You. Amen.

Young Adult, Remember Your Creator

O Lord, I've trusted (remembered) You from my youth.
—Psalm 71:5

Read Ecclesiastes chapter 12.
Young adult, remember God. He is your Creator. Because of Him, you are here. He designed you and planned you to arrive at this time and be in your specific family with its interesting ancestry.

You are so special. God chose to bring you on this scene. Don't forget your Creator. Honor Him in your youthful todays before those latter years arrive and your living gets altered.

Those days come upon one quickly when

the eyes grow dim,
there's no silver lining future to wish for,
limbs become tired and weak,
the body aches and stoops,
diet becomes unappetizing,
teeth problems occur,
hearing loss occurs,
one loses height,
there's many health issues, or
one becomes fearful of much.

Young adult, remember your Creator today while you are still young.

Spend time with Him
Get to know Him
Read His Word
Accept His Son Jesus as your Savior

Allow Him to lead you through today and on to those up-and-coming days and then into the older years.

Don't wait until it's too late for you to remember God when there would be no return. Young adult, you need God now to walk with you to maturity and beyond.

Dear Lord, I am young. Time does pass quickly. Walk with me each step of my life's way. Amen.

Because God Said So

Being certain of this one thing, that He which
began a good work in you will continue it
on through to the day of Jesus Christ.

—Philippians 1:6

All my small flower garden's perennial and annual plants began summer just fine. They blossomed well for a brief time. Then the appearance of death struck each one.

I considered removing them and replace with another choice. But I didn't take the time to shop. For that I am thankful.

A couple of weeks later, I noticed one white blossom on a dark stalk. It was amazing. Soon my entire circular garden was again full of color. It was like God intervened in my little garden.

When our loved ones walk away from their commitment to Jesus and their relationship with Him appears to be dead, this promise in Philippians reminds us Jesus will indeed do the work needed to bring each one back to Himself. Jesus will intervene in their lives.

Dear Lord, this scripture reminds me that You had drawn my loved ones to You at one date in time. Today You know where they are right now, what they are doing, and the why. You will intervene and bring each one back to You. I only need to keep praying, trusting, and knowing they will return to Jesus. Because You said so. Amen.

Our Flag

In the name of God we raise our banner...even to the top of
any high mountain...for His banner represents His love.
—Psalm 20:5; Isaiah 13:2; Song of Solomon 2:4

Our country has a flag. It has been designed and sized to represent what we, as a people, are.

Each flag is to be treated with highest respect in its display, on special occasions, folding and storing, and not to be soiled or torn. Never, never treat this flag, our banner, with disrespect.

Many wonderful brave men and women have given their time, health, and lives so we can enjoy freedom in our USA. That sacrifice only provides for on-this-soil life. Beyond that, it does not help.

Jesus offered His time and life to provide us life beyond our on-this-earth years. His sacrifice gave salvation to all repentant hearts, regardless of age, gender, or locale. His death brings us freedom from sin.

There has been a Christian flag designed to represent what Jesus has done for us. That flag is an emblem of the Lord I love, and He loves me. This representation beams with cheer, impressive courage, and solid and unyielding faith because Christ lives in my heart.

Raise our hands in praise to God in church (Psalm 134:2), in the evening (Psalm 141:2), and at any time or place (Psalm 63:4). May we lift our hands that hang down (Hebrews 12:12) and raise them high (Lamentations 3:41) unto God in heaven relaying our gratefulness to Him.

*Dear Lord, by raising my hands, I lift up my banner
in praise unto You. They are my flag telling the world
of my love and allegiance to You. Amen.*

Happy Father's Day

Urge and comfort...as a dad does for his children.
— 1 Thessalonians 1:11

F amily provider
A ttentive to his children
T eaches by example
H onors his children
E njoys spending time with them
R elies on God's Word for instruction

A father is to "work by the sweat of his brow to supply bread for the table" (Genesis 3:19). Through this effort, he maintains the care of his children.

Each of his children are unique. Their personality needs Dad's individualized interest, concern, and notice.

Whatever Dad does or plans needs to reflect what he is. Mr. Dad always supports his own words and requirements through his own way of life, the way he lives out his days, and responses he displays.

Whatever these young ones are or progress in their growth, Dad is available with support and continuous encouragement.

Mr. Father finds his children fun. He loves being with them at home as well as on vacation. He takes pleasure in their at-home antics and performances at school and church.

This dad finds his strength and wisdom to be a godly leader in the home and to his children by reading the Bible. He spends daily time with the Lord. Here he seeks and learns how to be a Christian role model to his children. After all, they are gifts from the Lord entrusted to Dad.

Dear Lord, the responsibility assigned to Dad is big. God knows, with Him, each Mr. Father can do the job. Amen.

Shattered

It's best to trust the Lord, than put confidence in people.
—Psalm 118:8

What do you do when your immediate expectations are shattered? You looked and found what you needed but had to wait to receive and got stuck in the on-hold status. Then that unexpected happened. Readily it was available. "Surely this must be God's will. His response to my prayer," you tell yourself but did not double-check back with Him.

The date was set for you to take possession of your choice object or position. With excitement, you go see, and in an instant, you realized this was *not* God's best choice for you. You had hurried the process and got its results.

This was my "oh no, this can't be the one for me" story. After a serious heartfelt conversation with me, I sought the Lord. I needed His Words to get me over this hurdle.

He came through, loud and clear, leading me to two similar scriptures just a few verses apart—Psalm 42:11 and 43:2. "Why are you dejected, disappointed? Why are you discouraged? Now trust in God" because "God has provided something preferable" (Hebrews 11:10).

When your hopes get shattered, remember God's written encouragement. He knows best. He has the best. Trust Him.

Dear Lord, You are there to pick up my self-caused and impatient broken pieces. Thanks for Your condolences and continuance to carry me on to Your perfect answer. Amen.

Let Us So Shine

Let your light so shine...that people sees
what you do so God gets the glory.
—Matthew 5:16

We have many solar stake lights lining our sidewalk. These small summer lights remain unnoticed during the daytime. The bright sky with its brilliant sun, or one filled with clouds, even dark clouds do affect our summer's evening outdoor lighting.

Sunny days give them the best boost. The gray, dreary, or rainy day display a luminous power radiated though with a dimmer light. Either way, they display a sidewalk safe for use.

Negative nature does its best to remove the light's faint or bright glow. Remember, at the back of the clouds, the sun is always shining. Its ultraviolet rays feed solar lights on bright summer days. Those lights would not be put out. Though harder to do so, they push on and do their best. Nighttime's darkness shows those efforts.

Life's sadness, disappointments, illnesses, and harassing days reveal one's light. It might have gotten a bit faint, but they're there nevertheless.

Life does lay shadows and dullness across our way. Those Christlike paths we walk will shine on; even to us, they seem lessened. They are not put out.

Tough times still bring light
Remembering God's cloudless constancy
This light continues throughout life's darkest night.

*Dear Lord, may the light of Your presence never
leave my countenance and witness. Amen.*

Reap

Say to the righteous, it shall go well with you, for
you will eat the benefits of your efforts.
—Isaiah 3:10

We often quote the scripture "One will reap what has been sown" (Galatians 6:7).

When I plant a garden, I will reap maturity of the seed placed in the prepared ground. I will get more and greater of what I had planted.

A tiny, almost insignificant-sized seed is laid in a dug-out row. It's watered and left to do its thing.

Days pass. Nothing is noticed. Then the seeds beginning is very small. But it grows and grows until the matured vegetable is ready to be harvested.

What I am able to take from the garden has become multiple sizes larger than planted. But I get to reap the delicious vegetable.

And then there are our words and actions that produce positiveness or negativity. But as we plant those seeds and they, too, do their thing, sadness or gladness comes forth. It's so true that all we've said or done will develop into the results of what was planted.

Its beginning grows to a fulfillment of what was sown. We get to eat the fruit thereof. May it be helpful and favorable. Good tastes best.

Dear Lord, I get to reap the fruit of my hands, words, and attitude. May it bring glory to You and blessing to me. Amen.

Strawberry Test

I hear Thy voice in the morning. For in You I do trust.
—Psalm 143:8

It was the season to pick strawberries. Rain had been forecast for this day—70 percent. I felt the urgency that God was directing this time-slot trip, yet I was concerned about the weather.

Our many a mile drive to the strawberry-picking-fields continued off the expressway. Two lanes into and through small towns required slow speeds for umpteen miles. With rain scheduled to arrive, it gave the desire to hurry the trip.

I hate getting behind vehicles larger than mine. Sure enough, for most of the route, we saw the backside of those extra wide and high. We couldn't pass and were forced to drive at a crawl.

I was stressed. The sky showed clouds. We tried to encourage each other with little success. The only encouragement I received was the Lord reminding me to trust Him. I couldn't see any sun but could almost see God's smile. I tried to believe all would be fine.

By the time we arrived, the sun was bright. The fat strawberries were plentiful. Within a short period, we had our thirty-two quarts, paid our dues, and left for home.

The promised rain did arrive before we entered our hometown and stopped before we got to our driveway. It was only after our strawberries were unloaded did the rain return, and it did aplenty.

God sent this test our way. He had everything under control. We were only to trust. He comes through every time.

Dear Lord, I passed the test. This makes me
stronger for next time. Amen.

Unplanned

That way seems okay to me, but its conclusion brings death.
—Proverbs 14:12

Taking the wrong medicine, eating the wrong food, and connecting with the wrong bee can be hazardous to one's health.

Results will swirl us out of control, hurling every cell and fiber in our bodies to the sphere of trouble, rearing our heads into a dizzy spin and soaring our physical system toward a violent collapse. How long would it take before our heart flatlines a disaster?

The inner parts of our body may feel the ensuing tragedy, or that sudden destruction may appear without advance notice. Emergency response must be on the scene, or life's pronouncement may not be favorable.

We dabble in passing whims that expose hidden passions. This itch urges our weakness to yield to its allurements.

Surrendering to the inclination of some type of self-promise may produce an unflattering single punch causing humiliation, embarrassment, or a critical, grim, and sobering downfall.

This can injure more than health, like marriage, family, friendships, finances, employment, privileges of varied interest, when we allow ourselves to go, do, or take the incorrect, inappropriate, or ill-advised route. This we may have unintentionally titled "My Personal Unplanned Road to Self-Destruct."

Wrong that is consumed or experienced can be deadly, not worth its taste or touch.

Dear Lord, too often I'm convinced I know what's best for me. You know my opinion and what it'll do to me. Please take charge of all my decisions. Amen.

Riches

Accumulate no treasures on this earth, for moth
and rust destroys, and thieves steal.
—Matthew 6:19

In our area, tornadoes are not a normal issue. One came through anyway, causing much property damage.

Explosions as well are a rarity. Unfortunately, this, too, took place locally. It happened to the home of a friend. Their house was flattened.

And then there's my son with the loss of his house. His family had just moved into their new apartment when a fire destroyed the building and all its contents.

Along come accidents that abruptly destroy our very special or expensive vehicles.

We never know when the unexpected will hit us. It could happen anytime. The loss of belongings brings on an *oh my* and a *why*. Things are gone, rarely to return. Replacements are often impossible or too costly.

I have heard it said. "Riches may come," but I add, "may quickly go." How would we feel at the loss of our possessions? Empty-handed, I'm sure.

Because of Jesus's love, only people get to go beyond this world. Now that's true riches. Such value is so out of this world which no earthly hazard could ever destroy.

Dear Lord, help me to be ready when the unexpected comes. Amen.

Marriage—Uneven Is Evened Out

Love is strong…marriage is honorable to each partner…
God made them husband and wife to become as one.
    —Song of Solomon 8:6; Hebrews 13:4; Matthew 19:5

One is in love with money, position, location, and recognition and then decides to get married to a person. That marriage put One together with Another, which now wears the name Spouse.

The relationship was fine until Spouse expected to be One's first love. But alas, the heart of One belonged to selfish financial benefits, job promotion, prominence, or some preferred status.

Spouse had to take second, third, and even fourth place in the heart of One.

Spouse hurt. Words came. A rough path grew. The debate progressed.

"Oh no. Oh my. Oh dear. Why?"

No solution came until One admitted and repented to Spouse and to Jesus for their selfishness. With Jesus now allowed to be at the very top of their marriage, true unsubstituted love begins and reigns.

When Jesus became number one in their relationship, when both partners became a willing second love "of each for the other," any and all other selfish loves became non-tempting.

Dear Lord, after our love for You, You made us as One and Spouse,
and our love of each for the other to be and remain Mr. and Mrs.
Unsubstituted Couple. For that we give You praise. Amen.

Cuddles's Favorite Chair

He chose us to be His own.

—Psalm 33:12

I have a narrow second-floor room I call the Upper Room. Here I spend many daily minutes alone with God. At some point during devotions, my dog Cuddles joins me.

Two folding lawn chairs are set on either side of me. A pillow and small afghan are placed in one chair. A larger afghan blanket, folded many times, is set in the second one.

Either chair, to my assumption, was soft and cushy. These comfortable chairs are readied for my spoiled dog. He uses both.

This particular day, chair 2 was needed to be used outdoors. It had been taken with plans to return. But that didn't happen in the same day.

Next morning arrived. Cuddles came in to join me, and he noticed the chair with the afghan blanket was missing. He was beyond confused. He looked, smelled, and walked around the area many times, looking for the chair.

He did jump up into the other chair, turned around, and jumped back down. He was back to the second chair's area and stood perplexed.

Carefully, I laid out the afghan blanket for him to snuggle. After giving it a full once-over, Cuddles settled into this blanket.

He chose that chair and its blanket. A substitute would not do.

God has chosen us. We're created to do what God planned for us to do. We're His choice for that specificity. No one else can do the job quite like us. We're designed for it.

We are His choice.

Dear Lord, with Your help, I will accomplish
what You created me to do. Amen.

Vow

When we vow a vow before God, and lack to come through
with it, for God requires it of us, we would have sinned.
—Deuteronomy 23:21

At some point in time, we stand before a minister, a judge, an official, or some group leader and say, "I will," "I do," or "So help me God."

Some of these promises are easy, difficult, or lengthy. They may be as basic as a committee member accepting a position or an elected political candidate swearing in to office. Each stands at attention and raises one hand, consenting to uphold the assigned job with sincerity. Whatever the reason to vow, the individual must keep that vow as stated.

When that situation or opportunity presents itself for our approval, we answer with yes or no. If we have any hint that agreed arrangement will not be in our best interest or is not God's will, we should not do the pledge.

The choice is ours. Either way, let's be remembered as a man or a woman of honor, a person of our word living truth before God.

Do we vow? Do we say I approve, swear, promise, or shake hands in any flippant manner? Do we assume it's no big deal? We may, but God does not.

When we say we will give or do or go or speak or accept, we vow. God hears. He expects us to come through or provide to the specific process negotiated.

What we say we will do, let's do it. Period!

*Dear Lord, I am guilty. I will be careful what
I commit myself to do. Amen.*

Trusting Chipmunk

Be sober, be vigilant, because your enemy the devil is like a
roaring lion, sneaking around seeking who he can destroy.
—1 Peter 5:8

Our large open feeder offered bread, popcorn, birdseed, or any
appropriate food to make a meal for small animals.

One particular chipmunk made regular visits for food pieces.
These, I assumed, were taken back to his home. I enjoyed watching
the small animal do his thing to provide for his family.

After many of these trips, I saw a stray cat crossing the backyard.
He had a wiggling little creature in his mouth. Brazenly, that cat had
grabbed the chipmunk to devour. I was helpless to do anything for
the defenseless critter. This chipmunk had become too comfortable
with the seeming safety of the feeder.

Clearly that cat stalked the trusting chipmunk. He had not
been watchful to possible danger lurking about. Thus the chipmunk
was caught by his enemy.

If we are not alert, the same is possible for us. We can't become
comfortable with life as usual. Our enemy has his eye on us. At the
most unexpected and vulnerable moment, he will latch on and bring
us harm.

Dear Lord, keep me aware of all that's going on around me.
Thank You for true security I have in You. Amen.

Life's Journey

The thoughts of the Lord's heart goes to all generations.
—Psalm 33:11

Our life's journey began in the heart of God. He carefully assigned us our family to prepare us to be the very people we are.

He planned our parents and theirs and what qualities they had to pass on to us for our travel in this our life's journey.

We may be disappointed or pleased with our formative years or the bone structure to which we're framed, but they are ours nevertheless and will serve us well. We've been given what's needed to step out and do our life's journey.

We're here right now, better for what our childhood was back then. Whatever those upbringing years may have been, they provided experiences to share as an encouragement or an opportunity to teach.

Many people will come our way because they knew us back then, or new acquaintances and friends having never known us in those past years. These people, of all ages, will be affected, impressed, or blessed by our having lived and learned practical knowledge.

The Lord was then. He is here now. He will be in our future. Our life's journey can fulfill God's plan for us and bring on the best of His smiles, or we can go our way and be unhappy, discouraged, or sorry with that choice. The decision is ours. The journey is ours.

Dear Lord, I choose You and what You in me via my family will produce what is needed as I walk out my life's journey. Amen.

Type of Harvest?

The Lord will give to each one according to their needs.
—Romans 2:6

I love my garden producing well from what I had sown. It's fun to harvest the vegetables for immediate or future use.

It takes time, after seeds are placed in the tilled soil, for beginning growth to be seen. I water and weed as needed. I enjoy watching my self-planted garden to fully develop. Its rewards are tasty.

Now if my negative opinion gets planted in some juicy gossip soil, seeing it grow and spread will not be as complimentary as my vegetable garden.

Insensitive words and untruths produce pain and separation with heartbreaking sadness. Sorrow and anger can rise from such erroneous remarks filling open hurt with tears.

When I plant corn, I will get corn. But if I plant scorn, I will get scorn.

Corn is yummy and fresh from the ear with salt and butter. But scorn leaves a bad taste. Until repentance and forgiveness happen, no healthy relationships can surface or proceed.

I love corn. I hate scorn. I want my plantings to have worthwhile benefits and offer delicious, mouthwatering, positive harvest for anyone (including myself) near or far from my garden.

Dear Lord, I want no bland or insipid harvest from me.
Instead, I want Jesus to be seen in me. Amen.

Sandwiched Wisdom

Whoever looks on a man or woman with lust in
their heart is already guilty of adultery.
—Matthew 5:28

Proverbs chapter 8 and more than half of chapter 9 speaks of wisdom. This is sandwiched between parts of chapters 5, 6, all of 7, and the latter end of chapter 9. (Check them out. Don't be confused.)

Here God expresses His objection to adultery. (He placed this sin as number seven in His top ten laws/commandments.) Adultery, regardless of who tantalizes, a mister, missus, or miss brings distrust, heartache, and disease. No one involved comes out at the other side truly pleased with his or her action or proud of what it brought to themselves and other people affected by that choice of behavior.

So God slipped in instruction of wisdom for the benefit of both the man and the woman. He includes an *if* in verse 12 of chapter 9. "If you are wise," this verse states, "you'll be wise for your own best interest, but *if* you scorn, you stand alone."

No one can pass the blame for their adultery. Temptation can ride heavy and is always available, but the yielding is of one's own choice.

Wisdom rewards. Scorn hurts.

*Dear Lord, so much seen, read, or heard offers temptation. With
Your directed wisdom, I will resist and remain pure. Amen.*

Following Correct Route

> There's a route people think is their preferred way
> to travel, but its destiny brings destruction.
> —Proverbs 14:12, 16:25

There's only one way to heaven no matter the individual wish or education. One means one, not two, three, or as many as can be invented or decided. One way plus zero remains one.

This message was made clear as we were traveling. The expressway we were on had upcoming construction signs in advance. It described our lane as closed. We had to merge to the left. There was no choice. Merge or hazard awaits.

Orange barrels and cones were positioned to show us the path to remain on. If we insisted on staying in the right lane despite those warnings, there would be damage and we could be hurt, maybe seriously, maybe fatally. The signs were posted for our safety.

The Lord said He is the One and only Way to salvation. No one can get to God or heaven by any other road, except through Jesus (John 14:6).

Those attempting to do their own driving and manage their own route will find themselves slipping, wavering, weaving, or rolling over some embankment or other unwanted collision resulting in eternal loss.

There stands that lane changing requirement which says, "Driver, you can't go other than the laid-out route and expect safety to your journey's end."

A self-determined route brings doom. Following Jesus's directed route today will prevent eternal decay from the disarray a wrecked life's willfulness brought its way.

Dear Lord, there is only one way to be with
You forever. I will take it. Amen.

Which More?

Do you love Me more than all this?
—John 21:15

It's there. I'm tempted. I yield. Not too bad. I do it once more. Then again, "it's just this time," I tell myself. The more I succumb, the stronger the influence.

Temptation is always there and will be upon me from the time I put my feet on the floor at the start of the day until I place them under the covers at night.

Even in bed or sleep, temptation doesn't forget me. It's there—thoughts, wishes, plans, and dreams. Temptation doesn't sleep. It's there to tease, tempt, then trap to gain success.

Temptation continues to overwhelm me and draw me under its spell/control. Then I'm bound, stuck, and drowning, unable to find my own bootstraps and try to pull me out of the mire in which I'm sunk.

Oh, I wish I hadn't done that, taken that, said that, or eaten that plagues my mind. Excuses are there. Each time, they make sense. They seem to have wisdom, education, and value. But they all end with me being the loser.

Now this me is repenting. "God help me. I don't what to do it anymore. I'm out of excuses. I got myself into big trouble because I wanted more. All the saw, heard, touched, walked, tasted became a yum-yum, I wanted more than I had before. Now I'm stuck to the floor, too heavy to move anymore."

Dear Lord, speak, for this me is now listening. Amen.

Hole Truth

But revealing the truth with love, we'll grow up in Christ.
—Ephesians 4:15

Thrift stores and rummage sales present interesting shopping. At one of these adventures, I found a pleasing and comfortable top.

After this purchase was laundered, it displayed two sets of tiny holes. They were stitched up. Proudly, I wore this light-yellow top. It fit good. Following its second wash, another hole arrived.

Most every time this article of clothing was laundered, little holes appeared. Sewing them shut helped, but soon those many mended spots were obvious. Hiding the holey problem was impossible. Their location and size became evident. The process continued.

But this unique top of mine remained because I liked it. I chose it for myself.

We were chosen by our Lord (John 15:16). He sees the many holes of imperfection in our lives and loves us anyway. When asked, God will not just mend, He will show us how we can eliminate our flaws. Then He gives encouragement and sends us on our way. That's the hole truth.

Dear Lord, when I ask You to forgive me of my fault, You don't do a temporary repair job. You forgive and help me remove that unwanted hole from my life. Amen.

God, Have Mercy

> I will give mercy on those I chose.
>
> —Exodus 33:19

When God decides to destroy a nation but its people turn from their wicked ways, He will not destroy it as planned.

However, if God chooses to make a nation prosperous and those people turn to evil and refuse to obey the God they know, He will change His mind and no longer bless it (Jeremiah 18:8–10).

These verses speak about any nation. It also speaks to the people, for a nation is made up of them. But if each person gets his or her life right with the Lord, then the nation will become upright.

Nineveh was destined to be removed off the planet, but God was merciful. In that mercy, He sent Jonah to preach to the sinful Ninevites. They were given forty days to repent or die.

Upon hearing such a message, immediate repentance and fasting began. God then changed His mind. Nineveh was saved.

But those in Sodom refused to repent. They were annihilated (Genesis 14:1–28).

Many times throughout the Bible, Israel, blessed of God, became rebellious with a "we'll do it our way." God would lift His hand of blessing on His own chosen people. These Israelites suffered materially and died.

When each national resident repents, the nation receives mercy and blessing. No repentance. Loss is certain. Maybe one's own life.

Dear Lord, I repent of my willful ways and ask for Your mercy. Please, Lord, save me and my country. Amen.

America's Change

> If My people, which say they are Christian, will humble themselves, pray, and seek Me, turning from their wickedness, I will hear, and forgive their sin and heal America.
>
> —2 Chronicles 7:14

America's real lasting change will not come from programs, politics, or pundits but through and by genuine Christians living out their salvation.

This remains to be the truths of the gospel of Jesus Christ and exemplified by repentant and yielded hearts to the Lord.

Each one of these individual's action and speech will reflect what the Bible says. Actually behaving in a "Christ has forgiven me of my sin" manner in itself will bring conviction to many observers, wherever they may be.

Then if you, me, we, us, the church humble ourselves, admit, and confess our sins before Almighty God and pray for a countrywide awakening or revival that leaves no one untouched, it will come. Unquestionable heart transformations will then be seen in men, women, boys, girls, and even teenagers, and then real change will take place in our beloved country.

Humankind's designed efforts often produce failure. Education, with its many years and lots of dollars, have brought little success. Permanent results will only come from God, when His people get serious with Him.

Dear Lord, it's us Christian, Your saints, that need to humble ourselves and seek You that will make the difference in America. Touch lives through me as I repent of my sin. Amen.

America, God's Idea

Remember when you were in your homeland of
difficulty, and the Lord your God brought you out from
there with His mighty hand and loving arms.
Remember in all those olden days
(ask or check out its history)…therefore bless the Lord.
—Deuteronomy 5:15, 32:7; Psalm 34:1

America
God's idea
For the weak, the worn,
Worried, and forlorn.
People of all types to
Make a home in the hills
Or in a city with lights.
America's meant to be
A place that's free
For you and me
To live our lives
Till eternity.
God has blessed
All of us.
It's our turn
To bless Him.
Let's give, do, and pray
Ev'ry day for our USA.

*Dear Lord, help me to remember where I came from and
what You have given. May I humbly repent before You
and get involved with people wherever possible. May I
bless and encourage to bless You at all times. Amen.*

Our Good Land

The Lord God has brought you to a good land.
—Deuteronomy 8:7

We live where we do. We have what we have. We plant and harvest, when possible, where we can.

We have soap and water, dishes on which to prepare and then serve food, beds for sleep, vehicles for transportation, with all their accessories, plus clothes to cover our bare and unprotected personage.

Have we noticed what we do have? Do we appreciate what the Lord has given us?

We have glasses for eyes, dentists for teeth, grass to mow, flowers to enjoy, leaves to rake, snow to shovel, books to read, and games for fun.

We have telephone for use, loved ones for family, music to soothe, camera to catch a memory, education to learn, experience to teach, home to shelter, and Jesus for salvation.

We get to roll over in bed, rise out of our chair, put our fork down at the completion of dinner, and clean up, wash up, put up, and store up all those extra things we have around the house, garage, shed, or barn.

The Lord has not just brought us to a good land, He's provided for us abundantly. God has given much more than we could ever list. God has been and is so good, so very good all the time.

Dear Lord, You have provided well for me and
mine. I give You thanks. Amen.

Naomi

A grandson was born to Naomi named Obed.
He was the grandfather of David.

—Ruth 4:17

Read the short book of Ruth.
Naomi was angry of what life had dished out. Her husband and both sons had died. Naomi felt empty. She had nothing.

Her widowed daughters-in-law were also sad. Orpah and Ruth were their names. They were respectful ladies willing to stay with Naomi and be an encouragement.

I'm sure she was blessed knowing these young women were sacrificing their feelings to be available to her. But she chose to send them back to their families. Orpah agreed, with tears, and left for her childhood home. Ruth would not leave.

What a woman Naomi must have been for Ruth to love her so much. Naomi had to have been humbled with such devotion.

These ladies left for Naomi's hometown. Soon after arrival, they needed to find means of support. Ruth offered to glean in the field and provide for their livelihood.

Within this process, Ruth met Boaz. He was a kind and honest man. After a series of events, they wed. As time passed, they had a son. He was named Obed and given to Naomi to repay for her deceased sons.

She was blessed beyond measure. Words must have escaped her for having received this loving gift.

Naomi did not live to see and know her great-great-grandson David, man after God's own heart.

God returns much from our efforts. He has blessings beyond our imagination.

Dear Lord, what You have done for others, You will do for me. I may never see it, but my family will know. Amen.

Second Chance

In confidence I remembered...that
you may have a second chance.
—2 Corinthians 1:15

I was there and I did that thing. Today I'm ashamed to admit my foolish decision. Yet God gave me a second chance.

No, I'm not going to reveal that ugly and gruesome detail of my past. It was dumb.

Yes, I have many excuses but not one valid reason to the why I was so empty-headed.

All every Christian does reflects the Jesus we say is our Savior and what He has done in us. What we say we are and what we actually are can be two separate things.

We profess and confess and even digress on the value of being a real Christian and then do the most unintelligent possible.

We stand with empty hands and shamed faces before people and our Lord. Jesus is merciful. He knows we are human and capable of blowing it big time, making one serious mess.

I admitted my foolishness and was given a second chance. How grateful I was to receive forgiveness on all fronts.

We're all guilty at some time in our lives of doing something or forgetting to do that thing, overlooking an individual, making an inappropriate remark, or being where we should not have been.

It all gets noticed. God holds His hand out to lift us up, dust us off, and send us on our way with a second chance. Praise His glorious name.

Dear Lord, nothing feels quite as bad as having been stupid. Thanks for Your forgiveness and allowing me a second chance. Amen.

Commonplace

It is common to man.
—1 Corinthians 10:13

Commonplace is where we all live. The ongoing realm of the miraculous is routine in this our human living process. We all get the same twenty-four hours every day.

God is in our commonplace. Look for Him in nature. Squirrels of the trees, birds in the fields, deer through the woods, sun rises in the east and sets in the west. Plus a planted seed has to die before it breaks open life to grow. It's then nourished by healthy soil. All are common yet miraculous.

And us, look at us. We breathe oxygen using our lungs. Our hearts pump blood, keeping all organs and limbs operational.

Our fingers write, toes wiggle, knees bend, and our seat sits. Daily sleep refreshes our bodies, food gives energy and growth, and hands can clap and praise the Lord.

We can drive a car, fly a plane, mow the lawn, cook a meal, and drink hot coffee or iced tea. Imagine it.

We have strength to carry a child, hang clothes, tote a filled toolbox, and lift our arms to blow our nose.

Our world operates through education of the mind, wisdom to understand, and ability to apply. People can't do anything special unless they use commonplace miracles. We take them for granted. Each and all are God-given.

Dear Lord, I'll look around, give a listen, use all
my senses, and notice they're not just commonplace.
They are miraculous. All from God. Amen.

Fresh, Clean Wash

Wash me from my sin, and make me clean again.
—Psalm 51:2

I like clean. I like its smell. I like its feel. This ranks highest with my bedsheets. Outdoor clothesline drying makes fresh air fragrance penetrate within each fiber of these sheets.

Tomorrow's busyness and issues are faced best after an invigorating shower and a refreshing rest between smooth and tidy sheets. Come what may, fresh and clean energizes the body to meet it straight on.

To keep my bedsheets in the fresh and clean condition that I love, they must be washed every week. This repetitive process is but a temporary fix with no end in sight.

Clean is a must for the heart as well. Soap and water or fresh air will not cut it when God looks on the condition of the heart. Will He find it clean or heavily soiled?

A complete wash job to the heart makes for an eternal clean. No weekly repeats necessary. The only way that can happen is by repentance. The heart is full of sin, and sin is not pretty. It's black, dirty, very unattractive, and stinks.

With genuine sorrow for our dark heart's condition, we cry out to Jesus. He alone can wash the vile and crusty accumulation from our hearts. When Jesus washes away our sins, we will love what the fresh and clean smell does to our person.

Dear Lord, You provided the answer that washes my heart
all the way through, from now through eternity. Amen.

King Amaziah's Idea

God is able to do so much more than I can ask or think.

—Ephesians 3:20

Second Chronicles 25 records the history of one of Judah's kings. This young king Amaziah was heavily prepared for any potential battle. He drafted many soldiers.

This chosen military force of three hundred thousand was filled with men twenty years of age and older. Many were made officers. These leaders were assigned separate units. They consisted of hundreds and thousands of qualified troops.

King Amaziah wanted more men for his self-asserting army. Thus he hired one hundred thousand from Israel. The equivalent of $30,400,000 was the silver paid for their co-operative service.

King Amaziah convinced himself this decision was correct, even honoring to God. But God was not impressed.

He sent a prophet to inform the king that God said no to this employed army.

"But...but," King Amaziah stuttered. "What about all that money I paid to rent these men? That was one huge amount of silver. How do I get back what's rightfully mine?"

Maybe God smiled at this immature response from Judah's twenty something leader, or not. We'll never know, but we do know what God's positive answer to King Amaziah. It was "The Lord is able to give you so much more than any of that amount you spent."

With our assumptions, we often put God in a box and forget His promises and godly abilities.

Dear Lord, through my understanding, I limit what You can do. Starting now, I will remember You said You would provide so much more than my request or understanding could theorize. Amen.

Thanks for Water

The rain and snow comes…to water the earth, makes it bud
and blossom, provides seed for the gardeners and food.
—Isaiah 55:10

Water is a requirement. It's used for drinking, cooking, cleaning, and growing our food. It also provides beautiful landscapes.

In many areas, water flows free. At our geographic locations, we are able to use it with regularity. Little thought is given about those who find themselves in a drought. Lack of water cracks the soil, kills plants, limits food supply, and affords no moisture for gardens or fruit trees. No water destroys cattle and poultry farming.

Showers, bubbles baths, shampoos, or simply brushing our teeth become nonexistent. And then, of course, mopping floors, doing laundry, washing dishes and countertops, even vehicles, with no water becomes impossible.

Water is necessary no matter the situation. It's basic. Without it, we could not take pleasure in that cup of coffee or tea. Water is essential for living.

The Lord has blessed us with so much. Water is just one portion of His bounty. Give God ongoing thanks for water from which we all get to receive its benefits.

Dear Lord, thank You so much for water. With each glassful of clean, safe drinking water and the most welcomed shower, plus every morsel of food I'm privileged to enjoy, I am blessed. Amen.

Mountain or Valley

Let everyone be fully convinced in his or her own mind.
—Romans 14:5

The mountaintop is high and spectacular. It spans unlimited range of vision, a victorious sweep of the horizon.

The valley grows fruit, vegetables, flowers, trees, opens paths, displays creeks, and rivers. All are filled with abundance of good things.

The mountaintop has its mountain goats, briars, and rocks amid barrenness. Yet its invigorating and vitalizing many a thrill of an uplifted spirit draws one close to God.

The mountaintop can be glorious, overflowing into deep and majestic waterfalls. From the valley, we observe such splendor with a mouth wide in awe.

The valley is open to ambition for satisfying self where varied opportunities are available for the taking.

The valley can hide wrong thoughts attempting to dominate over others. Such greed is most unwelcome. People can be caught in its grips or reject such efforts.

Mountaintops are not as able to hide ugly truth. Eventually, it's noticed and exposed.

The valley of our lives may get muddled and confused, easily strayed by circumstances or temptation we've allowed to hang around.

Mountaintop clears the thinking and seeing, causing us to admit our actions. Through our repentance and learning what the valley has taught us, we're now prepared to carry on.

Our assigned time to be on planet earth requires that we must deal with both the valley and the mountaintop.

How shall we respond?

Dear Lord, may my life be a time of seeking and reflecting You wherever I must be. Amen.

My Body

You are not your own. You were purchased with
a price. Honor God with your body.
—1 Corinthians 6:19–20

It is my body. So what does my body express? What appearance am I displaying? What have I allowed to happen to my body, deliberately caused or orchestrated and then paid to have done to me?

How do I dress? Does it reflect my Christian life? How about the cutting, body piercing, or those indelible colored marks on my skin? What beverages and food do I consume? Tobacco and drugs? Do they keep me healthy, sensible, and in my right mind?

I reside in this house called my body. It is all I have got to take me from that fertilized egg to death. I have no choice but to live in me.

The Lord gave me this human frame for my place of residence on this earth. Parts of it can be repaired or replaced, but there is no full body replacement.

This, my dwelling place, God gave me, and then He bought it through the blood sacrifice of Jesus. I am to take care of me. I am to provide proper nourishment and exercise to keep me in good physical form.

This home of my figure, with its inside and outside permissiveness, is seen and heard. How does it honor my Owner who paid an expensive price to buy me?

*Dear Lord, I consecrate my body to You that it will
glorify You in all I wear, say, and do. Amen.*

CH__CH

Do not forsake to get together with fellow
believers, to exhort one another.

—Hebrews 10:25

What's missing in the title? Are we willing to fill in the blanks? Only we can answer those questions. Many excuses tend to exonerate us from filling in the blanks.

Yes, there are hypocrites in the church. They're also in the workplace, shopping center, and our mirror. Hypocrites are everywhere. People often present themselves to be what they aren't.

Yes, the idea of worshiping God in the great outdoors is interesting. When my husband and I were in the Great Red Wood Forest, it seemed like we were standing in a cathedral. But we didn't do any worshiping of God, even though His presence was felt.

Yes, television, computers, and radios do offer many Christian programs and live services. They're good…if watched.

If one is physically unable to attend a church, these opportunities are essential and God-approved. However, those pieces of technology are impersonal.

Attending and becoming part of a local church brings the human touch with hearing ears, caring words, helpful hands, and even a hug. People care about people.

The blanks in CH__CH are *UR*. You are most welcomed and invited to church. Go this week. Meet other Christians. You will be blessed. People coming together in a church is God's idea.

Dear Lord, I will find a church and attend. I need those
people. They need me. We all need You. Amen.

Ruin the Rut

Obey My nudge. I will be your God.

—Jeremiah 7:23

Has your daily outlook been unchanged? Do you feel that inner nudge gets ignored?

Have you a tenacious spirit that struggles to get out? Maybe you are stuck in a rut. For some reason or excuse, you don't allow yourself to listen to God's voice in promoting and encouragement with His "yes you can" or "My will for you."

May today, begin the ruin of that rut. That change starts in your own corner by stepping aside from familiarity and moving into the "new to you" God's clean and reshaping state-of-the-art usable witness of His love and salvation to all, wherever is His direction for you. Dare to trust God.

So what is your rut? Is it routine, regular schedule, expected plans, or that's the way it's always been done? Or is it that you simply can't leave your comfort zone?

Now is the time to leave all the above and allow God to have His way, His will, His plan in what's to be done through you. It can be most challenging but satisfying.

Back off from self and allow God. See what He will do through a yielded you. The benefits will be lasting, continuing on into God's eternal reward.

Whoa! Now that will beat your rut. Ruin it today.

Dear Lord, take me and use me in whatever way I can be
used for Your glory. I leave my rut behind. Amen.

Day's End

Blessed are those who follow my ways.

—Proverbs 8:32

Daytime hours have been spent. It's bedtime. As I crawl between soft sheets and settle into the comfort of my deliberately chosen mattress, I sigh with satisfaction of the day.

It was well spent. Work was completed, shopping was accomplished, family time was rewarding, visiting and witnessing opportunities were worthwhile, meals were satisfying, and even the emergency produced an appropriate outcome.

Now the day is finished. All that's needed to be done was completed. The family, coworkers, acquaintances, and strangers played a part in the day's results.

The Lord was with me through it all. I invoked His counsel in each minute. He responded, and I obeyed.

This day began with its regular routine. Morning devotions opened the upcoming hours, with Jesus and me together. I made time and set aside minutes to be alone with Him. I wanted and needed His blessing on all this day would hold. Its planned schedule was understood, but the unexpected could have happened at any time. It might have brought forth something serious or difficult, yet I knew, with His help, I would have responded in a Christlike manner. I walked the responsible line everywhere my steps and responses were required.

Now I get to lay my head on my fluffy pillow knowing my life is all right. Nothing is quite as great as being able to go to bed knowing I am blessed.

Dear Lord, the day was long. It came to an end. I reflect back. You were there and took me through it all. Truly I am blessed. Amen.

Fear

God…is help in trouble. I will not fear, even when…
mountains shake and fall into troubled seas…
neither will I fear what people can do to me.
—Psalm 46:1–2, 118:6

Cuddles, our dog, wears many irrational fears. He shakes at the presumed sound of any something. It could be a loud noise or the quiet fall of a book on carpet. Then comes a camera flash or quick shadow movement that send him in a tizzy.

Thunderstorms cause a hard panting panic. At its slightest hint, Cuddles will shiver, do circles, and stop eating. Attempts to console him are rejected. Cuddles believes he's heard, seen, or thinks that unknown is destined to injure him. Fear overwhelms him, and he freaks out.

He is a dog, comprehends like a dog, and reacts like a dog. Then there's you and me. We see, hear, and surmise what's happening around us. Some things we understand and much we do not. Nevertheless, we shouldn't get overconcerned.

If we do have a cause for fear, we talk to and trust God. He's here right now, at this minute, and each moment to follow. He promises whatever the trouble, He is our refuge.

We try to calm Cuddles's fears. They control him beyond the point of reassurance. Let us not allow ourselves to get engulfed in something that triggers an alarm. It may be a hunch or full knowledge of danger. Remember, God *is* there and everywhere the air bears any layer of a scare.

Dear Lord, potential of harm reigns all around me. I trust them in Your hands and me in Your care. Amen.

God Knows

I have called you.

—Isaiah 49:1

The Lord called us while we were still in our mother's womb. He spoke our name. In recent years, the medical field has developed an ultrasound. This piece of equipment shows a child's development. Some of these machines are so intricate they can display color of the preborn's hair.

Through this, no child has privacy. It's thumb-sucking, rolling over, kicking mom actions and even gender can be observed. The boy or girl images are displayed.

While this little one is growing, God sees him or her too. He knows the physical makeup, challenges, and potential they own.

God already has their days numbered and knows what each one will hold for them. God is and will be on the scene through them all.

Nothing in our lives surprise Him but can surprise us. We shortchange ourselves by not using all our capabilities in our daily lives. God knew they were ours before we were in our mom's womb.

God is well aware of our heritage, immediate family, growing up and older years, and what their influences in this life offers to those around.

Regardless of our lifestyle
God placed His call on us while
His design for us was on His mind.
He gave aptitude, leaving nothing behind,
On how to use our talents, knacks, and abundant skill,
Even when we were in our mother's womb still.

*Dear Lord, when Mom was pregnant with me, You
had chosen me to be alive today. May I use what you've
placed in me to the best of my ability. Amen.*

Brief Life

Which is here today and gone tomorrow.
—Matthew 6:30

Insects, plant life, rainstorm, snowfall, even an ocean wave survives mere moments to a few weeks. Then they're gone. God designed shortness of life for critters and things. Yet He talks to us through their brevity.

Fruit and vegetables are grown to be eaten for our health. Caterpillars eventually become gorgeous butterflies, reminding us we, too, can be born anew when we're born again through salvation in Jesus.

Look around and notice all that God has given for our benefit. Each has but one brief life. It last only so long and then is gone and replaced by another. The original never returns.

People too—men, women, even teenagers, and children. That's all humankind's bodies will end at some age. It's our bodies that die. They get to house us while we are residing on this planet, but our actual life continues forever. No end comes to human life. Bodies, yes. Life, no.

Earth and all it produces is short-lived. Pesky bugs and flowers become fertilizer for future growth. But we—you and me—go on into eternity. The question remains, where will that be?

May we be prepared for which afterlife, of our choosing, we will get to live.

Dear Lord, I am here longer than they, and still my years are brief. Nevertheless, I am ready to face my life after death because I've been born again. Amen.

Born Again

Jesus said, "Except a person is born again,
he or she cannot see heaven."

—John 3:3

Jane said, "Yes."
John said, "No."
Sally didn't know
What it meant to be born again.
Was it a birth or a process to relieve stress?
Or could it be some fairy tale
As one may over the ocean-blue sail
With romance
For their dance?
No?
Then a doctor allows one to see what happens
At the birthing thing.
Is that being born again?
No.
It's of the heart
It's of the soul
Both must be made whole.
Oh.
As I say,
"I know I've sinned, needing to be clean within."
So
Open my eyes
I need Jesus to wash away my sin
I've confessed from sin, I will be set free
Born again
Reborn anew.
Do you understand, Lew?

Unless a person is born again
He or she cannot go to heaven.
That means me
That means you.
We each need Jesus too.
Repent it today
Don't delay
Be born again.
You, me, and all our friends.

Dear Lord, come into my heart, save me from sin so
that I'll be born again, ready for heaven. Amen.

Cry Out to Jesus

Each cried out in fear.

—Matthew 14:26

Read Matthew 14:22–32.
Jesus had finalized the feeding of five thousand men plus the women and children with one boy's lunch. (This miracle is recorded in Matthew 14:15–21.)

Jesus may have become fatigued, for He sent His disciples on a short boat trip to the other side of the sea. Now Jesus went into the mountain for some R and R.

While He was there, a serious storm, with all its high waves, arose upon the sea. It tossed about the disciples' boat. They were scared. Jesus saw them, and for a while He allowed them to struggle. He waited and watched their actions.

Then He began to walk toward the disciples on the stormy waters. (No problem for Him. He had created them.) Was Jesus going to pass by the men? We don't know. He did make Himself available for each to see. All these men needed to do was cry out to Him. They did so. Immediately, Jesus responded and provided the needed answer.

That's all Jesus wants from us today—cry out to Him. I'm reminded of a Christian chorus I've heard. "Reach out to Jesus. He's reaching out to you," it says.

That's what the disciples did. We must as well. Jesus is also watching our every move. Let us cry out to Him. He's waiting for that cry.

Dear Lord, life's storms rage all around me. I cry out to You, "Help me, please. I need You." Amen.

Prayer
Talking with God

When you pray, go to your private space,
close the door, talk to God in secret.
He'll reward you openly.

—Matthew 6:6

When we spend time with people, we talk, laugh, disagree, and compliment each other. Prayer is the same. It's a one-on-one conversation with God, a time set aside for speaking what's on the heart with whispers, tears, and cheers.

That's what God wants. Matthew 6:33 says God asks us to share all our whatevers with Him first. He'll supply answers.

His request is for us to choose a set-aside time slot to be alone with Him to help us develop a God-time habit.

We may choose some room, corner, or chair in the house. Additional prayer time can be in the car, at the market, when taking a test, or any place needed. With a bit of privacy, location can be anywhere.

Our all-important minutes spent with the Lord, will, in His time, bring results, responses, and rewards, even publicly.

Dear Lord,

I want to spend time with You
Because I want to be with You
You're the One that knows me
And all that's messing with me
You can bring about solutions
To calm my heart's palpitations.

So here I am in this place, You and me.
As I share my heart with You, may I listen as You talk to me. Amen.

Prayer to Answer

In the very day of my trouble I will pray, for You will answer me.
—Psalm 86:7

Somehow, God's going to do it
Somehow, He's going to bring it on
It could be today
Or another day further on
It could be as expected
Or may be in the unplanned
Yet God will provide His answer
The answer that's perfect for me
God oversees the process
Bringing questions to an end.
No more wondering
No other query.
To a where or how or when
God will bring it
To our attention
In His scheduled perfect now
Trust and know
Believe to receive
God's promises.
Will be fulfilled
According to His Word
We'll trust and believe
And always receive
'Cause God said so
Thus is so
Which puts us in the know
Our request God has heard
Our thoughts,

Our tears,
Our praying word
We'll rejoice
With great joy
And much thanksgiving
God is faithful and true,
With all He says, He'll do.

Dear Lord,
I've prayed
You heard.
I've cried
You saw.
My needs
You know.
I yield my
Faith to You
And Your
Answer to
My prayer.

Amen.

Doin' the Work

Preach the gospel to everyone.

—Mark 16:15

There's that lawn

Just a growin'
I'm a knowin'
It's a showin'
Time for a mowin'

It's not a fakin'
As it's a waitin'
Time I'm a takin'
To smooth it a makin'

What are we a doin'
Eternal souls a savin'
We must be a bravin'
So they go to heaven

We must be a tellin'
People that's a needin'
Their souls long a lastin'
Didn't count the costin'

Weeds are surroundin'
Truth fast a chokin'
Let's do the cuttin'
Time now's a shortenin'

Cuttin' grass to smoothin'

'Cause people's a waitin'
Jesus their soul a fixin'
Today we be a tellin'

Brings the answer

Dear Lord, no matter how it's said, people need the Lord.
May I do my part in tellin' them of Your love. Amen.

Feet

Wash your feet, take a rest.

—Genesis 18:4

We have feet. They may be large or small, because we're short or tall. Our feet must be the sturdy foundation to hold us up.

Feet are well used. They take us to work, car, store, church, or the kitchen sink. To go from point A to Z, we must walk those steps in between.

Our feet may be soft and smooth or rough and calloused. They may smell sweet or not. Still, these right and left feet will walk us to good or evil places. They'll keep us standing or running in whatever we do or wherever we go.

There are places and people that don't give or bring glory or allow any reference to God. Nothing about them is Christian. Yet their feet carry them in the direction of no interest in God. Do ours?

How about that avenue where God is honored? Do our feet work their way there?

At the end of the day, our feet are tired, dirty, and maybe sore. Where have they been? Where have they taken us? What did our feet's movement permit us to do while we were there? Questions aplenty about our feet are left unasked.

Take note of our feet. They're needed to hold us upright. May each one of our steps be acceptable in God's sight.

Dear Lord, I ask my feet, "Where are you taking me today? May it be to reflect Jesus all day long." Amen.

Beautiful Feet

Beautiful on the mountains are the feet of those that bring good
news, with words of salvation saying, "Our God reigns."
—Isaiah 52:7

Feet bring us to and fro, carrying all the weight we've grown. Here
we are. There we stand.

King Solomon said in Song of Solomon 7:1, "Feet are beautiful
with shoes." Some stores only sell shoes. What a range of style flow
from ugly to lovely do fill these store's shelves.

God promises to keep the feet His saints (1 Samuel 2:9) and our
feet from falling (Psalm 116:8).

Often people give little consideration to their feet. Ingrown
toenails, scrapes, cuts, beestings, bruises, bumps, lumps, or a simple
ache draws attention to the feet. Yes, we do dress our feet to meet the
occasion from flip-flops to tennis shoes to an evening out.

Our feet cover but a small part of our body. Yet God has spoken
more than two hundred times about our feet. They're important to
Him. Feet walk the direction we go or stay. May our heart's desire be
to move our feet, toe jam and all, on the road God has planned for
us to trod.

Let's take excellent care of our feet. They're important to God
and special to us while we walk His designed course of action we're
to tread.

Dear Lord, I ask for Your blessing upon my feet
as I walk a life reflecting of You. Amen.

Feet of Truth

How often must I plead with you to tell…nothing but the truth.
—1 Kings 22:16

There are things in this world that're wished to become a requirement thus presented as fact. No matter how they are debated, they're not true.

Do we know the difference between authentic accuracy and prejudiced agendas as we do our right foot from our left?

Both feet are needed to walk from here to there. If we decided to treat one foot independent from the other, we're in for a fall.

Now what if we choose to remove the shoe from our right foot and leave the left shoe untouched? The naked foot becomes vulnerable to all weather and surface conditions. The left foot is kept safe. This shoe's heel and sole will elevate itself above the bare foot. It's like the insisted false attempts to stand higher and make a bigger impression, hoping for immediate obedience. Such an unbalanced condition will eventually cause injury.

Just as there can be no changing of truth in law or life, both feet must be treated with honesty to keep the body's frame in line.

Feet can wear shoes or not, but truth cannot be on and off. It is what it is, not what it is wished to be.

When pressure gets put on you, remember your feet. One is not better than the other. That's the truth.

Dear Lord, so much is out there messing with my convictions. With Your help, I'll not step aside from that which I know is true. Amen.

This My Prayer

God's Word lives in you.

—1 John 2:14

I will...live godly in this world.

—Titus 2:12

I want to be one with You, Lord, in all I say and do. So when people see me, they'll see me as Christlike. If I don't have any of resemblance of You coming from me, it's not You but me. It's only me trying to have and speak as Christ would do. But that's impossible, when I allow me to display myself.

May the Christian life I wish to present be one of genuineness. I do want Christ in me and my life daily, living that out as a reality. That's a tough call requiring a twenty-four seven responsibility to be in tune with God. No spare time. No vacations. No taking breaks. Always in contact with the Lord. I will talk with Him and listen as He communicates back to me. May my ears and mind be open to hear and my mouth ready to speak forth truths of instruction, wisdom, and discipline.

I was blessed to receive words of guidance from a caring family member, friend, minister, or a passing someone somewhere.

Yes, You often talk through them. After all, they, too, are living out and experiencing life and could have the very advice that I need to adhere.

When I use the helps You have provided, the action of my heart, words of my mouths, and the life I live reflect continuous purity.

Dear Lord, may this my prayer remain true
as I yield my all to You. Amen.

Worship God

The Lord is... God.

—Psalm 95:3

Read Psalm 95:6–11.
Let's worship the Lord our Creator. He is our God. We His people must listen to Him speak. He is talking to us. Will we hear Him? Will we care or walk away or say He is but a crutch? That we can do just fine on our own? That we have a good education, job, heritage, and have a recognized position? We are okay.

Let us not harden our hearts as the Hebrew children did in the desert. They saw the oodles of miracles God had done just for them. Yet they decided God was unnecessary and they could do all right without Him.

This very attitude gave them extra years to trek out their time in the wilderness. Stubbornness in their know-at-all pride left all over the age of twenty, from their slavery via Exodus, to meet their demise within the forty years. Those people never got to see or experience the many benefits of God's promises (Numbers 14:22–23, 29).

He is God. There is no other for man, women, sister, or brother.

God and God alone wanted us, planned us, created us, and placed us in the geology that best suits us. We, people, human beings are His idea. Come give Him worship!

Dear Lord, anything similar to what those Israelites suffered because of their disobedience, I don't want to experience. Willingly, I bend my knee, lift my hands, and worship Thee. Amen.

Be Vigilant

Be clearheaded, be alert, your enemy Satan, like a
lion, sneaks around seeking to consume us.

—1 Peter 5:8

We must have continuous consciousness that our enemy Satan is slithering around trying to consume us. In every minute, his attempts are to use us up, eat us alive, wipe us out, exhaust our attempts, delete our energy, or squander our funds. Whatever will take us down and out of the picture, he'll do.

It could begin with a small possibility. This could be just the test that would move us off course. It grows daily, weekly, monthly, and maybe yearly. That shift has encompassed our livelihood, hindering our Christian walk.

Current trends pull us in. Popularity is temporary. Through it, our enemy distracts us. We like, we love, and then we lose. This was always his plan. Our enemy won't stop until we are stopped. His process is sneaky. We must be vigilant. We *must* spend more time with the Lord and His Word.

How much of our daily twenty-four hours does He get? That amount will feed and grow our spiritual life and biblical understanding, and we become alert to anything trying to smuggle harm into our lives.

Putting and keeping God first in every moment of each day will keep evil away.

We can't afford it. We don't want it. Hanging with Jesus is insurance against it.

*Dear Lord, teach me so I'll become more like You and be
able to recognize the enemy's sly maneuvers. Amen.*

Strength to Success

God is my strength. I can do everything
through Christ who gives me strength.
—Isaiah 12:2; Philippians 4:13

The thought of pushing the lawn mower around my uneven, hilly half acre yard one more time was beyond what my tired body could conceive.

But push I must and did step by step, even with the sweat rolling down my face nearly blinding me. A long sleeve worked well to clear eyes and my grass-cutting allergy drippy nose.

The sun's angle changed as the summer months progressed. This made the mowed line harder to find. So a wiped out me made many extra steps removing what I had just done. Finally, this tough summer chore was finished for this week.

At its conclusion, I dragged myself indoors to a chair for a small salty snack and iced tea. Minutes passed before my overexerted body could stand and face the shower and the remainder of the day.

Success happened again. The lawn looked good. I was freshly washed and pleased.

Strenuous work was hard in my younger years. Now that I'm considered a senior, I find such physical effort difficult, almost beyond my ability to fulfill.

But God's promises are faithful regardless of the years of my life. What God has said He will do, God will do. That I can depend on and receive strength for success every time.

*Dear Lord, I'm most grateful for Your strength that
pushes me onward to success. Thanks. Amen.*

Our Shepherd

The Good Shepherd.

—John 10:11

Read John 10:1–14.

Sheep are timid, with no leader they are
defenseless and wander aimlessly.
When a leader is on the scene, they follow willingly.
Sheep do not force, push, drag, or demand their way.
They are meek and sometimes rather stupid
Even among other sheep.
Some of them buck like a goat, scattering the rest of the herd.
Other sheep shove around with their hollow horned bullying
Causing unsettledness to the entire gentle flock.
God relates us to sheep, helpless and foolish, needing a Shepherd
To guard us from elements and protect us from all harm
And lead us to safe grazing and calm water,
eventually to a secure shelter.
Wolves and robbers will come to steal, kill, and
destroy us haphazard and silly sheep.
But when Jesus is allowed to become our Shepherd
He will be there to rescue us, mend our
wounds, and provide necessities
If we will accept Him and allow Him to lead us safely on.

So what kind of sheep are we? A butting goat, bullying others,
self-absorbed wanderer, or accepting the Shepherd that will
walk with us and take us through this life and into the next?

Dear Lord, You are my Shepherd. I need no other. Amen.

God Hears and Answers

Trust the Lord.

—Psalm 37:3a

I say wait on the Lord.

—Psalm 27:14

I love the Living Bible paraphrase. With it and the King James Version, I obtain a well-rounded understanding of the scriptures. Most of my own paraphrase stem from these versions.

My one Living Bible remained in a separate room for my devotions. The living room didn't have one.

A year ago, I saw one Living Bible at a rummage sale. For some reason, I chose not to purchase it. Later, I prayed, *God, please forgive me for not having bought it.*

A full year had passed, and this very location had another sale. I went hoping to find that the Living Bible would still be available.

I walked past many objects to the tables packed with books. I looked. No Living Bible.

Lost in thought as to what to do, I was greeted by Bill and Brenda. We chatted. I told them why I had come to the sale and expressed my disappointment for not finding the Living Bible.

I continued to shop. Then Bill approached me with "Is this what you are looking for?" He held my desired paraphrased book of scripture. With many thanks and near tears, I said it was and gratefully took what I had waited a year to receive. This precious book was now mine.

I nearly had a "Hallelujah fit" right there at that rummage sale. Praise God!

God hears our prayer. We may need to wait and wait to obtain His answer, but answer He will.

Dear Lord, I nearly forgot that prayer. You did not and provided. Thanks. Amen.

Praise

You praise the Lord.

—Psalm 117:2

What a time of rejoicing it is when we read God's Word. It's full of history, teaching, warnings, and encouragement. Any area of our lives is dealt with through some measure in the Bible.

While I was relaxing and sitting before the Lord, He drew my attention to Psalm 115:12–14 then across the page to chapter 117. Excitement grew as I read these verses.

Wow! Even though in our day-to-day life we can get lost, hung up, confused, used in some circumstance, go on a blah, or receive that exciting report or sad news causing many tears, God knows about them all and is on the scene.

Through whatever it is or meant to be, let's give God praise. He is aware of us and constantly thinks about us. He promises blessings to us regardless of our position or location in life. Plus He will bless our children. The King James Version says, "God will increase us more and more" (Psalm 115:14). There is a catch. We must reverence Him no matter who or what we are.

Are we still sitting quietly when we know God sees us right now, right where we are, and knows all that concerns us? He will bless us anyway, including our kids (and their kids). Jehovah God said so. Come on. Right now, let's just praise the Lord!

Dear Lord, to think You single in on me twenty-four seven is beyond wonderful. I give You praise. Amen.

Sneakers

With God everything is possible.
—Matthew 19:26

I have a set of tennis shoes that resemble the older type of sneakers. They were purchased at a local thrift store. I was pleased with my choice. I love sneakers.

It took a few walks for me to realize something wasn't quite right with them. Upon inspection, I learned they were a set but not a pair.

The only thing that matches is their color—white. Their liner is different. One has four sets of eyelets, the other three. Even the shoelaces are not the same length. The left sneaker has a higher arch than the right. Neither did their soles match.

But they worked just fine. I walked many a day and lots of miles wearing them. They cooperated just fine. No argument between them.

The left did its thing. The right did too. They did what they were designed to do—be someone's sneakers for whatever purpose the wearer needed.

People are equally different and are expected to work side by side to complete a job, an arrangement, or hold a marriage together.

It's true they see things and life from opposite angles, direction, opinion, and hopes, but by working and talking, they learn cooperation is doable.

They begin to agree even though they are opposite. Deliberate willingness produces progress. One right. One left. Yet they join forces as a team and work with combined effort toward the responsibility at hand, side by side.

Sneakers can do it. So can we.

Dear Lord, whatever is required of us, with
Your help, we can complete. Amen.

Dance Alone

Let them praise God in the dance.

—Psalm 149:3

It was early evening. I sat watching the outdoors. Birds sang their cheerful song. The breeze blew upon the leaves of the wood's trees facing me. It was a gentle wind moving all leaves, except one.

This leaf danced alone and with noticeable enthusiasm. It was out of rhythm with the others. Up and down, back and forth, and all around it swirled. This leaf was unafraid to be singled out.

It was as if the lone leaf was giving God praise. Every opportunity that leaf could move, this one did, excited and unashamed to do so. The rest of the leaves remained unimpressed and uninfluenced. This brave leaf continued.

When all around us the presence of the Lord is unwanted and discouraged, will we allow ourselves to be seen and heard as a Christian? Regardless how the wind blows, will we remain true to the Lord no matter how obvious and different to those around?

We do our job. We live our lives and raise our families, teaching about Jesus in the process. When we're alone, people notice and remark.

What will we do? Will we encourage God's breath to breathe on us again so those people will truly see the Lord in us? That leaf did. Again, it danced. Those other leaves did not move. A single leaf continued to dance to the Lord and not the world's opinion, interest, or culture.

Dear Lord, I will dance for You, even when others see me. Amen.

What Will We Do?

But if not.

—Daniel 3:18

R ead Daniel chapter 6.
    In today's world, things are changing. Morals have gone with the wind. We are put into places and among people not of our preference. Here we are pressed to embrace what we know is incorrect, even a sin. Nevertheless, we are expected to abide by the decision of a few.

We feel abandoned as we stand, maybe alone, facing the leader's requirements. What do we do? What do we say? How does it all make us feel?

The answer is expected to be forthcoming by our believing, accepting, and taking on these new laws as our own.

But if we refuse to participate in that direction, what would they say? Are there consequences for not going along with said stipulation? What would be our final decision?

Daniel met such a law that said, "Bow to no one but the king." Daniel would not budge on his belief to daily worship God. Daniel remained firm, knowing the outcome would be personally painful and maybe fatal.

Daniel spoke of his faith in Almighty God, period! If the leaders complied with Daniel's conviction, good; but if they would not, they could do whatever they chose to do to him. Daniel did not move.

What will we do if that expectation becomes ours to make or break?

Dear Lord, it's just me. I'm only one, but I do trust You to take me through whatever and all comes my way. The results I leave up to You, for I know I'm in Your hands either way things may go. Amen.

Remain True

True Christians are bold as a lion.

—Proverbs 28:1

Daniel remained true in his captivity through. Because of his consistent life, he was watched. Jealousy brought legal action. Men wanted Daniel of out of the picture. They looked for any way Daniel was illegal. None was found.

These men approached King Darius with a plan. If anyone "ask petition of any God, except you, King Darius, that person shall be thrown into the den of hungry lions." King Darius was persuaded to sign it into law.

These men watched Daniel continue his daily prayer routine. They tattled to King Darius. Daniel was arrested and taken to the lions' pit.

King Darius was sad for the outcome of this law. He liked Daniel, but he had to be thrown in anyway. King Darius said, "May the God you serve deliver you."

Daniel was pushed out of sight. King Darius worried. The King didn't eat, drink, or sleep for his concern over Daniel.

But Daniel landed safe on a soft group of lions. He slept comfortably because he wasn't alone. The Lion of the tribe of Judah, Jesus Himself, was there with him. Thus, hungry beasts kept their mouths shut.

Morning came. King Darius hurried to call out to Daniel. He answered. God had taken care of Daniel.

However, his accusers and families didn't fare so well. They received the same fate contrived for Daniel.

God was on the scene and protected Daniel. He'll take care of us as well.

Dear Lord, I'll stay true my life through. As You were
with Daniel, You'll be with me too. Amen.

Truth versus Lies

Speak truth to everyone.

—John 8:32

And ye shall know the truth and the truth shall make you free.

—John 8:32

If the truth shall set you free, what does a lie do?

Oh my
Why would I
Tell a lie
Instead
Speak the truth
Lying is uncouth
It brings
Dishonor
Dirty shame
Shady smears
Humiliation
When
Honesty speaks
Accuracy
Validity
With truth-filled
Reality

Lies produce wounds and a penalty
Truth generates favor and a blessing

A lie requires the mind to remember its dishonesty
And forces the heart not to care about its effect.

Truth liberates the soul with pure integrity
And releases honorability unto righteousness.

So brothers (sisters), if anyone of you errs (lies)
from the truth and someone converts
him/her, the person that brings him/her back
to the truth rescues them from
certain death (James 5:19–20).

Dear Lord, lies are negative (false witness). Truth is positive (a just witness). One heals. The other hurts. May I be a truthful witness at all times. Amen.

Cleanup Is Needed

Nothing is hid, that shall not be seen, nor
kept secret that will not be known.

—Mark 4:22

After washing dishes, cleaning off the counter and the stove's glass top, I considered my job done. And then the *but* showed itself not once but twice.

But as I ran my hand over the stove's surface, unseen and still dirty spots were felt. These unexpected sins exposed themselves to my experienced fingers. Having done this kitchen process many times, unclean couldn't hide long. It was discovered.

But again, as I turned to leave the kitchen, my well-trained eye gave a second glance to the countertop. Oops. Wet splatters and some missed areas were exposed.

My job was not finished. I couldn't walk away. These areas were not to be ignored. It's now double back time for me to do the required touchup.

And there we are, as well, overlooking our "oh well, no one will ever see or know" neglect. Eventually, it will be made known to our embarrassment. Facts confirmed. Evidence bears witness in our attempt to ignore the truth. Cleanup is essential.

God's observing eye has been aware all along. Thankfully, He's provided an answer using that very conjunction *but*. This reference is found in the book of 1 John 1:9. It says, "But if we confess our hidden sins, God will forgive and wash us clean."

*Dear Lord, You know me so well and will still forgive
me for my willingness to disregard those hidden
things if I but ask. I do so today. Amen.*

Safe with Jesus

Whoever trust the Lord shall (will) be safe.
—Proverbs 29:25

Everyone, without exception, needs to use the bathroom. Whatever process must be accomplished, parts of the body get disrobed, desiring total privacy.

When emergency crews arrive to help from an unexpected accident or illness, one becomes helpless to protect self-dignity.

That was me. I woke with intentions to bake for a bake sale. Cookies, zucchini bars, breads, and a pie were my baking plans. All preparations were readied for a day of baking.

Soon after the second sheet of cookies was taken from the oven, a serious illness came over me. I rushed to the bathroom soon to become as helpless as a wet and limp dishrag.

I was in an inconvenient position, too weak to do little to help myself. Consequently. I fell facedown on the ceramic tiled floor. With God's help and my determined effort, I got back up on the toilet, blood pouring from my nose.

By the time my husband found me and tried to help, I could not respond. He called 911. Soon I was surrounded by men and a woman getting me up and out. I was transported to the emergency room. Five hours later, I was discharged to go home.

A grave and severe injury could have happened in my untimely, undignified, and unwelcome event. And then what?

Dear Lord, because I accepted You as my Savior, I was prepared for whatever sudden incident or tragedy could make my life very different, or take it from me. I was safe in Your arms. Amen.

Broken Walls

He or she that doesn't control their own spirit is
like a city whose wall has broken down.

—Proverbs 25:28

In Bible times, cities had walls. Each city was surrounded and enclosed in their protection. These durable thick walls provided safety for the residents. They appreciated the security that wall gave them.

But if that wall got broken down, its citizens were in peril. It would bring great risk to even get up in the morning. The city could be invaded that very day.

If we, too, don't keep an unbroken wall around us, whatever our problem or temptation might be, we will be captured and lose the battle.

With the wall broken down, we find ourselves in a fight. A grave struggle will present itself when our wall of defense is not kept intact.

Many areas in our lives present conflicts such as immorality, addictions, bullying, politics, technology, or that pesky individual. Each requires safety measures be kept intact.

The only permanent response to freedom, from whatever it is that can cause us harm, is to "cast our care on the Lord. He cares" (1 Peter 5:7). Trust Him to secure us in His protection and direct us to an *if* or *when* we should respond.

Dear Lord, You know the struggle I continue to face. I give it to You and believe You're on the scene and will take care of me. Amen.

God Comes Through

Give and you will receive.

—Luke 6:38

Read 2 Kings 4:8–37.

Elisha came to Shunam. One local woman was concerned for his health. She and her husband opened their home for this prophet.

After frequent trips using the offered relaxation and study opportunity, the woman and her husband added a room to their home. It was an efficiency with a bed, chair, table, and candlestick. Elisha was appreciative to have privacy.

What could he do to repay the couple for their kindness? After inquiry, he learned the childless woman wanted to be a mother.

Elisha predicted a year later, she and her husband would have a son. That prophecy came true.

When this son was young, he suffered a serious head pain. His father sent him to his mom. She held and comforted her son until he died.

This woman didn't panic. She laid the boy on Elisha's bed and went for someone to drive her to the prophet's house.

Elisha hurried to the boy. After praying, he stretched from nose to toes on the young lad. Soon the dead boy's body became warm. He sneezed seven times. This grateful mom hugged her resurrected son.

This woman gave out. God gave back. Her trust in God and His servant proved to be more than enough.

That same God is here today. He will give us much more than we could give to Him through our donations and help to Christians, needy situations, and ministries.

Dear Lord, I am thankful I can take You at Your
word. Your promises are sure. Amen.

1,000 Years

Dear ones, realize this one thing that with the Lord 1,000
years are as one day and one day are as a 1,000 years.
—2 Peter 3:8

How long is one day in this earth? No matter where we live, what
time zone we're in, or the season of the year, one day reigns in
a twenty-four-hour period.

Parts of this time slot has daylight, darkness, sun, warmth, snow,
and blistery cold. Still, each day holds only twenty-four hours. No
more. No less. No matter the wish. While we are here, twenty-four
hours surrounds us everywhere we walk, talk, sing, dance, entertain,
or sleep.

Twenty-four hours is all we get, whether we're tall or short, rich
or poor, worker or royalty. We are all allotted the same amount of
time every day.

But in God's eye, each day we live is worth one thousand years.
What we are doing values well beyond twenty-four hours. What
accumulates in our day stretches into the worth of one thousand
years. And those hours that seem to grow long here are filled with
one thousand years of meaning.

Our daily twenty-four hours on earth to God magnifies to one
thousand years' worth of significance. The usefulness of these hours
is maximized consequences benefitting to the gain of one thousand
years.

What a treasure to understand our days are not accepted at face
value, but with a one-thousand-year price tag. Amazing.

*Dear Lord, You've increased my twenty-four-hour day with people,
livelihood, and witness to a thousand-year boost. I pray the quality of
this day conveys the grace You've given me, and I freely share it. Amen.*

Availability

I will behave myself…and will allow nothing bad before my eyes.
—Psalm 101:2–3

What is allowed before our eyes? What do we do with the image that flaunts itself with its availability? Do we drool? Plan expensive excursions? Design wardrobe ideas? Layout what's unaffordable? And then allow circumstances to force open closed doors to step into the beginning of an available temptation, certain no one will be the wiser?

It's true there is availability. We all get the availables available at most any time, day, or place. The privacy of our vehicle, office, or home can be persuaded to serve that availability of most any type.

Technology's doors are always available. We all use them. Often it's necessary. Maybe this availability is used as an excuse to type or say or watch or submit to its user's appetite.

We read articles or hear about an individual yielding to an available temptation. In doing so, they are embarrassed because they got caught. Some remorse, sorrow, or apology is made available to soothe over the information. Is there real repentance? Will there be true change? Available opportunities in time will tell.

God said behave and do what you know is right. Remember the old-time Christian child's song, "Be careful eyes what you see, ears to hear, hands to touch, feet to go, 'cause God sees and knows the facts of that availability and us."

What and who do we allow us to go to or see, allow in our homes, allow us to socialize with? Do we take un-Christlike advantage of the opportunity its availability allowed?

Dear Lord, may all parts of me keep themselves focused on
You and not yield to wrong availabilities. Amen.

Laying on of Hands

Forget not…to do the laying on of hands.

—1 Timothy 4:14

Moses was exhausted from trying to carry all the burdens of the Israelites. He needed help. God instructed him to find seventy men. They would help him to carry the heavy responsibility of caring for God's people.

Levites were chosen to be spiritual ministers to the Israelites. In front of the congregation, Israel's leaders laid hands on them to consecrate them before God (Numbers 8:9–10).

Jacob laid hands upon his grandsons, Joseph's boys, for each to receive a special Grandpa God directed blessing (Genesis 48:14).

Jesus laid His hands on children, prayed for them, and passed on a blessing (Matt. 19:13–15).

Acts 8:14–17 records Peter and John laid hands on the Samaritans. They received the Holy Spirit.

The twelve apostles couldn't stretch themselves to care for all the church's needs and prepare to preach. So seven Spirit-filled men were selected to help. These men stood before the apostles. They laid hands upon the seven and prayed for them (Acts 6:6).

Paul and Barnabas were to be used of the Lord. People from the Antioch church laid hands on them, prayed for them, and sent them off with a blessing (Acts 13:2–3).

Deacons, elders, and other Christians may receive the "laying of hands." That's good and biblically demonstrated.

But often, there's a but. This but is explained in 1 Timothy 5:22. This scripture tells us to lay hands on no one "suddenly." The receiver must be a pure Christian before God, or we partake in their sins.

Dear Lord, I'll know they're a believer and spiritually qualified before I lay hands on them. Amen.

Examination Time

Examine ourselves to see what are we.

—2 Corinthians 13:5

Does haughtiness, lying, murder, plotting evil, being eager to do wrong, being a false witness, or willing to sow discord among some people describe us? If so, God hates them. In Proverbs 6:16–19, He calls them an abomination.

Do we have love, joy, peace, patience, goodness, meekness, or self-control within our personality? If so, the apostle Paul calls them "Fruits of the Spirit" (Galatians 5:22–23).

To help us make right responses within life itself, we need to adjust our thinking. Paul wrote to the church in Philippi, Philippians 4:8, with a list to guide that thinking process. He said we must fill our thoughts with truth, honesty, impartiality, purity, love, good report, virtue, and praise.

People are all around. Wherever we are working, shopping, schooling, eating, watching, and hearing, people are there.

In what manner do we place all aged people, the ones we do or don't like, cute or ugly, rich or poor, smells pretty or not? Yet they are all out there, everywhere we are. How then are they perceived?

It's certain what we see in them is seen in us by someone. This day is our time to check out the what and how of us. It will expose the truth that most resides in us.

They, you and me
Are as imperfect as can be
Yet Jesus loved us enough
To have died on Calvary's tree.

Dear Lord, what am I? May I becoming more like Thee. Amen.

Love

There will always be a time to love.

—Ecclesiastes 3:8

Want love? Need love? One rarely takes place without the other. Love is an interesting word. It can be used in many instances of excuses that push forth will, or it describes God's affection for us.

The words *I love you* are easily flipped out, but proof of their validity remains in the deliverer of such words. What was meant in the use of this triple-word phrase?

The fruit of the Spirit speaks nothing of any form of being self-absorbed in the word *love*. The actual description of the reality of love is in facts, not our fancy.

Genuine love is not the mushy, smoochy, hot breath, buying flowers or chocolates, or the aftereffects assumed from a paid for dinner out expectation.

True love endures, is warmhearted, and is not resentful, pushy, demanding, or uncouth.

It shows full self-respect, one not easily ticked or automatically thinks bad or is selfish.

Love trusts, believes, hopes, and accepts the whatever. It hangs on praying for God honoring results (1 Corinthians 13:4–8).

How do we measure up with or describe the tender feeling, admiration, enthusiasm, desirous thoughts, words, and actions of love? How do they flow from us?

Dear Lord, love *is a word often used and expressed in varied ways. May love from me reflect You. Amen.*

Joy

That Jesus's joy stays in you filling you full of joy.

—John 15:11

One of the fruits of the spirit is joy. This full and ongoing experience floods our being, even in sad and difficult times.

Joy radiates the presence of the Lord that reigns within our lives and lifestyle regardless of any kind of circumstance.

Joy captivates the spirit and gladdens the heart with adoration. Troubles will come and troubles eventually do exit, yet joy remains.

Joy should not be compared to or equalized with happiness. They are two separate conditions.

Joy does not leave. It's always there, maybe briefly hidden by some situation, but it's there nevertheless.

Happiness comes and departs. If and when happenings do go my way, I will then be happy. If they do not, I will not be happy. Happiness demands affirmation. Joy accepts life whatever it may present, because it triumphs in the continuance of Christ's eternal love.

Outgoing, friendly, and sunny disposition is joy's deep abiding attitude captivated by the presence of the Lord, our source and cause of delight.

He is there in the good, bad, and ugly and will take us through them all. No wonder joy reigns in our lives. We hang onto Jesus because He's got a hold of us today and forever.

Dear Lord, joy floods my soul, for You have made me
whole. You promised and that makes it so. Amen.

Peace

> We will abide in perfect peace, when our minds are
> focused in the Lord, because we trust (fully) in Him.
> —Isaiah 26:3

Peace is a soft, contented word. Just speaking it flows out truth of itself. Say the word *peace*. Hear its calm and soothing syllable slip between your lips. The word on its own is nonviolent.

Jesus used the word *peace* often:

Peace I leave with you (John 14:27).
Peace be still (Mark 4:39).
Peace to this house (Luke 10:5).
That you might have peace (John 16:33).
Go in peace (Luke 4:48), and after His resurrection He said, "Peace be unto you" (John 20:26).

Life is full of living. It can have good times, but often an overwhelming amount of sad, difficult, trying, and painful days, months, maybe even years fill our eyes with tears.

Frustration, anger, and upsetting occurrences roll its heaviness across our hearts, attempting to rob us of our peace. If we do not give all these burdensome incidents to Jesus, they will steal that peace.

He may not take these hard times away from us, but He will be with us through them all, providing His peace each moment of the passage. We will then find ourselves on the other side of those issues, wallowing in Jesus's perfect peace.

Hmm, blessedness is peace given by Jesus. Whisper, "Peace." Accept Jesus's peace. It's ours for the taking.

Dear Lord, Your peace displayed through me is a vital
fruit of the Spirit. Thank You for peace. Amen.

Patience

The Fruit of the Spirit is…long-suffering.

—Galatians 5:22

Pregnancy takes nine months. Its length seems unending. The further along in the gestation period, the growing baby makes Mom uncomfortable.

Some gals suffer sickness the entire time, and others not as much. Cravings of the unusual can overwhelm Mom. Her energy and clothing size can display an emotional change affecting everything and everyone surrounding her. This mother-to-be endures it all for the benefit of her developing child.

Long-suffering describes this uncomplaining lady as she does her daily routine, because she has resigned herself to the amount of time required, to carry through to the delivery of her child.

Life places all of us at some time or another with the need for patience. We rarely know the date of completion for that issue we are forced to wait. While doing so, remember that God is at work in that very trial and hardship in which we seem to be stuck in.

It'll take time to ready us for its birth. Immediately prior to this due date unknown to us, things can get most painful. Yet this may be the very process needed to bring us on through and to the joyful greeting and acceptance of that very "babe" we desired.

Waiting can be long and difficult.
Its arrival is well worth the patience.

Dear Lord, patience is one fruit of the Spirit fully illustrated by the pregnant woman. I trust You with the long-suffering patience I need to wait for my answer. Amen.

Gentleness

God's servant must be gentle to everyone.

—2 Timothy 2:24

Have you ever needed an ambulance? Or maybe you are an EMT or paramedic that cares for patients or potential patients.

At some time, you have been to a doctor or some type of a medical caregiver. In all of these situations, whether receiving or giving the essential medical attention, it must be done with gentleness.

Each and every time I have needed a medical professional, their voice, words, and touch were always gentle. This well-trained personnel never gave cause for complaint. They were all top-of-the-line gentle.

The life we live is not always gentle. It can be tough and at times maddening. Yet we are to respond with gentleness.

That person, coworker, fellow shopper, or a relative can make things stressful for us. It is certain problems will arise or already has taken place, and we are forced in the middle of a controversy.

We have heard the quote "Life happens." True, and life is filled with people of all ages, personalities, and attitudes. God placed us here to live that happening life among them.

We all have troublesome issues, but more often than not, it is that other person that has the serious difficulty. As we appreciate the understanding and gentle care of the medical workers, we, too, are required to be available with gentleness. Let's get involved where God has placed us. We're needed. Be gentle.

Remember, gentleness is welcome. Harshness is not.

Dear Lord, may my response always be gentle. It's best for them and reflects You living in me. Amen.

Goodness

Most people display their own goodness.

—Proverbs 20:6

What is goodness? The dictionary describes it to be a state of being good. What is good? The same dictionary devoted nearly half column to its explanation: favorable, sound, true, free from sorrow, and so many other words were applied to the noun, adjective, and adverb of the four-letter word good.

It does not need to take so much expansive page space for us to know *good*. We do recognize whether good is there or not.

The question remains, Are we good? Do we give out good? Do those others see good in us? If so, to me, that would spell goodness.

One of the fruits of the Spirit is goodness. To display this very attitude reflected in our behavior, we must be honest, virtuous, honorable, respectable, high in integrity, and fully worthy to be called a Christian.

Christ is good, period! The Bible concordance lists goodness with many references of Christ. We are His, and His goodness should be clear in you and me.

What do we do or say or speak of the goodness of Christ living in us? Thus the answer we give ourselves to that question *Are we good?* reveals the truth about us to us.

One less *o* in the word *good* spells out God. May God shine through and make us good.

Dear Lord, I want Your goodness to be seen as the good in me so people will see You in me. Amen.

Faith to There

Faith, by itself, is dead, if it doesn't include works.
—James 2:17

You say you believe you have faith for that position or to receive certain recognition or win a race. That could very well be your calling, but it will never take place without advance preparation.

You know you heard from the Lord that such a *there* will happen to you. Excellent. Faith to believe is noteworthy. *But.*

But to get *there* from *here* you have to add a *T*. To get that promotion or accolade, you must begin somewhere at some time with you doing something. You've got to do the work to acquire that *T*.

Get the studies needed and work hard to learn and prove your ability to perform well toward the *there* you wish to attain. To be so noticed for that specific award, recognition, or position requires one starting from its lowest point and moving up. To achieve anything of value, one begins with work.

Yes, if one wants to run a marathon, it must begin with the first step. Sweat, tears, and lots of grunts are required for many days, weeks, even years to be able to complete such a goal.

Faith to believe you'll receive is wonderful, but to do so begins at point one. We have faith to sit on a chair and have it hold us up securely because someone worked to put it together.

Faith, yes, it's essential. Work is the engine that provides the *T* to the fruition of the wanted *there*.

Dear Lord, I assumed I've enough faith for You to drop my there *in my lap, pronto. That's just not so. I must put faith into action to deliver desired results. Amen.*

Meekness

If that person is angry, have a quiet spirit.
It will soothe their bad temper.
—Ecclesiastes 10:4

People can speak forth and demonstrate their disagreement with a bad mood, flare up, or simply lose their temper. When this happens, what do we do?

Some person might get bent out of shape, demanding their own way, their opinion, or they just want to be noticed. Another individual might become upset or get absolutely livid. If so, how would we react?

And then there are those living with, working alongside, passing someone in the store, on the street, or just by watching an action which can set them off. And there we are.

What type of a spirit do we display?

How are our viewpoints expressed?

Will the truth of our hearts display a spirit of meekness?

Allowing spiteful injury or insult without resentment will express meekness and reflect the compassion of the Lord Who reigns within.

When brought into an unwanted or an unwarranted situation, flee. If unable to leave, wear and speak meekness. When possible, respond as an unaffected teddy bear—undisturbed. Your meekness can soften their foolishness.

Dear Lord, may Your life be seen in me when all that
unkindness happens my way. I want meekness, so
flood my spirit that would calm theirs. Amen.

Self-Control

The Fruit of the Spirit is…temperance.
—Galatians 5:22–23

Through decades of calorie counting and scale watching, I prayed and prayed. Success came when I listened to God's reply to my urgent "I need to lose weight" request.

Food is plentiful. I enjoyed it, but I had to learn to think, believe, and understand eating is to be done in moderation.

Most valuable of God's instruction I received was to exercise most by restraining my impulses, emotions, and desires.

Such temperance or self-control I learned played the biggest part in me becoming smaller in size.

The same formula, straight from the Lord, will work in all areas of our lives from a candy bar to that deep temptation.

In all those minutes and hours we deal with people, admittedly they can be most frustrating and self-excused. Yet we need not come out on the negative side. We can be constructive and cheerful with heartening encouragement for them (and us).

When we develop a bad relationship with food or that other issue, we must have a one-on-one discussion with the Lord. We'll then be ready to take authority over ourselves, with each portion we consume, places we go, actions we do, or whatever battle happens along our way. Each opportunity remains with us, as we get to express temperance and display self-control in it all.

Dear Lord, help me to be determined to say no where
I should and a yes when appropriate. Amen.

Exactly—Come to God

Come boldly to God.

—Hebrews 4:16

In Whom we receive forgiveness of sins.

—Ephesians 1:7

We imperfect humans are guilty of many things from our earliest years to now. We have done and still do what we know is wrong, improper, unpleasant, disrespectful, hateful, and maybe suspicious. It doesn't really matter what it is or was. We do remember the *exactly* of it.

People we know and some we do not know are affected by the *exactly* of our actions and words. They may respond in emotion, pity, or nothing. That reaction can be kind or hurtful. So whatever we aim to do back to that one or more persons will make a difference to others who know us *exactly*.

We may still continue to do something else dumb, bringing its results upon ourselves. That outcome will not be flattering, but there it lies because of our own decision.

With all the above and more makes no difference, when we cry out with genuine repentance to God, He always welcomes us regardless of what was or is the *exactly* in our past or present.

God offers forgiveness. In all times of our need, forgiveness is available. We just need to ask God and His abundant compassion for His forgiveness for all our misbehaviors. He is there for all the *exactly* that is in us. Come to God.

Dear Lord, I have done, said, and been unkind too often.
I do repent of all those wrongs and am very grateful for
Your forgiveness. May my exactly *reflect You. Amen.*

Potter

We are clay... You are the Potter.

—Isaiah 64:8

The Lord intentionally wanted us from our beginning. He molded us into a particular frame. Here we are poised like that glazed vase being proudly displayed.

That particular vase caught our eye. We liked its design and color. It was beautiful. Then we envisioned where it could be placed in our home. The style, with its flair, would grace some specific table, adding pizzazz to its surroundings.

This lovely vase had an inventor who formed it with caring hands. That vase might have had many forms before its maker settled on the special shape it now wore.

Creator God is our personal Planner. We were in His heart and on His drawing board well before we became clay in His hands. The decided model for each of us was that we would be conformed into His "go into the world and live the gospel" image. God our Potter's results produced you and me to be a specific designed vase. With our unique and Christian character, we've been placed in our job, neighborhood, home life and all that's happening around us. Others will then see the remarkable vessel Jesus made us to be.

Dear Lord, I do not see me, where I am, or what I do as a handsome, fine vase. In Your eyes, I am just that. You molded me to be the actual me, exactly as You planned me to be. Amen.

Repentance, Day 1

You God created the earth, laid its foundation.
—Hebrews 1:10

Repentance means
Turn from sin
Turn to Him.

Who is Him? What is sin? Where does
one begin? It started with God.

He was before it all.
The earth, the sky, and the sea.
He created this globe
For plants, critters, you and me.

This dirt-covered sphere
Was filled with bubbly life
Enjoyment for its residents
Until selfishness brought strife.

Those first created persons
Named Mr. Adam and wife Eve
Cared for God's perfect garden
He designed for their leave.

Until one day, Ms. Eve
Had an idea. She tried it out.
Mr. Adam joined her effort
Curious what would come about

Like a loving parent
To this couple, God gave
Everything that was there, but
From two trees they must behave.

These were a no-no to them
Do not go near, no touch, no eat.
Mr. Adam, Ms. Eve were tempted
A no-no to them was a treat.

So Ms. Eve slowly approached
That forbidden pretty tree
It was full of tasty fruit
She must have a bite to see

Mr. Adam stood by, was there
When he saw her disobey
Father God's rule—don't touch the tree.
She, with Adam, did it anyway.

Dear Lord, You were there and saw what they did.
You see me too. May I obey You. Amen.

Repentance, Day 2

While we were still sinners… Jesus died for us.
—Romans 6:8

God said no. They said yes.
This rebellious behavior
Was deliberate and self-willed
Causing sin to open its door.

All people born from then
To now and years to come
Adam and Eve us sinners made
Tallying us out one hefty sum.

But God had the solution.
He sent His Son Jesus,
To come as a babe to earth
Then grow up to die for us.

What a price to be paid
To salvage our needy souls
From facing hell's flames
Those sins have eternal tolls.

Jesus's death and resurrection
Bought you, me, and others to be
Our only escape from all this
Spawned by Ms. Eve and her he.

We must accept Jesus's love
Displayed on Calvary's cross
As He died to set us free
From sin's resulting loss.

Repent today
Don't delay
Jesus is the way
Holds sin at bay.

Dear Lord, thank You for saving my soul that I may live better on earth and forever in heaven with You. Amen.

Don't Get Frosted

When it's sown in tears, joy is reaped. Those who steps out weeping and living a witness of God's truths, will come back rejoicing bringing their sheaves (others) with them.

—Psalm 126:5–6

We just had our first frost of the season. My flowers were not covered. Yes, they were killed. The begonias became as mush.

No life left in a single one. Our beautiful flowers did not survive, but the weeds did. They retained their summer lush, unaffected by the damaging frost.

An available, involved, or a caring Christian can get caught up in a determined frost that kills their genuine efforts. The frost makers' well-timed attempt to produce destruction brings success.

People do cause hurt to other' hard work and intentions. To destroy their witness is the desire. However, results of their planned frost bring momentary happiness.

We must remind ourselves those benefits are temporary, because a new season begins now. Pray for a new direction or different process to grow in the garden.

God produces great things through faithfulness. Our efforts do grow much in the hearts and lives of onlookers.

Then comes another life-giving season. Spring starts, summer matures, harvest reaps care to share everywhere. But that frost will continue to harm our plans any day of our agenda.

We must be prayed up and fixed up with preparations for any unexpected frost.

Dear Lord, I trust You to lead me to reap a colorful harvest as frost free as possible. Amen.

Pippin

You will help me from getting into trouble.

—Psalm 32:7

An absolute Pip is our kitten. He was hiding in the weeds of a ditch. His loud meow and bright eyes caught our attention. Securing my hand around this big-eyed noise maker, I lifted him out of the ditch.

He was a small wiggly kitten and seemed to be okay. There was no evidence of injury. I carried him home.

After consulting with an animal rescue facility, we chose to keep him. Health checkups were done. This presumed eight-week-old kitten became ours.

What do we name him? Our teenage granddaughters chose Pippin. It was a perfect choice. He's been a real pip.

In and out of trouble, this active kitten displayed need of training. Instructions fell on deaf ears. Maybe that was why he'd been "thrown away."

How many times are we rescued by our Lord? We, too, have a strong will, are hardheaded, and become self-insistent to do *it* our way. But that *it* often brings problems. We maneuver, trick, bribe, even push our determined will on others or some issue. Hurt then follows by a brief regret, only to do something else equally selfish.

Will we ever learn? All our actions are known to the Lord. Still He provides care.

We are fond of Pippin and try to teach him proper behavior, preventing harm to himself, people, or things. Our Lord guides our way of life so we won't become a pippin.

Dear Lord, thank You for consistently rescuing me
from my own actions. I give You praise. Amen.

Rest for the Test

I went to bed, slept, and awakened.

—Psalm 3:5

And maintained an honest life.

—Titus 3:14

God gave us human flesh to house our bodies. We have twenty-four hours in each day. Within this amount of time, we are to work, play, and sleep.

Work takes eight plus hours most weekdays. At home, we deal with housing and property upkeep. Then comes family time.

Each member needs attention in individual ways. Of course, meals are essential to nourish and sustain our continuance of life. At some point in the evening, relaxation and maybe a bit of entertainment is expected.

Finally, it's to bed we go. How much time has to be allotted for sleep? This day was busy. Tomorrow is scheduled with more of the same—busy.

All that is expected of grown-ups presses our buttons with tests. They never stop. All waking hours are filled with one test or another, at home, at work, or at play.

The busyness of each week's routine tests proceed, whether we take time out each day for private time or not.

Too many tests fail when we do not put God first and allow for proper rest. Both are of His original intent.

Sleep
Sleep today
Just now

To be rested
For life's tests
Lord, Help me sleep, I pray.

Dear Lord, I'll take time for You and allow time for sleep.
Then my life in health will meet all daily tests. Amen.

Prepare You

Prepare you.

—1 Samuel 7:3

God is going to use you. It's in His will for you to step in among people. You will represent Him. Others will appreciate your efforts or not.

They may believe you presume too much of yourself. They may become jealous and display it. You can be compared to that special person and come up short. Negativity will probably arise around you. But remember, God has called you.

Prepare yourself in the manner fitting where you will be used. Prepare you in the most productive way possible. Ask the Lord for direction in other ways needed to be prepared.

He will answer that request.

When God is asking you to be prepared, He is also speaking to other helpers that will be for your encouragement, support, and maybe even assistance.

Whatever the plan, whatever the future, wherever the destination, God says, "Prepare you."

Today's world is filled with a lot of *iffy.* True enough. Nevertheless, we are to get ready, prepare to work through, or simply deal with difficulties that may pass along our way.

Your call today is to be prepared so you will be ready and able to face tomorrow.

God is already there.

Dear Lord, You want to use me? Oh, wow! Help me to know how and where to begin and prepare for Your use. Amen.

God's Instructions

The path of the disobedient is darkness,
they can't see why they stumble.
—Proverbs 4:19

Read Exodus 7–11.

Lions and tigers and bears, oh my, were stated back then. What about blood, frogs, lice, flies, disease, boils, hail, locust, darkness, and death? And oh my, these ten troubles were experienced by Pharaoh, the leader, when he refused to release God's people, the Israelites, from slavery.

Pharaoh wanted to use every ounce of their strength in his service. He didn't care about their health or concerns. They were in his property.

But these Israelites cried to God. They knew He was their only escape. He could provide a rescue. God heard and answered.

He sent Moses to meet with Pharaoh and told him to "let God's people go." Pharaoh said no. So God sent all ten troubles, one at a time, to get Pharaoh's attention. He was stubborn. It took all ten until they got personal before he let God's people go.

Then Pharaoh insisted Moses and those people get out, like now. God's continued toughness got Pharoah to finally take note and admit defeat.

God still reigns over all. His will is for us to listen, obey, and yield to His voice. He knows the way we should go.

Let's not wait for lions and tigers and bears or more to come knocking on our door. God will work with us whether we are willing or encouraged to be willing.

Which way shall it be, the Lord's way or mine?

Dear Lord, oh may I listen and follow Thee. Amen.

Cleaned-Up Tomato

You (we) look like cleaned up sepulchers with
beautiful exteriors, but yuck fills our interior.
—Matthew 23:27

In late summer, northeast tomatoes are ready for picking. It's this season's routine for me to gather a full bushel of this ripe red fruit.

The large open field of my destination was full of many hearty tomatoes. They looked well worth the effort: fat and beautiful.

One by one, they were thoroughly checked. As each tomato was picked up and examined, many were returned to the ground.

It's amazing that an ideal shaped and colored tomato can be worthless. At its first appearance, a flawless looking fruit hides its lie. Upon closer investigation, reality glares back.

These particular tomatoes were cracked, had bad spots, or were just rotten with an accompanying gross odor. Nothing from its original pictorial assumption was useable. That view was deceptive. Truth got exposed. Only so long could these damaged tomatoes hide their inner decay.

We, too, walk, talk, and dress appealingly. How lovely we present ourselves when we want to make an impression. We can become rather captivating and well-groomed until our inner person is exposed. Then it becomes more than an oops when the ugly and smelly truth falls out.

"Oh, why did I reveal the real me?" we ask ourselves. As our own truthfulness is exposed, we become aware of our own authenticity.

Dear Lord, forgive me for the yuck I allow to remain in my heart. Help me to be a rot-free tomato, offering functional use. Amen.

Christian Fruit

Jesus was hungry. He saw that the fig tree far off had leaves,
but upon arrival He found there was nothing but leaves.
He said, "No one will eat fruit from you again."
—Mark 11:13–14

As Christians, are we covered with leaves? Do we wear an appearance of being fruitful? Has our upbringing, training, church attendance, and church activities camouflaged us to think we look all right? Do we speak with Christianese?

There are many questions we can ask ourselves. But with truthful honesty, do we admit whether our religious preparedness has produced Christian fruit of any kind, size, or amount in us?

Does all the above cover us with fluff? Reality is what we need. Fluff never works. The question glares. Will God cut us down if we do not produce fruit?

Such a thought is sobering. May we not be just leaves but lives filled with nutritiousness reflecting the love of Christ. That's accomplished when our actions show and offer fruit within our Christlike lives. As Christians, we must produce beautiful fruit. This should be made available to everyone today and every day with their life-giving eternal destiny in mind.

Dear Lord, with all the biblical truths and Christian information I have learned and even taught, help me become a valuable witness to all I contact in person, by phone, through mail, or any type of social media and simply to whomever or wherever they may be. Amen.

$10.00

Everyone shall give as they are able.

—Deuteronomy 16:17

As we left the morning service, the Lord told me to give money to a certain young man. No urgent need had been mentioned. He didn't look needy or ask for financial help. Still, the Lord turned my attention to this person. I didn't know his name. He might have just strayed into the service.

All I know is God told me to give this man some money. So I did. My wallet contained one $10 bill and one $20 bill. I gave this man the ten. His radiant smile and kind words expressed gratefulness.

While we were driving home, I told my husband what I had done. I was pleased with myself for having obeyed God's nudge. I opened my wallet to further expound on my generosity. There was one $20 bill and one $10 bill.

"Huh."

How could that be? I gave away the only $10 I had. There was no other. Yet $10 was there. I touched it. It was authentic.

Immediately, the Lord replaced my $10. I was amazed AT what God had done. Why did I shortchange that young man and give him the least that I had? Why did I not give away the best? The same God that replaced the $10 could have replaced the $20.

Dear Lord, I also shortchanged me by not having a more caring heart for this man and limited my trust in You. Amen.

Respect Mom and Dad

Respect your mom and dad. This is the first
commandment with a promise.

—Ephesians 6:2

Rachel was a dear Christian woman I had the privilege to know for thirty years. This lady lived to be 105. She wore those years well.

I often remarked about the blessing of her advanced age and good health. This, I believed, was her reward for respecting her parents. God's promises such a plus in the fifth commandment.

We all have parents. We are here because of them. We are not responsible for their past and the way they treat us. We are only accountable for the way we react to them.

Whatever they are (present, absent, or deceased) is whatever they are. We are to do what ought to be done. That is to bestow great regard, high esteem, and full courtesy to our moms and dads.

Our reward is a long life on this earth and a loving care for those who gave us life. And may it be so that our children will honor us with genuine concern, as Rachel clearly received throughout her long life.

Dear Lord, thank You for the parents You gave me. Who they are made me what I am. What I lack, You will complete in me. Amen.

God Knows Best for Our Project

The Lord said to David, "It was in your heart to build Me
an house. You did well to have it your heart's desire."

—1 Kings 8:18

We come to the end of our career and have not received God's directive to go ahead with our desired project.

This has been in the back of our minds, front of our wishes, and heavy in our hearts for some time, but God gave no permission to design the plan. God may have agreed it was an unselfish suggestion, but He hasn't allowed us to do it.

Disappointment was big. We don't understand. We've lived a godly life. Plus we're qualified and capable to accomplish the project. God still said no.

Maybe it's because currently, our plates are full.

Maybe He sees something ahead and keeps us away for our best interest or safety.

Maybe this isn't the proper time for the idea to have best value.

Maybe there are reasons—our past, for instance—that wouldn't work best with us leading the project.

Maybe God has chosen someone else to do the job, and we'll be used elsewhere.

The question and possibilities to the whys and why nots grow with each passing day. We are at a loss for an answer.

Yet that answer may never be known. We must let go of that hope and let God do what He knows is most fitting for all involved.

*Dear Lord, You do know me best and my future. I'll back
off and trust You with my desired project. Amen.*

Manasseh

We declare peace to others but hold mischief in our hearts.

—Psalm 28:3

Read 2 Chronicles 33.

Manasseh was twelve years old when he became king of Judah. This proud young man soon became wicked, vicious, and murderous, as well as an idol worshiper using witchcraft. He did all that God hates. Manasseh, Hezekiah's son, knew better but didn't care. He pushed his agenda anyway, no matter how many warnings God sent his way (verse 10).

After many years of his grisly treatment of God's people, even encouraging them to sin, God sent the Assyrian armies. Manasseh was captured and suffered gruesome affliction. Finally, he came to his senses and cried out to God, "Help" (verse 13).

Why must humankind need to be in grave danger before they turn to God or get serious with Him? Many people have known God, as Manasseh did, in their childhood. Why then must they ignore God for so long, maybe to the point of causing hurt in others?

Unfortunately, it happens. Eventually, the repentance begins, but not always with an honest heart. Secretly, a little desired something is kept active. "After all, God will not know. Even if He does, He'll understand" is quoted to cover up the very understanding that the knower knows the truth.

Manasseh's repentance was genuine. However, the people were not 100 percent in tune with God's directive. They kept a bit on the side (verse 17).

God does know the heart. What is He seeing in ours?

Dear Lord, I give You my whole heart. I want
nothing hidden or left behind. Amen.

God's Abundance

Now God is able to do more abundantly
beyond all we can ask or think.
—Ephesians 3:20

Early autumn found us waiting in line at a local ice cream stand because, as a gift, my husband and I were invited out. Summer was gone, but its warmth was not.

Our turn arrived. I ordered a small ice cream cone in my favorite coffee flavor.

"This is a small!" I announced when the completed cone was given to me.

I repeated several times, "This is a small!" My question brought smiles on the other waiting customers.

But I was embarrassed for the size of this small coffee-flavored ice cream. Three large scoops stood on top of a filled cone. A good five inches tall that frozen treat had grown.

My ordered cone was more than what I asked, more than what I thought, and more than what I needed, but not more than what I wanted. I love coffee-flavored ice cream. It's a rare treat. I enjoyed every lick of it.

If God can give a free and abundant-sized ice cream cone, how much more will He oversize the answers to our prayers?

Ice cream to a bill payment, ice cream to needed school clothes, monthly groceries, household appliances, or even a job to God is no problem. Abundance at all levels is equal to Him.

Any simple prayer request we submit to God will be answered. He may provide us with a triple-scoop response. Its size and appearance will be given in our favorite flavor to fit our specific situation to perfection.

Thank You, Lord. I can trust You to answer my prayer request with Your abundant love and provision. Amen.

Imagination—Starved

The Lord God has made the expanse of heaven and earth
with His great power. Nothing is too difficult for Him.
—Jeremiah 32:17

How starved is our imagination? Is it set on our presumption, our daily lives, how far our money can go, or view of others?

Check out the bright or night sky of our "over world." Regardless of the season. it goes infinitely beyond our eyes or magnificent telescope. So much more is out there and beyond all that's seen and understood.

How about the depths of earth and sea's underworld? We know there as well is much out of range of one's vision.

God, too, has instilled within us a great and productive imagination. How about our imagination? It stretches. But not to the extent God has planned for us.

When we get in that spot and are stumped, our imagination is spent. It has gone dry. Everything seems dull. Our imagination has come to an end.

Then God may say in one simple word, "Finally." It is now time to trust in His eternal creativity to work on our behalf. He has directions, positions, possibilities beyond what we could ever have thought, let alone dreamed, could be there.

When our wonderful imagination gets reinvigorated, we'll say, "How come I didn't think of it already? Amazing. Thanks, Lord."

*Dear Lord, my imagination is starved with no answers for
my dilemma. I know You have my solution in Your limitless
imagination set to arrive in perfect time. Amen.*

Rescued

When we were quite helpless with no way to
escape, Jesus came at the very time needed and
died for us sinners who had no use for Him.
—Romans 5:6

We wander, flounder, and wallow in this world and its distractions. The we get lost, hungry, or something happens, and we come to an end.

All hope seems gone. Desperation kicks in, and we feel about to drown. "Help," we may whisper. Then a hand reaches down, lifting us up and out of the mire of which we have sunk.

Yuck drips off in clumps. We look, smell, and feel gross. Our life seems to be ebbing away. That hand pulls us to Himself. Steadily, He holds us, even to the point of rocking us.

We cry and moan. We hold tight then begin to relax, settling in the embrace in which we are most grateful.

What and who has us now? flows through our foggy brain. Brief memory of how we got to that low point and questions to why it was allowed slides in our brain.

There we were. Now we are here, secure in the arms of Jesus. Just in time, He rescued us from despair's deadly grip.

When something tough happens, pray and trust Jesus to be there. He is and will stay.

Dear Lord, with my own permission and action, I got desperately low. Your loving mercy came and rescued me. Amen.

Billy Goat Christian

The Lord is good, a strong help for those in life's
difficulties, and knows those that trust Him.

—Nahum 1:7

When I was a child, I asked Jesus to come into my heart and be my Savior. He did. I'm now a Christian. I trust Him for my eternal life. I have no doubt about the permanency of my salvation.

Yet when life presents the difficulties, I kick in with a *but*: "I understand, but…," "I hear you, but this is my situation." Yes, God said He would supply, but… And so go the excuses. But you don't know what he or she is like or my financial and health responsibilities.

My billy goat response keeps a-kickin' in. I can't see or believe beyond my limited and self-focused narrow tunnel. I've convinced myself that the God Who gave me life after death in eternity, can't provide for my now.

Sounds rather silly. Billy goats are silly. They can't see because their heads are down. They're looking at the ground and assume things are what they presume them to be.

God says, "Look up." He has our solutions and will lay them upon us at the proper time for our best interest and benefit. He alone knows all the circumstances that surround us from every direction. And God will do what He says He will do—provide.

Dear Lord, forgive me for being a billy goat Christian. Help me to become a sheep that follows You, my Shepherd. You alone know best and will take me safely through. Amen.

Are We Ready?

Are we ready to worship the Lord in His holiness?
—1 Chronicles 16:29

Church time. That weekly scheduled hour to attend a service has come. Are we ready?

What have we done, said, watched, touched, or where have we been within the past week? A lot of minutes have enveloped our attention while walking through our weekly routine.

Has God been first place in our days and thoughts? Was He consulted in every decision? Did we exercise our knowledge of God's commandments or apply our understanding of His Word or even last week's sermon to our daily activities?

The finality of all these questions come from what we have cultivated all week. What we allowed into our minds and hearts, we take into the service.

As we enter our church's doorway, are we ready to be there? Psalm 100:4 instructs us to enter God's house with gratefulness and into its sanctuary with praise.

Our attitude after an hour or so of worship explains whether we were ready or not to be there. We can't function in any other avenue of life without being ready. This remains true for every church service we attend.

Getting ready for service includes spending daily minutes with the Lord, reading the Bible, hearing/singing hymns, spiritual songs, and choruses. Plus any radio or TV's Bible teaching program would be advantageous to our preparedness if we listened.

Church service comes around at least once every week. This week, are we ready?

Dear Lord, I will be ready this week and every week for service.
I want to be prepared to receive as I worship You. Amen.

God's Driving

Commit thy way unto the Lord. Trust also in Him.
—Psalm 37:5

It was on a recent Gaitler's radio program I heard Gordon Mote speak about his daughter when she had her driver's permit. His wife asked him to ride with his daughter to show her 'your faith and trust in her.'

Finally, blind Gordon Mote was convinced to do so. It was a-sit-on-the-edge-of-the-chair experience. His daughter did just fine.

Life has many, and often seems like most, days our unseeing eyes are committed to trust in God's safe driving. He will take us from here to there, safely maneuvering around each curve, over all bumps, up the mountain's scary heights, down those difficult steep, heart-wrenching inclines, and through all of the unknown, uneasy, discouraging, and heartbreaking intersections.

We are blind. We cannot see. We do not know what's in front of us or coming at us from any direction. But we can today, at this moment, and that tomorrow, trust in the Lord to drive us carefully forward, because He said so.

Dear Lord, I don't know, I can't understand. Admittedly, I am scared. Please help me to fully commit it all to Your safe driving. Amen.

Prepared?

Ezra prepared his heart to seek and understand
God's law, and to do it…

—Ezra 7:10

How are we spiritually prepared? What does our time reading the Bible look like? Do we pray?

Now three plus times a day, we feed our bodies. Those meals and snacks are our daily habit. Feeding our bodies bring energy for us to accomplish our responsibilities. Food is needed. It's a must. We can't survive without it.

So what would happen if we fed our spiritual lives as often we do our physical bodies? Would we be strong enough to face the anti-God issues that swell around us?

Would we know exactly what the Bible states and how it's to be applied in our personal and public lives as well as the ongoing global events? Would we know God's direction in dealing with such concerns of the day?

If we physically eat as we do spiritually, what would our bodies look like? Would they be malnourished? It's like if we have no food and have no umph, we'll become unusable for any physical or spiritual value.

To be worthwhile, we need to spend alone time with the Lord, in His Word, plus praying and listening to His personal responses to us. They prepare us for what's up today, tomorrow, and life.

Dear Lord, so much is happening all around. May we make time to prepare ourselves and to help others as we spend time with You and the Bible. Amen.

Preparation

Prepared for every good work.

—2 Timothy 2:21

The apostle Peter spent time with the Lord and learned from Him. Thus Peter was prepared to minister to anyone along his daily route.

Acts 3:1–11 report the event of one particular morning. Peter was going to church to pray. A disabled beggar was sitting on the side of that road. He was begging for money. Because of that infirmity, he was unable to get a job. Begging was his means to support himself.

Peter saw this man. Peter had no money but was prepared and gave what he had. In Jesus's name, Peter spoke, giving healing to this lame man. Immediately, he got up, leaped, and praised God.

How we prepare ourselves today is how we will be able to be used tomorrow. We don't know the how or where it will be needed, but if we are ready, we can give what we've gleaned from our preparation.

A well-prepared Christian is ready for that whatever. That can be a wide range of needs or issues. The greatest answer we can give is Jesus.

As the beggar was outside the temple, many people today are outside of Christ. In their own way, they are begging for someone to notice, care, and help.

These people are not inconveniences but opportunities for us to impart results of our preparation, providing in their desperation.

Dear Lord, I want to be there for those needing attention. May I be as prepared as Peter was for that down-and-out person. Amen.

Prepare for the Fox

We must wear the armor of light.

—Romans 13:12

Early in the evening, a red fox with a long fluffy tail takes a frequent trip in front of our house. He steps from the dark woods a short distance to the left of our front window which faces our house, and he works his way down the country road, reentering a short one hundred or so feet later.

This sly critter moves into the open, cautiously observing each step he takes. He's very aware of us and watches our activity, giving us side glances or a full-face view. What is the wily fox up to? We may never know. Nevertheless, he's there. He's slipped his cover. Our alert has been raised.

Temptations, distractions, smooth speakers, and many others work in their cunning to trick and draw unsuspecting people their way. These people may take training by watching the fox. It's certain these people are aware of us.

Our defense is to be awake, informed, and full of knowledge from God's Word. Every day we must read the Bible and learn its answers, directives, and warnings. They will make us aware when some fox comes our way.

We need a full-bodied armor (Ephesians 6:10–17) to protect us from his or her craftiness. This safeguard is essential when that foxy person sets us in their sight.

Dear Lord, help me to take the time to become
prepared and ready for any such fox. Amen.

Different

Shout with joy…come before God with singing…
comprehend the fact He made us, we are His people.
—Psalm 100:1–3

You are different from me. I am different from my husband. We
are different from our neighbor. But we are alike in many ways.
We all have feet, hands, ears, noses, and can communicate and eat.
Our food and creative tastes can be as different as we are in appearance and hair color. But through it all, we are unique. Your abilities
are given to you for you to accomplish in life which you are gifted
to do.

God singles each of us out for His purpose. We were planned to
have our family of heritage. They have prepared us for life. All that
we are is God's individual design from the billions that have, do, and
will walk on this planet we call earth.

He has filled this globe with a variety of people. A full assortment of us folks cover this world. We are a beautiful, colorful, and
interesting creation of God.

Yet we are all so unlike, even poles apart, specifically distinct,
worthwhile, valuable, simply priceless men, women, boys, and girls
created to reflect our spectacular and awesome God.

Different is good. That's God's idea. I like it that way.

*Dear Lord, thank You for making me and all those human beings
around me. How much You must love us to make us so different. Amen.*

Choices

For I know the plans I have designed for you, says
the Lord. They are for your peace and not for harm,
to provide you with a blessed conclusion.
—Jeremiah 29:11

You had no choice:
When, where, or by whom you were born.
Your inherited shape: is it apple or pear?
Your family: your mom, dad, siblings, and all.
Your natural talents and personal whims.
Whether you are hyper, strong-willed, or not.
Because you are a gift from God planned by Him a long time ago.

But you can choose:

What your body does or where it goes.
Your attitude: does it stink or shine?
If you share or don't care.
What you reflect: good or ill.
What you see, hear, and consume
What you will do with God.

Summary

Ancestry: you did not choose,
Genetics: your birth design.
But what you do with what you got
Is up to you at every stop?
Dear Lord, as You said in Your Word (Joshua 24:15),
I am to make a godly choice. Today, I do choose to
serve You in every avenue of my life. Amen.

Proverbs 2

Hear instruction and wisdom, do not reject them. For those who accept wisdom love their own soul.

—Proverbs 8:33, 19:8

Listen

1. My son, if you will take My words and place My laws within you,
2. So that you will turn your ear to wisdom and use your heart for discernment.
3. Yes, if you desire comprehension and speak your voice to understand,
4. And if you search for wisdom as you would silver and hunt for it as you would hidden riches.
5. Then you will have fearful respect for God and become more aware of Who He is.

For the Lord

6. Gives wisdom. Out of His mouth comes learning and understanding.
7. He gives soundness of mind to the godly and protects those that are upright.
8. He guides the results of decisions securing the paths of His saints.

9. You will understand righteousness, justice, and fairness, knowing right from wrong.

Because

10. When God's wisdom connects with your heart, you will have delight in being you.

Then

11. Discretion will preserve you and understanding will possess you,
12. And you will be delivered from the wiles of evil persons and from being disobedient.

These will save you from

13. Leaving the paths of the godly to walk with the godless;
14. Revel in doing wrong and join in the disobedience of the wicked
15. Whose lifestyle is ungodly and pathway obstinate.
16. To hold you from the seduction of a prostitute and all her flattery,
17. Who walked away from the vows of her younger years and the covenant she made with God
18. For her practice and health leads to disease and ultimately to death.
19. No one that goes unto her will return the same. Neither will their health be the same

Then you

20. Will walk the life of a godly person and remain morally clean in all your doings
21. For good people will be the ones to live full lives, and the healthy shall enjoy it
22. But the immoral shall lose the good they once had; violators of godliness shall be the losers.

*Dear Lord, may what I take from this chapter
help guide me daily and beyond. Amen.*

Believe

Not one word of His promise has failed.

—1 Kings 8:56

"But God promised. He said He would do it. He said so." We complain because God did not come through in the way we assumed He would.

Material and financial needs, physical health, or loved one's salvation has not yet happened. We guess we had given God plenty of time for Him to fulfill His promise. It has not arrived.

What do we do now?

We should begin by reminding ourselves of those times our children wanted something so bad, and we didn't get it for them, not then.

Also, when we wanted something equally and it didn't occur. Today we are *so* grateful it did not come. If it had, it would have been a serious hindrance.

And there's that fellow employee who aimed for an advancement that could not be achieved. He or she tried hard and longed for it anyway, and it still didn't come through. Instead, they received something better.

There are many instances we have known and experienced God's outright provision via an ordinary routine or a complete surprise. Let's remember them when we question God. He does know what's going on and will do that which is perfect for us in His time, way, and manner. We just bide our time and wait.

Dear Lord, I do believe You do know best and will wait, because what You said You will do. How dare I doubt. Amen.

Teabag Message

I do hope for what I don't see…with patience I wait.

—Romans 8:25

I put a cup of water in the microwave for tea using an already used teabag. It was coming to the end of its assumed value. Nevertheless, it was put it in the water.

The microwave's heating process would take out the last amount of tea remaining in this teabag. When the microwave's set time was completed, the water was hot, but it was barely tea colored.

The teabag was left in the hot water. A few up-and-down dipping with this teabag improved its color a little. Off I went with my cup of weak tea.

By the time I arrived at my destination, this cup of weak tea had gotten rather dark. It now held a much tea-flavored value.

The tea's first appearance was incorrect. It was wrong. The teabag eventually did its job, and it did it well. I had a serious cup of tea. I just simply needed to wait. That waiting wasn't long, though I was impatient.

God will bring forth to me what He has promised. Sometimes a waiting process is necessary. The answer needs time to be at its best for us. And I need to practice trusting in the Lord while I am made ready for that answer. The entire process displays God's never-ending faithfulness.

The wait will always be worth its time.

Dear Lord, I continue to wait for Your solution
to my request. You're never late. Amen.

God Already Knew

It shall be...before they ask Me, I will answer.

—Isaiah 65:24

God has everything under control, even before we know there could be a complication.

As a house cleaner, I have the ladies I work for arrange their day and time slots to fit with my schedule. That arrangement is set weeks at a time. Then something happens that these gals need to make a time line change.

It was this week that adjustment was essential. I was to work for Lady A on Tuesday. She called last week and needed to up me to do the job a few days early. That would be this very Friday.

Then scheduled Monday's Lady B gal had to postpone me to the now opened Tuesday.

I was on my way to our Sunday evening's church service when my cell phone rang. I didn't realize my phone was on. (We live in an area where there is no cell service. When at home, the phone is shut off.) Thus I was surprised to receive Lady B's call for the date change.

Amazing. Without the Lord's prior knowledge and intervention into this situation, someone would have been left on the extended waiting list, inconvenienced.

As I reflected back, it brought a chuckle. God already knew the situation with both ladies and my availability and had everything all set up so everyone was satisfied.

Tuesday was back up to the emptied Friday.

Monday easily slid into that Tuesday.

Dear Lord, what a blessed assurance knowing You will work out my needs for me, even before I know I have them. Amen.

Offer Out

Stuff of this world passes away…but Jesus's
Words will not pass away.
—1 Corinthians 7:31; Luke 21:33

It's true this world we live in has lots of pretties. It can dress us up, slim us down, give us a mortgage or rent an apartment, design our vehicles, advertise vacations, offer a job even to some prominent religions or political position.

We provide for our children with as much as possible. We try to afford the perfect college for their desired career and expect us to achieve our own goals as well.

Much of the above is routine in this present age. We do need a home, education, food to eat, and clothes to wear. The rest that we load upon ourselves are simply God's blessings. He's generous.

At death, what happens to all that made up this our fortune we've worked, struggled, and pushed to attain? Those people left behind gets it all. No one travels with us. Those previous, present, and presumed to come days are just a few compared to the afterlife that follows our passing.

Having Jesus as our lifelong preference fills us up and into eternity. The path we travel to that point should be filled with more than these earthly benefits. God's very presence, conviction of the Holy spirit, and forgiveness of sin through Jesus's love at Calvary overrides any gold, silver, possessions, and recognition we accumulate on this planet. Plus we get to have an everlasting, never-ending life spent with Jesus our Savior in heaven. Wow. This offer outglitters them all.

*Dear Lord, I get to have Jesus today, tomorrow, and
all through eternity. Nothing beats that. Amen.*

Thoughts to Words to Response

The tongue can spill hurtful words or speak sweet
to that one hiding spiteful thoughts.
—Jeremiah 9:8

How do we greet that coworker, churchgoer, fellow shopper, or family member? Are we full of kindness, helps, promise, and encouragement? Do we share, provide, inform for that individual's benefit?

Do we search ourselves to know the truth of our motives? Would we admit it? Our thoughts hold many things. They may be bitter or sweet. Too often words spill out with no advance thought. After they have been said, no retrieval is possible.

Our inner wounds and deep-seated dislikes can be exposed at the least desired moment. Then we try to push that anger, frustration, or hurt out of sight. Yet those existing feelings, not dealt with, allow unkind thoughts to linger. Unfortunately, they can move us into an unwanted response.

Pleasant words bathed in vinegar gets absorbed. Then sour pickles develop. They reveal the contents of the heart.

Nothing can be hidden indefinitely. In time, the heart exposes answers to the questions: How do we? Are we? Or would we?

What then are we?

Oh,
May we like Jesus be.

*Dear Lord, it's easy to get upset and harbor those feelings.
May I settle the issue quickly and forgive. Amen.*

Circumstances

The Lord sees the righteous and hears their petitions…
no one that trusts Him will be sorry.
—Psalm 34:15, 22

Circumstances that happen to other people brings a sigh or "sorry." When they come to me, it's another story.

They get jobs, new cars, and good health. But I lost my job, car needs repair, and surgery is needed. Yet I understand when it seems they get all the pluses and I'm stuck with minuses. In every respect God knows each of us.

The Lord takes full responsibility for all that happens—life or death, wealth or poverty, homelessness or royalty. He can also change one to the other at any time.

The permission for my situation was granted by God. Sure, they may plant bountiful gardens, can afford to travel, or lose weight. When the deer ate *my* roses, no vacation was possible, and I'm overweight. It comes down to it's a *they* are them and I am just me. I cannot have what they have; it wouldn't be me. I know if I had to deal with what *their* life includes. I would be uncomfortable because that's not the way God designed me.

Yes, they may have plenty, but they have issues too. God is with all of us and will provide for daily requirements.

Life is God's plan for me. I must trust Him while in the midst of my circumstances, 'cause God *is* up to something.

Dear Lord, help me to be grateful and remember You are
bringing good out of my predicaments, difficulties, incidents,
and that matters to me—those circumstances. Amen.

Circumstances—Listen In

Because you do rely on the Lord. He will deliver.
—2 Chronicles 16:8

Circumstances are everywhere.
    Circumstances can put one on a dare.
Circumstances might become an *it* providing excuses such as the following:

It was. *It* wasn't.
It did. *It* didn't.
It could be. *It* may be
Because of some set fee.
Or
I saw *it* fall
At the corporate ball.
Then watched *it* rise.
It was, I surmised,
Seemed to be okay there.
And
Yet *it* appeared unfair.
'Cause
It said. *It* did.
It was not hid.
So
Is *it* true? Is *it* not?
Depends on what *it* has got.

Circumstances can ride on a single situation, an *it*, unexpected occurrence, unrelated factors, and then a complete turn of events can change *it* all around.

When all particulars fill in the context, *its* finale produced confusion. Did the *it* score?

Don't get caught in circumstances. They could be an *it*.

Dear Lord, I do know circumstances are not always trustworthy. There will always be an it *in* it *somewhere. Without reluctance, I will rely on You and not be concerned about any* it. *Amen.*

Jesus Was There and Is Here for Us Too

The Spirit of the Lord…is available to
comfort me in my mourning.

—Isaiah 61:1–2

At the death of a special person, one may need to be left alone. In this privacy, the brokenhearted can spend time with the great Consoler Himself, Jesus Christ. He soothes the wounds of the grieving.

When Jesus learned that John the Baptist had been beheaded, Matthew 14:13 tells us He took out a boat alone and went to a place of solitude. Jesus needed to be by Himself.

Upon His return, people were waiting for Him. He had to go on with life, even though He anguished over the loss. He continued ministering to the people's needs.

But then at the tomb of Lazarus, Jesus openly wept (John 11:35). Everyone around heard His cry and saw His tears. He was sorrowful at the death of this friend.

Death of someone dear brings on varied reactions. In any loss we face, Jesus does understand and will be with us through the sad and lonely hours, days, and years ahead.

When we ask, Jesus will hold us in His arms and allow us to lean against Him and receive strength to go on.

He promised He'll never leave, walk away, forget, overlook us, or get too busy to be aware and concerned for our aching hearts and earthly needs.

Jesus was there in John's and Lazarus's death. He is here for us in our loss too.

Dear Lord, when You were on earth, You were human and experienced sorrow and loss and felt the pain it caused. I'm comforted to know Your understanding love is here for me today. Amen.

Need

> If you see your brother and sister (or anyone) in
> need or hungry and you say, "Best to you,
> trust you find what you need," but do nothing
> to help, what good was that?
>
> —James 2:15–16

We all know of some need but don't get too concerned because we are okay. Our lives are settled in a safe and comfortable order.

Yes, we did wish that person or ministry the best and said we would pray for them. We shook hands and walked away. The need was forgotten.

Hence the injured, sick, and financially depleted people remain out of mind, and that Christian organization might have to close its doors from lack of funds or personal assistance. Nothing changed in their circumstances because nothing changed in us.

Then our conscience gets tweaked. "Come on," we console ourselves. "We did pray those few words in passing."

Our inner voice persists. We stop long enough to hear God talk to us. Then our hands, feet, and words work together, giving what we have available toward the very need we were aware.

Everyday suffering happens, and the everyday kind of help can be used and accepted if we do our parts. That will settle the conviction of the heart.

Dear Lord, when a needy situation is brought to my
attention, I promise to provide what's possible for
me to do. Yes, sincerely, I will pray. Amen.

A Big Head

The judgment of worldly people rejecting the
Light, is that they prefer darkness rather than
the Light, because their deeds are evil.
—John 3:19

What a sad story is recorded about King Jehoram. This young man was the son of Jehoshaphat and grandson of Asa. These deceased men had been godly leaders. They loved God and obeyed Him in all actions.

Then it was Jehoram's turn. He was raised with righteous influence. He, too, knew about God and His commands. But Jehoram got the big head.

The entire chapter of 2 Chronicles 21 describes the life and outcome of Jehoram's kingship.

This thirty-two-year-old king eliminated his brothers so he would have no competition. His reign remained unkind. He believed he knew better than his dad or grandpa. They were the old people.

Jehoram must have complete control. After all, he assured himself that his progressive method to lead was best. He would run God's people in Jehoram's know-it-all-way. And he did.

But the end results of King Jehoram's reign was both physically devastating and publicly embarrassing. His big head produced heartache aplenty for his short eight-year rule's pathetic climax.

Dear Lord, I don't want to reap judgment for selfish demands. Help me to keep my thinking and decision-making Christlike, completely with Your guidance. Amen.

Bribery

> You shall not take (or make) a bribe, it blinds
> eyes…and cause untruthful words.
> —Deuteronomy 16:19

It must be done to get what I want wrapped up to my way of thinking. Come do it my way. You'll be paid well to get it accomplished. When the offered and approved financial amount is received, there would be no changing of the mind on said arrangement.

The bribe was set between two or a select few to produce the mastermind's desired effect. It was to be the initiated way, at any price, to get the job done. The bribe must bring its organizer's plan to fruition. That was the purpose of paying money.

Bribes, large or small, God sees them all. He was in the know from the get-go. We might try to conceal it. Eventually, someone will squeal. Fingers will point back to the originator's strategy.

Bribery eventually gets exposed. God says no on bribing to achieve our selfish intent. If the desired outcome is best for everyone, God will hear our prayers for His assistance. Then we listen to His answer. That response will show His way to be the better way. He'll receive credit for its success.

Seek God first. Be honest. He has the perfect solution. Bribery is never to be involved. Bribery is never included. Bribery would never be necessary.

Prayer changes hearts, mostly ours, to be willing to hear God's voice.

Dear Lord, I will reject all offers to be dishonest at home, work, play, politics, or church regardless of the reason. Amen.

One Small Stone and One Big Dude

The battle belongs to God.

—1 Samuel 17:47

It began when the young adult David took food to his older brothers in the army. As he approached their campsite, David heard loud and mouthy disrespect pour from one extra tall Philistine. This man named Goliath was defying Israel and their God.

David's brothers' military company didn't like the negative remarks and threats coming from the giant but did nothing about it. Instead, they ran in fear.

Now some years before, David was given instruction in God and Israel's history. David had been a good student and knew God to be who He says He is.

So David got permission from the king to confront this vulgar fellow and did so. Goliath was one big dude (9'3"). David was but a youth. Yet he remembered the God he had studied and trusted Him for direction and protection. Bravely, David ran toward his opponent, carrying his faithful weapon—a slingshot and one small stone. Goliath was armed to the hilt plus had a bodyguard to boot.

David looked straight into his enemy's eyes as he ran toward him. "I come to you in the name of Israel's God," David said. He swung his sling. Goliath's irreverent words were never again heard.

We may know someone carrying an intent to cause us harm. David left with one excellent example. He spoke God over the situation. God did the rest. He's the same God here, right now, available to help us. Call on Him today.

Dear Lord, I give it to You. Tell me what I should do. Amen.

Meet with God First

David asked the Lord...the Lord said, "Go."
—2 Samuel 5:19

David had been anointed king. This didn't sit well with the Philistines. They were ticked and accosted David.

The valley of giants' Rephaim, was the location chosen to meet David head on. He was to be put out of the picture as soon as possible.

David heard of their planned hostility against him. He didn't attempt a rebuttal. He met with God first. God knew the in-depth battle schemes of David's opponents. He wanted God's perfect direction.

David asked, "What should I do?" God said to go ahead and He would deliver the Philistines into David's hands.

It happened. The enemy was beaten. David named the battle Ba-alperizen, meaning "place of breaking through."

Yet the defeated Philistines chose to try again and stretched their troops over Rephaim. Their expanse was impressive. They would win this time around.

David said, "Wait," and asked the Lord what to do.

God said, "Don't go to them yet."

A special tune was to be played in nearby mulberry trees. When it was heard, they made their move, for God had already gone before, opening the path against the Philistines. David and his men followed God's instruction. Victory was theirs.

God directed the battle. God produced success. Today He is aware of each unkind intent pinned against us Christians. God has the perfect answer. We're to ask and respond accordingly.

Dear Lord, too often I plunge ahead to do what I think is best. This can bring a serious oops. Now I will consult You first. Amen.

God in Our Situation

They cried to God in the midst of trouble and He
rescued them from their situation. He brought
them out of the darkness…setting them free.
—Psalm 107:13–14

We got us a situation. We are in the middle of something serious, confusing, or momentarily exciting. Part, or maybe all of it, is of our own doing, or none of it came about by our actions. We could very well be the innocent party drawn in without our control, or because we just did not say no.

Whatever or however it happened, we feel we are now in the depth of darkness with that unexpected pregnancy, family friction, identity theft, ill child, no electricity, false accusation, employment disagreement, or a refused loan application. We see no exit.

The sovereignty of God has permitted this darkness. He is aware of all that is involved with us. The question is, Are we prepared to allow God to do the work in our lives as He chooses? In all likelihood, we will be separated from seeing God's process. We will be confused.

When we do arrive to where He has been working to place us, it will be okay. Its purpose may then be made clear why we encountered such a situation. God will remove the darkness and set us free.

Dear Lord, when I don't know, I know You do know,
and You are working on my behalf. Amen.

Colorfulness

Gray or white hair is a crown of glory. It's often found in
those that have walked upright in the way of the Lord.
—Proverbs 16:31

So what color is your hair? What color is your life? What color does
your heart express through thoughts, attitudes, and behavior?

A lady teller at my bank dresses in vivid colors. She wears appropriate color makeup that sets off her beautiful smile. She is a color-filled lady.

Color describes us too. We may not choose brilliant reds, greens, and blues to dress for the day, but we do display some degree of color.

Color is worn on our bodies through the pigmentation of our skin and color of our eyes, as well as our hair. We complement them with the choice of our personality.

I don't know that particular bank teller. I've not had private conversation with her. I've not been in her home, shopped with her, or even attend church with her. Truthfully, I don't know anything about this woman, except her first name (because of the placard) and the colorfulness of her dress, speech, and mannerisms. She seems equally lovely. I have no firsthand knowledge either way.

It's what's inside people that works its way up and onto our physical appearance. Maybe that's why the inner beauty of this woman becomes visible through her colorfulness.

Having family and walking through life and age does give color. What shade will that be?

If we're to have color, may it be the Jesus in you and me glowing through and shining all over us.

Dear Lord, may the world around see Your radiance.
Color me from my hair to my flip-flops. Amen.

Don't Put God in a Box

Do not wound the Holy Spirit or extinguish the Holy Spirit.
—Ephesians 4:30; 1 Thessalonians 5:19

We pray for the Lord to work in our church, speak to the congregants, and bring conviction on each one.

Yet when the service begins, we have our format program arranged the way we decided it should be done.

My question is, Where is God permitted to do as He sees fit? He alone knows all hearts, minds, and lives in attendance. He knows the when and way He would want to move.

He may speak to a certain someone about something, and that person hears and is willing to respond, but we've given no opening and allowed no space of time for that one to find God.

After the organized church service is over, so is the conviction in that individual. We've put God in a box and said, "If You want to work among the people, this is the time slot open."

And yet in many of our services, we feel God's presence in us and know we should back off and give the Holy Spirit space to work. Instead, we say, "No, there's no time. We have our own after-church plans."

In other words, don't put out the Holy Spirit's fire. Let God move at His will. This is not for just our church services, but it is to be applied in our personal lives as well.

Dear Lord, I can critique my church services
just fine. But I must do the same in my life and
see where I've put You in a box. Amen.

God Has No Lack

Every beast in the woods are Mine, as well
as the cattle on a 1,000 hills.

—Psalm 50:10.

God said, "The silver and gold are Mine."

—Haggai 2:8

Gold or silver
Dollars and coins
Houses and lands
Earthly toys

Are just a few
We think we need
To care for us
In our life's greed.

For patience
Faithfulness
Mercy
And love.

With answers
And direction
Come only
From above.

God's got it all
It can be ours too
If we but ask
He'll give to me and you.

He does not lack
He has no need
Only for us
To follow at His lead.

*Dear Lord, my son needs shoes, my daughter a coat, the bills
must be paid, and I am broke. Help, I cried, and thanks for
Your supply. You've met my needs because I applied.
You're always there for each of us, if we would but ask, and we
would plead, knowing You will provide for our every need. Amen.*

Moods

One must be willing to accept what is and not what it isn't.
—2 Corinthians 8:12

Moods are not caused by condition but by our willingness to express a desired state of mind and attitude.

Are we in a bad humor, low spirits, or down in the dumps? Do we plan to stay in such a disposition? Are life's doldrums offering an excuse?

We can choose to be sulky or spiteful to a family member(s), but when an admired and more welcome visitor knocks on our door or makes a phone call, instantly our mood improves. We become chipper and upbeat to that person. But when they've said goodbye, our mood goes back to the "woe is me and bum on you."

At some point in time, we all can get in a negative mood. It happens, but we do not need to hold onto that unattractive and ill-desired grumpiness.

Such atmosphere can be dark and envelop us within it, or we can decide to say, "Enough already" and put on a cheerful tone. We can decide on a mood. We can deliberately, with actual thought, adjust or change the mood.

The nature of our feelings is portrayed in our vibes. Let's make our manner matter and reject the blue and choose to smile through whatever besets me and you. God is waiting to help us. Call on Him. He's there.

Dear Lord, oh that person or job's decision does upset me!
But with Your ongoing encouragement and faithfulness,
I will wear a genuine smile through it all. Amen.

Standard Time

Recall how brief is my life (time).

—Psalm 89:47

In past time was summer.
At that same time were longer day time hours.
At those times they were appreciated.
For the time being they're history.
From time to time one remembers those longer daylight hours.
In no time, they are gone.
In good time they will return.
In the meantime, we have a new time.
In time, it's hours will be filled with cold temperatures.
Many a time fun and celebrations will brighten those short dark hours.
On time starts and completes each day.
Time after time, Christian witnessing continues.
Ahead of time we pray, plan, and prepare to share Jesus's love with others.
It's time all of us who know the Lord tell others.
What are we doing with our time now that we're scheduled in autumn/winter's standard time?
Today is the time.
Tomorrow there may be no time.

Dear Lord, You have allotted me only so much time. Today I will use its time wisely. Help me to take the time to tell others about You. Amen.

Stepped On

I am forgotten as if dead; I am as a shattered urn.

—Psalm 31:12

In my upper room, I begin each morning alone with the Lord.
This day, I wasn't alone. A jumping spider jumped on the
scene. It went in all directions, as if it knew it had been seen. I stepped
on the insect. "I got it," I said. "Now on with my devotions."

Upon their completions, I took a facial tissue to clean up the
dead spider and discard it. But the spider was missing.

The presumed demise of this spider happened on the carpet.
The cushion gave only a hint of death to the jumping spider. It got
away.

How many people are ignored and presumed to be out of the
picture by deliberate actions of another? Life continues with these
bruised people no longer considered.

But they exist. They're all around, crushed by the behavior of
one or a few. Maybe one of them is you. It hurts.

Tears flow, sadness envelops. "Too much already" is said.

Like the spider, you feel broken, even cast down. Psalm 42:11
asks, "Why be cast down? Trust God. He will lift you up."

"Then *they* won't be able to rejoice over me" (Psalm 30:1).

Cast aside all intentional "get back at them" thoughts. Trust
God to work it out. Allow Him to heal and take you through to a
higher and better position.

Maybe that's what the spider did. Either way, he got out of my
line of vision to his safety.

Dear Lord, when I'm overlooked or unwanted, I'll
give You praise. You will lift me up. Amen.

Teach Our Children

Teach your children about God, when you are sitting,
walking, at bedtime and up and around time.
—Deuteronomy 6:7

If we have children, we do all we can to give them the best of opportunities, including talking to each one about God.

He said to teach them His commandments, scripture verses,
and biblical reports of facts. Our children need to see us living out
God's truths in our lives in easy or rough times.

Our Christian beliefs should be portrayed in holiday celebrations. Do we display, speak, share, attend church services, or visit
those in need? What about books, movies, or handheld tech items or
the regular computer we use or allow to be used? Do these reflect the
Christian teachings we are passing on to our children?

All that has happened in our community, country, job, and
church began in the home. Results of family life overflowed into the
culture.

Teaching our children when they are awake and even when
they're getting ready to go to sleep about God and His love for everyone is required and necessary. Singing praises, praying often, talking
of God and His Word throughout the day, whether we are at home
or not, allows our children to see and hear us practice what we teach.
Soon they will see and know God's Word is for real and make it a part
of their lives. So when they have their children, they will teach God's
truths to them as well.

Dear Lord, I will teach my kids (and grandchildren)
about You and Your Word. Amen.

Fragile Fades

People are fragile as grass…that withers and fades as dying
flowers, but the breath and Word of God stands forever.
—Isaiah 40:6–8

Our fresh, young, glowing, fragrant, and ambitious selves grow
up and older. Older slips into age. This process diminishes
our youthful vigor and beauty, but the radiance and vitality of our
Christian life continues on.

The witness we've carried and professed shouts the validity of
Christ in us. It either saddens the heart of God or brings Him a smile
to see what we do with what we say we are.

Wherever we may be, do we display the Jesus in us? We cannot
undo anything of those bygone years. But today, we can lift our chins
and set our determination to walk and talk and sing and shout the
very Jesus we're about.

When these our earthly bodies dim, shrink, and fade out, will
their once blossom be remembered and made a difference to the people we've known well or as brief as "standing next to in the supermar-
ket checkout line" unnamed listener?

The life and love of Jesus within us is alive and displayed to
the onlooker, whether they feel their life is most wretched or they're
doing just fine.

Jesus is there for them. Share His love no matter the brevity of
the moments allowed or the attitude carried.

For all too soon, our fragile lives shall fade away to memory.
Will our years have shouted, "Jesus loves you. Please, dear friend,
Jesus lasts forever, and so we will too. Come join us."

*Dear Lord, I'm here today, gone tomorrow. May I be the
witness to help bring someone to You today. Amen.*

Sticks and Stones

Vengeance belongs to God. He will pay them back.
—Hebrews 10:30

It's been said, "Sticks and stones may break my bones." This a fact if stones are thrown at us or we're hit by sticks. We'll be injured. The old saying continues with "words will never hurt me." Bunk! Isn't so!

Harsh and unkind words send pain to the very center of our being. Immediately, hurt is on the scene. It could double us up, bring tears, or stay dormant until something shoots it forth. And then pain could become a huge issue, bringing heartaches aplenty.

God does promise to mend the bruises to our person. He said to "throw our pain upon Him. He cares what was said and done" (1 Peter 5:7).

God will deal with those responsible for the pain we received. That response will be accomplished with the appropriate accountability in His way and His timing.

Right now, God's concern is for us and the hurt we've experienced. But the beginning of our healing process starts with us. Many scriptures refer to the hurting person to forgive the attacker (Luke 17:3–4; Ephesians 6:12–14).

Unforgiveness sends the wound deeper. Unforgiveness will not help or provide any real answer.

Jesus says, "We must forgive them so we will be forgiven" (Matthew 6:12, 14; Mark 12:26). He will deal with the culprit. His plan is to bring peace and joy and good health to us. First, if we just forgive.

Please, Lord, help me forgive that one who caused me pain so I may bring glory to Your name and trust You for justice. Amen.

Wait

Blessed is everyone who waits for the Lord.

—Isaiah 30:18

We hate to wait. We want, almost demand, a microwave/speedy internet result to everything that concerns us. To deal with wait frustrates our very being. We want and expect it now. Waiting is a tough request.

But waiting is a must.

We had to wait to grow up, get our first job, find our spouse, the baby's arrival, employment paycheck, and the planned and hoped-for bonus.

Birthdays, special celebrations, various holidays, and desired vacations call for the need to wait. Weather changes are as God directs not by our impatience.

Of course, that expected letter or package necessitates a wait, as does the consequence of that particular situation. Time drags on. We wish for it to hurry.

The biggest call for our need to wait is in the salvation of our loved ones. Here we have no choice but to practice patience as we yearn for each one of them to get saved.

Then we realize others must wait for us at every level of our living. We understand the why of us and appreciate people willing to wait.

Wait can be good, very good. God answers all prayers. We may need to wait for it.

Dear Lord, waiting is so hard. You say I will be blessed when I do wait. And so I will. Amen.

God's Word Holds

By and by Heaven and earth will end, but God's Word will not.
—Matthew 24:35

Many years ago, a full-fledged flood came to our area. Hundreds of people lost homes, their contents, and personal and memorable effects. Vehicles and outdoor equipment were destroyed. They floated aside or were never found.

The loss was huge and affected my family. My in-laws were rescued by boat through a second-floor window. All their possessions were gone. It was devastating.

Within days after my son and family moved into a new apartment, the house burned to the ground. Thank God no one was hurt, but everything was destroyed.

Earthquakes, tornadoes, and even robberies remove people from their property. These difficult occurrences are travesties cause rethinking in affected lives and their listening and physically helping-out traumatized people.

Yet we know these things in time would have become history. In due course, temporary things will be gone.

But God's Word will never cease to be, come to an end, come to a close, or vanish away. It remains forever. Its truths never change. They are permanent from way back then, to today, and onto the always—forever.

Lost personal assets can be many and huge but not worth concern for securing our future. Worldly goods will fail us. The Bible never will.

Dear Lord, I place my life, its knowledge, wisdom, and understanding in Your Word. It will take me beyond the loss of stuff, from floods to fires, and the loss of my own life. Amen.

I Work, God Rewards

Be strong, don't let your hands get weak, for your
work, all your efforts will be rewarded.
—2 Chronicles 15:7

Nothing significant is happening. You submitted to God's call. You planned, prepared, rolled up your sleeves, and went to work.

Now your body is strained, your mental readiness is stretched, emotions pressed as you daily do the responsibility God gave you.

You see no real results. No souls are saved. No lives rearranged. No visible evidence of anything of value has come from your faithful and continuous work.

It gets tiresome. You get weary. You carry on, for it is God's assignment, and you are obedient.

Sometimes that original calling seems distant, far back in your memory. Yet you do remember and carry on.

God didn't assure big-time earthly money, recognition, or salvation of a multitude of souls. He gave the ability and gut desire to do just what you are doing, keeping on reigns in your thoughts and energy. You get up and face another day.

God promised to be with you each step of your current "seeming to be an unproductive" mission. Faithful are the words and work describing a Christian following God's assignment.

You will make it. You will have success. You may not see it today, but it will come. Eternity will reveal the excellent results your efforts accomplished.

Hang tight. Persevere. Jesus is with you through it all.

*Dear Lord, You see my work. You know I'm tired. Give me strength
to go on. I trust all rewards for my faithfulness to You. Amen.*

Spark

I cried, I am a person with unclean lips. Then a
seraphim placed a live coal on my lips.
—Isaiah 6:5–7

I have no experience starting a woodfire or to keep it going. All I
know is I have watched the process being done.

A log or stick to be used must be dry or hold little moisture.
These pieces of timber await the slightest flicker of a match, and then
a small fire begins. No painted, varnished, or soaked lumber will
spark. They've become too hard to ignite.

When we start our day with the Lord, we allow God to spark
a work in us. Then we set aside time to spend with the Lord, and
His Word helps us grow the size of that spark. By the time we get
to go to a church service or Bible study, we should have a fair-sized
flame underway. As this desire continues week to week, we've ignited
enthusiasm, opening our lives to a Holy Spirit blaze.

Wherever our feet trod, voice speaks, or hands touch, that fire
can become one God representing Christian living, people caring
vital witness.

But if our spiritual life doesn't take time for the Lord, we become
hardened as an unusable piece of wood.

Today let's fan that spark in our hearts to a flame and then on
into a valuable fire for the Lord.

*Dear Lord, I want my life to be more than a spark. I
will spend extra time with You to become a worthwhile
fire that will begin a spark in many people. Amen.*

Living Life

The days and years of my life…few and evil
they have been and have not reached.

—Genesis 47:9

Babies come and babies grow
To become men and women you know
They serve themselves or God their Father
Who loves them like no other
And then one day
Her eyes wake she
His eyes wake he
Truth now they see

What they have lived
What they have done
Where they have been
Where they have come

Emptiness abounded
Selfishness overwhelmed
He and she brought on failure
Of their life's chosen tour

Lord, help, please rescue us
From all we've pushed and fussed
To have it all our way
We do give to You to stay

We've grown to adulthood
Now more is understood
Our Lord, our Father God

Take us, change us right now
With such value others will see
We finished well this life's journey

Babies come and babies grow
Which way will they choose to go?

Dear Lord, may I never forget I fail and You do not.
Remind me when I forget all of that. Amen.

No Easy Way Through

Work with your hands to do that which is good.
—Ephesians 4:28

Work with one's own effort.
—1 Thessalonians 4:11

We want it? We got to work for it. Paying the required dues doesn't provide immediate results. That fee opened the opportunity for us to get what we want.

We can walk through the doors, wear a smile, and have lovely words, but that will not bring about our aspiration.

If we want to lose weight or get that degree, it will not materialize with only paying the entrance charge. Effort and hard work pave the way to accomplish our hope-filled wish.

No one can have what is wanted by stopping at the door. Each person needs to get serious, go on in, and begin to do what must be done to reach the goal.

Some stuff can be received with little to no effort. But to have a job, college education, or lose weight, one must put in physical effort to obtain it. The ability to do surgery, write a book, or walk a mile goes beyond the first step. Determination encouraged with action by taking the next step and even on to a run, pursuing the call that began it all.

Nothing gets done when money is paid and no work applied. Get up, get busy, go after that God-given desire He placed in our hearts.

Dear Lord, from today on, I will put one step in front of the other and follow them with as many as needed to secure my sincere longing. Amen.

Stuck

Because sin entered into the world via
Adam, I was conceived in sin.
—Romans 5:12; Psalm 51:3

I was born with coarse hair. As a teenager, I would say it was like a horse's tail. I've had it cut, colored, and permed, bringing no change in its texture. After a generous amount of conditioner is applied, the hair softens. But it's only a temporary fix. Nothing can be done to alter the natural intent of my hair's roughness. I was born with it. Today it remains the same. I'm stuck with its originality.

As with my hair type at birth, I also received a natural bent to sinning. I had no choice for this inheritance either. This happened because of Adam's disobedience recorded in Genesis 3.

No matter how much makeup I apply, outfits I wear, or maybe a surgical conversion tried, my sin remains. There is no human solution to free me from what Adam did. I'm stuck.

Hair I can deal with. But sin, I don't think so. To answer the question of my sinful nature at birth, I searched the Bible. I found it in a conversation Jesus had with Nicodemus in John 3:3–6. Jesus explained I must be born again. This was not like my birthday that gave me the stubborn grain to my hair but through God's planned design that unsticks inherited sin.

No hair problem could compare with my being born again. This experience takes me out of my sin and gets me unstuck forever.

Dear Lord, thank You for forgiving me of the
sin in which I was born. Amen.

Enemies Tried but Failed Faithfulness Won

After Ezra prepared himself, he sought
God and willed to do God's will.

—Ezra 7:10

Read Ezra chapters 1 to 6.

A remnant of God's exiled people returned to Jerusalem. Zerubbabel was directed to lead in the building of the temple for worshiping God. Their enemies said, "No, I don't think so" and tried to slip in among the efforts to sabotage the work.

These opponents tirelessly pushed their opinion to be upheld. They whined to the king about the rebuilding that was underway.

King Artaxerxes stopped the work. He probably got tired of years of whining.

Two years later, prophets Haggai and Zechariah said that the temple would be built. This was obviously a public prophecy and the adversaries heard.

These complaining foes picked up where it was left with the past king and whined to King Darius.

This king said, "Let's check it out." Research discovered three kings back. King Cyrus had written that this temple was to be built in Jerusalem, and the government would pay for it by returning all the items King Nebuchadnezzar had taken from Solomon's temple (Ezra 1:7; 2 Kings 24:13).

Be persistent in the call God has placed on your heart. Opposition of all types will attempt to stop your work. Pray and trust God. Don't give up and don't stop, for the Lord is with you.

Zerubbabel was stubborn for the Lord. Zerubbabel knew what he must do and continued until it was done.

Dear Lord, may I, too, be stubborn for You as I proceed to accomplish what You've asked of me to do. Amen.

Comparing One to Another

Heart was lifted up…mind filled with pride.
—Daniel 5:20

I'm glad I don't look or act like that person. He's praying to God. Can you believe it?

That man is said to have pulled questionable schemes, is prejudiced, unfair, and known to cheat on his wife. Now praying! You're kidding.

Luke 18:10–14 describes one proud Pharisee comparing his believed betterment to that Publican over there.

This man may have been guilty of everything the Pharisee described. Somewhere along, this Publican was convicted of his sin. He compared himself to Jesus, not to the critic watching him.

The Pharisee saw himself preferable to society and presumed to God. After all, you see, he was the top of the line—a Pharisee. He believed he knew best and expected people would agree with him. He was higher quality than most, especially that foolish, blubbering man on the other side of the aisle.

This weeping Publican was ashamed and tried to stay out of the limelight as he cried out to God. He wouldn't even look up toward heaven. His sin overwhelmed him in regret. He couldn't raise his eyes. In humility, he pleaded, "God, I'm a sinner. I ask for mercy."

Mr. Pharisee compared himself to another man and believed he was okay.

Mr. Publican compared himself to Jesus and knew he was not okay.

Dear Lord, I cannot compare me to anyone. I only compare myself to You. For You alone can make me to be more like You and of value to that someone else. Amen.

Rescued

When we were quite helpless with no way to
escape, Jesus came at the very time needed and
died for us sinners who had no use for Him.

—Romans 5:6

We wander, flounder, and wallow in this world
and its distractions. Then we get lost, hungry, or
something happens, and we come to an end.
All hope seems gone. Desperation kicks in, and we
feel about to drown. "Help," we may raspily whisper.
Then someone's hand reaches down, lifting us up
and out of the mire of which we have sunk.
Yuck drips off in clumps. We look, smell, and feel gross. Our life
seems to be ebbing away. Then that hand pulls us to Himself.
Steadily, He holds us, even to the point of rocking us.
We cry and moan. We hold tight then begin to relax,
settling in the embrace in which we are most grateful.
What and who has us now? flows through our foggy
brain. Brief memory of how we got to that low point and
questions to why it was allowed slides in our brain.
There we were. Now we are here, secure in the arms of Jesus.
Just in time, He rescued us from despair's deadly grip.
When something tough happens, pray and trust
Jesus to be there. He is and will stay.

Dear Lord, with my own permission and action, I got desperately low.
Your loving mercy came and rescued me. Amen.

Forgive

Before you pray, forgive anyone with which you have an
offense, if you don't, Father God will not forgive you.

—Mark 11:25–26

It's easy to get upset with another person. The disagreement may be long and harsh or as a simple tiff over some unintentional issue.

We've been hurt, vexed, disgruntled, insulted, treated wrongly, and the offender is unaware he or she did or said anything to upset us. So we hold a grudge against them, spitting fire at the thought or mention of their name.

The transgression wounded deeply, and we feel justified to be angry with *that* person. But it can place us in our own self-made prison, bound by the affront that continues to hold us tight. Our set jaw, piercing eyes, and determined intent displays our heart's attitude.

We have held ourselves captive by our own angry and rigid spirit, which may help grow ulcers, sleeplessness, changed eating habit, or some other ailment.

And then we read the scripture that we should forgive.

"Humph! I don't think so," we say.

Think again. Jesus said if we do not forgive them, He will not forgive us.

Now that is a risk one cannot afford to take. Forgiving others brings peaceful release, health, and God's forgiveness toward us.

Forgive. Do it today. Right now. Immediately. We can't afford otherwise.

No malice, no resentment produces sweetness and self-content-ment.

Dear Lord, You know that person. You deal with
them. I do forgive them completely. Amen.

I

Deception produces…pride of the heart…my sin is ever before me.
—Jeremiah 49:16; Psalm 51:3

The letter in the middle of the word *pride* is the same letter in the center of sin. That letter identifies the one responsible for both. It is *I*.

Each person reading and understanding such spelling reveals that the very I is I. I singles in on all human beings individually, specifically right in the location and time frame each twenty-four-hour day, seven days a week, twelve months per year, with its total of 525,600 annual minutes.

In every one of the 31,536,000 seconds alive in all 365 days, I remains centered in pride and sin. Its spelling does not change, but I can.

I can confess my sin and pride to Jesus. He then promises to forgive me of all the I problems and wash my heart clean (1 John 1:9).

Life with all its temptations, tastes, and testing the potential of that I is prominent. The I will never leave.

It hangs over our minds, memories, and actions to raise up huge I issues. In the English language, *I* will always be written in the middle of sin and pride.

But each time the I overwhelms, take a fast read back to 1 John 1:9 as many times a day, hour, minute, or even seconds that's needed. Jesus forgives every time.

Dear Lord, You know the I centered in the midst of my life. Help me keep I in appropriate boundaries so the effect of I will not overtake me. Amen.

I Was Wrong

Keep your heart with all diligence; for out
of it flows your values of life.
—Proverbs 4:23

Instead of shouting in the air
Words spoken with a flair
Proclaiming life's not fair

I fall down on my knees
With truthful, humble pleas
Of repentance to God, please

Saying, Lord, I have truly sinned
The world said I could win
If I would do this, their thing.

But I was wrong.
The world was wrong.
Ev'ything's gone wrong.

'Cause I listened too long
To their sinful selfish song.
Saying, "Join us. Come along."

Now I am in such a mess
For I have sinned, this I confess
My self-determined willfulness.

Lord, change my heart, fill my soul
That all the world will know
You've made me ev'ry whit whole.

Dear Lord, I blew it and am so very sorry. May all these I've touched by my sin be touched by the change You've made and are making in my heart and my life. Amen.

Past Forgiven

Who is God that forgives sin and transgressions
of His children? He delights in mercy.
—Micah 7:18

What have we done? What has been in our past that we wish
was not that? What were those remarks that can't be retrieved?
How far have they been pushed?

If we were put in a line up for sins and transgressions done, we
all would be pointed out as guilty. And we are. All of us are guilty.
At some point in time, we did make those comments, and we did do
that shameful act, but immediately or eventually, we were sorry.

Those unpleasant recollections flood back into our minds. We
repeat, "I wish I had not gone there, done that thing, or used those
words."

Whatever it was gets rehashed over and over again in our memories. The "why or why did I?" draws a deep and remorseful sigh.

But it is history, now over, never to be repeated. That is a certainty. Consequences of all that stuff are too great for our health,
thoughts, family, friendships, daily essentials, and everything that
concerns our Christian behavior.

All wrongful statement and exploits of bygone days given to
Jesus result in forgiveness of those sins, providing a clean heart with
renewed conscious and such a learning to make our future better.

*Dear Lord, I am so grateful of Your mercy and forgiveness
for those actions and responses of my past. Amen.*

Let Me Be Salty

> Salt is good, but if the salt losses its spice, how then
> will you season it? Have salt vitality in yourselves.
>
> —Mark 9:50

It had been many years since I made bread from scratch by dissolving yeast, kneading the dough, waiting for it to rise, and then baking it. I was drawn to attempt this process again. However, just when this batch was ready to be placed into loaf pans, I realized I had forgotten salt. At this point, it was too late to add it.

So the loaves were baked and eaten. They looked and smelled delicious but were rather unpalatable. Once more, I put together the same recipe. This time, I was extra careful not to forget the salt. This bread was m-m-m-m good. What a difference salt makes.

As born-again Christians, we represent Christ. If we live our lives without salt, our witness is bland, insipid. We must fill ourselves with truth and boldness of Christ. We become salty, tasty, and appetizing. The saltiness we exhibit will bring on real sanity and conviction to the world system. It draws unbelievers to Christ. All this attraction causes us, as old-timers used to say, "worth our salt"—a perfect loaf of bread.

Dear Lord, season my life with Your Word. I want to be so
flavored with salt that it will be drawn unto You. Amen.

Trust

The Lord said, "Let no professional person glory in his profession.
— Jeremiah 9:23

But trust the Lord to do good…in your
land, and you will be fulfilled.
— Psalm 37:3

I lack trust in this world
When
It's assumed I am to
Acknowledge,
Believe,
Understand, and
Rely on someone's words
Expounded
From
A professional person.

But by
Accepting life as
Uncertain,
Empty,
Discouraging,
Immoral, and
Brief,
Those responses just don't cut it.

Then
I found the
Answer to be in
Hoping,

Resting,
And
Residing solely
In Jesus Christ,
The world's Savior,
To carry me through.

Dear Lord, may I always share God's truth and faithfulness, in Whom I fully trust. Amen.

God's Reminder

Take heed and be diligent about yourself lest you forget
what you have seen, do not let it leave your heart.
—Deuteronomy 4:9

Read Deuteronomy 8:6–18.
When God says, "Beware," we need to sit up, take notice, and listen. The King James Version of the Bible begins Deuteronomy 8:11 with this single word of warning.

God rescued His people from slavery. Miracles and His constant attention were allotted to and for each one. He gave commandments and instruction to direct His people in a safe, healthy, and on into a prosperous livelihood.

He reminded them, "Don't forget from where you've been, when stuff comes on." When food, nice houses, livestock, silver, gold, and all you have multiplies, don't get proud thinking it happened because of your planning and doing and forget God.

For He alone delivered you from Egypt and loaded you with all these many blessings. It was God that fed you and kept you clothed and taught you in your time of struggle to be prepared for this very date and time.

Today, let us remember God is the very One that gave us the ability to learn and the knowhow for our sustenance. Nothing we have or will ever acquire is of our own doing. It all comes from God.

Putting credit upon ourselves sets us in the precarious position of God's "Beware" warning.

*Dear Lord, may I never forget that strength and
knowledge comes from You. Everything comes from
You. For that I do give You thanks. Amen.*

I'm Here—Ask

Give me your care. I'm here for you.

—1 Peter 5:7

Everything in my life is falling apart. Funds are dwindling. Family is self-absorbed. Government in my community, state, country, and other places on the globe seem to forget the individual. The little guy that struggles to hold all of life's pieces together is overlooked and even ignored.

I'm stuck over here, unable to change anything or anyone. From sunup to the next sunup like a daily whirlwind. Every day, normal rolls in its indifference.

Interests, agendas, influences, and schedules get knocked out of routine. You'd think I would get used to the ongoing scene adjustment. It doesn't happen. Yet it's my responsibility to be available and alert for and in any situation involving others.

Does no one see me and care about this daily weight I must carry? It's tough, it's heavy, and it grows.

"Hey, it's me. Did you forget me? Am not I always doing for you?"

Then to my knees I'm drawn. Down I go with tears flowing over my weary heart.

"Lord, help me," I cry. "No one remembers me."

God replies, "I have not forgotten you. I will not forget you. I am with you right now and will always continue to be here [Isaiah 49:15]. Give Me your heavy burden and I'll carry it for you. I see, know, and understand all you face each day. Ask Me and I will help you go through and do what must be done. I am here for you."

Dear Lord, I am being squeezed. You said You
hear my pleas. "Help," I ask. Amen.

Daylight Savings Time Ends

Remembering my time is short.

—Psalm 89:47

"This too shall come to an end." Often I have used this very phrase. Whatever seems to always be or is currently at work is only temporary. It or they will leave because it has its season.

Remember those desired longer daylight savings time hours. They allowed more time for the warmer temperatures and pleasant conditions to be available in each day. Early sunrise to later sunset hours were appreciated. More work and pleasure were accomplished within the extended daylight.

Eventually, daylight savings time slides into shorter cooler days and longer colder nights. Our daily routine takes on a distinct shift. That which was possible then today is not. Those weeks and months came to an end.

New and different now lie ahead. Exciting holidays and winter-time activities are in the near and future weeks and months. But alas, this season, too, shall come to an end.

It's a whatever we must face. It will as well come to an end. Ephesians 5:16 tells us to take note of *our* time. We're given only so much of it, and it, too, will end.

All we can count on that does not end is God's faithfulness. He is in today and will continue to be with us when "this too shall come to an end" happens to us, even in this season of our lives.

Dear Lord, things and time will end. You will take me through whatever they hold. Amen.

Rumor Mill

Sound words no one can condemn.

—Titus 2:8

Rumor mill's idle conversation is spoken by or obtained via a grapevine buzz to be accepted by some willing spirit. This one relishes the talk about someone, anyone, or any location.

If the story received is factual should be our first question before receiving such words. The report must be accurate. The "tell me so I can be in the know" or "maybe this topic will be relayed as a prayer request" are not good enough reasons to listen in or pass it on.

Excuses for accepting gossip are everywhere. They come from every direction. They are readily available and comfortable to share, especially in the manner we believe we have heard.

A truthful concern should become the real topic. Within our privacy, this need is presented to the Lord in prayer. We are commanded to pray for each other (James 5:16).

We do need to care and be available as much as possible. But first, let's be certain the information received was not from a bored busybody's tittle-tattle.

Give God that spur-of-the-moment ask before we speak such news elsewhere. He'll answer. Listen closely.

Dear Lord, it is easy to be a tale bearer or its recipient.
May I never be a participant of a rumor mill. Amen.

Election Day

When Saul was small in his own eyes…the Lord anointed him to be Israel's king…he feared the people and did as they wanted.

—1 Samuel 15:17, 24

Once a year, we have the privilege to vote. It's a right available to legalized citizens. The first Tuesday following the first Monday of each November provides that opportunity for Americans to vote for their local, state, and federal candidates for varied individual positions.

Results of the accumulated tally will have life-affecting ramifications. Those totals say yes or no to the person running for that specific office.

For all those choices, we need to become informed. It's our responsibility before God to be aware, as much as possible, about each person applying for the job.

To place that intelligent vote is essential for the benefit of everyone. Part of that is to receive clear instructions from God.

We must pray. God alone has all information. Some of which may not have been voiced, printed, or placed on line. Yet God is aware of the whole truth.

Before we sign our name to place our vote, let's plan to write in God's guided direction on that ballot. It's vital. God then will watch how we vote and why. Was it biased or God's choice?

The God Who knows the heart and knows what we did with our part to help bring America back to her start.

Elections do count
Conclusions we're stuck with
Accountability is ours
Answerable to God.

Dear Lord, I will prepare myself with available information and Your direction before I place my vote. Amen.

Your Trial

The trial of your faith...though tried by
fire will bring...glory to Jesus.

—1 Peter 1:7

Where are you? What circumstance are you stuck in? Has this happened because of your faithfulness to or belief in God or your Christian witness?

Time has been ongoing, and nothing has improved. The predicament seems to be going no place good for you. Fear enwraps you. Difficulties, with their headaches, fill your thoughts and words.

Stress grows. Health fails. Sleeps scarce. Appetite dwindles.

Please know God is aware of this struggle forced upon you. He is on the scene this moment and knows you're caught in the stranglehold of this situation's control.

Remember Shadrach, Meshach, and Abednego? They had been thrown into serious heat—the fiery furnace (Dan. 3:13–25). God was present in the lives and near death of these faithful and godly men.

Now King Nebuchadnezzar assigned such deadly fate for these men. But he saw a fourth man walking around in the furnace with these Old Testament Christians. That king said, "This fourth Person is like the Son of God." Yes, Jesus stood right there in the "seven times hotter" flames with those young men.

This very same Jesus is here with you this very day, this very moment, and this entire trial through, as He was with them, regardless how hot or long the process becomes.

*Dear Lord, I'm grateful You know the trial that's happening
to me, and You'll continue to be with me, bringing all
things out for Your glory and my best. Amen.*

Keep Your Cool

Gentle and quiet spirit.

—1 Peter 3:4

Wow! What was that your boss said? Did? That tone and volume used was unbecoming, impolite, and certainly not professional.

What did you do? How did you react? Was your reply as angry as his or hers? Did you reflect Christ in your manner?

Jobs are necessary. We eat, sleep, and live because of the income a job provides. Without it, we would be in a tough fix. God said, "If we don't work, we don't eat" (2 Thessalonians 3:10). Jobs are a gotta have.

You're like me. I like to eat. I like the comfort of my home. I want both, so a job is essential.

Bosses are as different as they are in number. Whether it is a mister, missus, or miss, each wears their personality and idiosyncrasies.

In contrast, we Christians are to be distinctive and unique. God tells us to "be holy, because He is holy" (1 Pet. 1:16). He is the One we represent when we encounter an unhappy employer.

When that individual gets angry, foolishness spills forth (Psalm 14:17). Don't let it upset you to the point of quitting your job. Instead, return with a quiet spirit. Your gentleness will soften the bad temper (Ecclesiastes 10:4).

Anger to anger makes anger. Heat to heat makes hefty hot. Extinguish the flame and speak forth a Godlike kindness, allowing His presence in you rule the atmosphere.

Dear Lord, only You can cool the steam of an angry leader. I cannot. I trust You'll govern the day. Amen.

Bumps

Put a watch, O Lord, on my mouth, control
the response from my lips.

—Psalm 141:3

What do we say when we're shopping and someone bumps into us? How do we react when a coworker passes an untruth about us or those hormones send a feeling through our bodies, bringing an unkind response? Or when our spouse makes an assumption, and of course, health, weight, finances, neighborhood, and other issues produce a range of bumps. How then do we conduct ourselves?

All these and more in our life's daily activities produce bumps. Bumps come to all of us. No one is exempt. We can't get away from them. Even alone we can get bumped.

When these bumps happen, we discover truth about ourselves. That which harbors in our hearts display itself from our lips. It's written in Matthew 12:34 that "out of the contents of the heart our mouth talks."

It's impossible to exist in life without encountering bumps. They will be on the scene to trip us up. We can't avoid bumps, but we can make praise to God number one in our hearts and from our lips. He asks us to always give Him praise (Psalm 34:1). When we do so, our lips will speak forth a genuine Christian response. Such words will be most pleasant to be heard.

Dear Lord, bumps reign heavy in my home and public life. When they come, may I speak a true witness to Your name. Amen.

Believe and Trust

God promised to make Abraham the father
of not just one, but may nations.
—Genesis 17:4, Romans 4:13

What has God promised us? What is our complaint? What is or is not happening that sends us to fuss, whine, question, and even to distrust God?

The situation around us or the one we are forced to reside in or work for doesn't change. Instead, it appears to worsen. We're stuck, thus ticked, cause it or they or that isn't going our way or doing our opinion.

So we get angry with God. Give Him the blame. Maybe we spit out words that don't compliment ourselves, let alone God.

What then shall we do? Check out that Romans. 4:13 reference. It says, "God's promise to Abraham wasn't because of his obedience to God's laws, but because Abraham fully trusted God to keep His promise."

God's promise to Abraham didn't take place then or even in his lifetime. God's promise still held and holds firm. Abraham believed, fully trusting God, because He is God. His promise is certain. It will take place. We must believe and trust.

God will come on through with the very best for us. In the meantime, occupy ourselves with the *else* God lays before us, allowing it to be a stepping-stone to the now unknown special blessing.

Who knows, maybe it will lead us to what we really want—God's perfect will.

Dear Lord, when I set my impatience aside and take up that something else available, I know I'll position myself in the center of Your will. That other thing may or may not follow. Amen.

Grace

Because of the grace of Jesus, we can be saved.

—Acts 15:11

A recent cartoon pictured a police officer talking to the driver of a stopped vehicle. This officer said, "No, there's no grace period after the light turns red."

That's true. A traffic light is the law without question. If we disobey, its built-in law says we pay the penalty.

Standing before the judge doesn't change the punishment for running a red light, no matter how excuses are whined out.

We must pay for our action. No second chances are allowed.

How different with the Lord. Humanity is full of sin and continues to express it. We come, go and be, believing we're okay.

At some point in time, we see the red light. We may give it a second thought and stop or not. When we are convicted and apologize, the Lord forgives. Then we continue on the same route as before.

Again, a red light glares it stop. This time we look around, see no enforcement, and we go on. This may be repeated only so many times until something happens.

When that moment arrives, genuine conviction sends us to true repentance. We pay the due, remembering God's grace remains still.

No traffic judge gives any grace, but God's grace is offered again and again because Jesus already paid the penalty for all red lights we run.

Dear Lord, I'm embarrassed for the sin I've committed.
I'm so grateful for your grace of forgiveness. Amen.

Precious Moments

I will not leave you or forget you.

—Hebrews 13:5

It takes but a brief moment of time to hear a one-on-one from the Lord to become a treasure beyond measure. This can happen when the Bible falls open to a specific verse or phrase, allowing a passing memory to float by. Or we might hear a tune from a song or hymn, or maybe it was a few of its words, or maybe it's overheard conversation from someone nearby that catches our attention. Whatever it may have been is meant to connect with us at that very moment.

However that brief moment with our Lord might make its way to our spirit is perfect. Those unquestionable clear-cut words or melodies settle deep within each fiber of our being.

Whether we're residing in quiet solitude or in a busy and noisy surrounding, God's short message is heard loud and clear.

This God-given answer or direction often brings tears or a heartfelt praise, but that instant belongs to each of us alone.

Things in life press upon us almost to the breaking point. Then God speaks individually and specifically. What precious moments we are then given directly from the Lord. Without them, overwhelmingness could overrun us.

God, in His infinite love and compassion, slips in these precious moments at the right moment that blesses beyond description.

Dear Lord, thanks for saving my day with those unexpected, most welcome, and precious moments of Your loving care. Amen.

Denomination

> Some say I'm of Paul, others say they're of
> Apollos, others say they're of Cephas,
> and still some say they're of Christ.
> —1 Corinthians 1:12–13

We say we're Baptist, Methodist, Presbyterian, Catholic, or Holiness. We belong to such and such church. It's located on that street or country road. We follow their teachings. Any other is brought into question.

Every group of people with a specific name above their door or on a front yard sign has their opinion. They believe their biblical interpretations are the correct ones. To be sure, not any denomination is exact.

When we divide scripture to position one's denomination over another, have we divided Christ?

Did that denomination's founder die for our sins? Scripture reads Christ alone provided salvation through His death and resurrection. It doesn't carry the name of any denomination to save us from our sins.

Thanksgiving is just ahead. Let's be thankful for the privilege to meet with other believers and worship Jesus in any type or titled setting.

It's to Jesus we give thanks. He gave us this life and offered salvation for eternal life. It's Jesus alone and our daily walk with Him from which we want to hear messages.

It's not or ever should be a denomination, location, style, or person on which we place our worship. If so, that's idolatry.

It's Jesus alone. Let's give Him thanks.

Dear Lord, if I want to brag, I'll brag on You
and what You have done for me. Amen.

Our Children Shall Be Saved

The children of the righteous shall be rescued.
—Proverbs 11:21

Our unsaved offspring shall be delivered from the depths of their sinful lifestyles and hellbent ways. Soon they will repent and walk with a forgiven heart, changed attitude, and transformed life.

Maybe our children are grown up with families of their own. Yet the understanding of God's truth and direction they should live is forgotten or ignored. They simply continue on the path that leads to their own eternal destruction. God is overlooked.

Nevertheless, God's promises never fail. What He says He will do, He will do. And He said our seed, that's our progeny, our children, will be delivered from their ungodliness and be saved.

So what do we do in the meantime? We just keep lovin' and carin' and be there when needed, where needed, as needed.

No pushing, no demanding, no shaming, no preaching, and no guilt trips.

We continue to pray the prayer of intercession, trust God for their salvation, and thank Him for the answer, even though we cannot see it.

So when we are asked, requested, invited, sought out, or wanted by our children, we respond in love and patience, trusting God for the answer. We do not force. God will bring each through today, or in some tomorrow, in His time and what works best for them.

Dear Lord, I will continue to take You at Your own
Word and know You will bring each one of my children
from their field of sin at the end. Amen.

Homebound

I will say about the Lord, He is my strength, my
hedge, and my God. I will trust in Him.

—Psalm 91:2

Are you stuck at home, unable to do what needs to be done?
Do you feel bound up,
    held up,
    or fed up
    with the slow medical process to get you up?
Are your legs kept up,
    you can't sit up,
    or lift a cup?
You've heard the sound
    that research will soon be found
    to get you moving around.
But here you stay
    today,
    waiting for them to say
    answer is on the way.
God's up to something.
    Why then are you down?
    Lift up your chin
    and cast aside that frown.
And use this time
    that's kept you in a bind
    to help you find
    what God has on His mind.
To be a blessing to your family,
    friends, acquaintances,
    And even an enemy.

All things and time
    God is aware
    of what's happening
    while you're in your chair.
Hang on to Jesus.
    Trust fully in Him.
    His plans are the best,
    whate'r condition you're in.

Dear Lord, admittedly, I'm confused as to the why of my physical health. But I will trust You, for You know all about me and my tomorrows. Amen.

Show and Tell

He went back home and told of the
great things Jesus did for him.

—Luke 8:39

You know the story recorded in Luke 8:26–39 about the demon-possessed man. This physically strong, dirty, and naked person wandered aimlessly among the tombs. He was uncontrollable and mouthy.

Then came Jesus, full of compassion and power to set the demoniac free. Jesus did. He cast out the demons and provided clothes for the grateful man.

Jesus sent this released man back home to show and tell what the Lord had done for him.

What did Jesus finalize for you? Have you told others of the wonderful works He accomplished in your life, your home, your circumstances, or in your body?

Jesus heals, rebukes, provides, and then sends His people out into the world to tell others of His personalized touch. You are one of these people and have a message to share with your family, church, neighborhood, community, and maybe beyond with the wonders and blessings of Jesus's care and individualized attention.

People will be impressed, inspired, and encouraged by the power of Jesus because of your very testimony. It draws many unto Him.

Declare the many answers Jesus has provided for you. Think of all of them. Be reminded that you are blessed. Give God frequent praise and continue to tell others all that Jesus has done for you.

*Dear Lord, You have done so much for me. I will tell
others of the same love You have for them. Amen.*

What Do You Have?
Use It Well

Whatever your hands find to do, do it the best you can.

—Ecclesiastes 9:10a

"That which is done by their word, feet, or pen will someday envelop them." It's my own little saying, yet it holds a message:

What have we been given?

What are we doing with it?

Are we holding it to ourselves or sharing it around?

We can bake, tailor clothes, crochet, knit, or do other handwork well. We paint pictures or walls beautifully. We know grammar and understand English or some other language. We can write it correctly or speak it fluently. Maybe we have excellent knowledge of music, reading, or writing it. Maybe we can play an instrument. Or our gifts fall into the bracket of building, contracting, mechanics, business, medical, and so much more.

Whatever we've been given, we need to be livin' it. We got it. Use it. Don't waste it. It's too worthwhile because it's God-given.

When we use the ability God has blessed us with, it will become us, wrap us in its understanding, move us above and beyond, or take us further up and further in. We can't afford not to use our God-given skills.

For there is no work, or device, or knowledge, or wisdom, we will be able to speak out about or produce after we're dead. (Ecclesiastes 9:10b)

Do your job. Use your gifts the best you can now.

Dear Lord, I will use all the abilities You've given me to benefit people and give You the glory. Amen.

Two Widowed Moms Receive

Not as the world gives give I to you.

—John 14:27

Read 1 Kings 17:8–16; 2 Kings 4:1–17.
Because of a drought, God sent Elijah to Zarephath for this first widow. When Elijah arrived on the scene, he asked for food. This mother of one son had just enough food for their last meal. Her cupboards were bare.

Yet this prophet wanted the first portion of that meager fare. This widow recognized the man of God and didn't argue. Elijah got his request and ate first.

To give back to this mom for her obedience, God, through Elijah, provided enough meals to keep the woman's barrel full as long as needed.

And then Elijah's successor, Elisha, was approached by the second desperate widow. Her husband had died. He left behind creditors. Her sons were expected to work off the debt owed.

This mom, too, recognized the prophet of God and pleaded to Elisha for help.

"What do you have?" he asked.

The answer was cooking oil. This required borrowing many jugs. God provided oil to flow from her near empty bottle and filled those jugs. Behind closed doors, this mother and her sons began the process. Upon completion, Elisha said to sell the oil. The total sales produced enough for the creditors and this family's continued livelihood.

Both examples describe miraculous solutions God did for each family according to their situation. Each provision was accomplished beyond what the world could do. God did it His way, through His people, and right on time.

Dear Lord, I, too, will trust You to supply what I need always. Amen.

11/17 or 11:17

Everything is safe...then sudden destruction comes.
—1 Thessalonians 5:3

Set between the first and last of November is 11/17.
Or 11:17 is late morning. Day's events are underway. Lunchtime is on the mind.

Afternoon's schedule is considered.

Or 11:17 is snuggling close to midnight. The day's well past done. Activities have happened, events completed, plans for another day put to rest.

And then this 11/17 can mean we're closing in on the finalization of planet Earth, as we know it to be.

The winding down of people living life as usual ticking away fast. Jesus is soon to come, and our world will change completely.

Those ready to meet Him will, and those not ready won't.

A shakeup of this globe will be severe. People's mentality will be enslaved, or they will be on the run for self-preservation.

At that moment, the enemy (antichrist) will appear to have won. He will, but only for a few years, then he's put out of dictatorship and put to silence.

Jesus will become king, in full control from then on into eternity. This 11/17 is vitally important.

At that 11/17 where will you be? Thinking, planning, regretting, hoping, or missing?

It's up to you to make the choice to be ready at 11:17 or whatever time God chooses to take us out of this life by death or (if saved) by rapture.

Dear Lord, eleven and seventeen are now a different set of numbers to me. The calendar's date or hour on the clock could be when You come for me or change this world completely. May I be ready. Amen.

Let It Go

Blessing of the upright exalts, but destroyed
   by the mouths of the wicked.
                                    —Proverbs 11:11

There we stand straight and tall
God's blessings overflow us all
Remembering our abundances
Cherished many assurances
We remain admirable and good
If undeterred by some annoying hood.

Our Christian life stays undashed
As weeks, months, and years do pass
Until one, just one, then more
Uncouth mouths readily tore
At my gut, feelings, and my heart
Undoing all from its start.

How could it possibly be
Those wicked voices came after me
To destroy all God's done
Replacing it with a ton
Of maliciousness
From their agenda's selfishness.

Yet you ought to have been there
When the Lord blessed my soul
Because I forgave them all.
Now Christ has made me whole

So from this day forward I will ignore
And not let them mess with me anymore.

Dear Lord, people with their words and deeds may try to hurt, but I give them to You for You to deal with each one, and I will just go on. Amen.

Time

It's time to seek the Lord.

—Ephesians 5:16

Here you are, right now. You're set in time. You've been given hours, months, years, even decades. What's been accomplished and of what value?

You're doing your thing. Then what? Life gets rolled into brevity. So much is wanted, but time is running away. Some desires are set aside, overlooked, forgotten, or finalized. Still much to be done, and life is moving on. What's yet to be stares you in the face.

Time is short. You've been given a fraction of it. The Bible suggest seventy or eighty years. Looking at these many years seems like a lot when you're young. The older you grow, the fewer they become.

But in the length of eternity these years, whatever that number, barely scratches the surface of what after-death time brings—everlasting life someplace.

That's the very reason God said to redeem time, be cautious, and not be foolish. Use wisdom to seek God while there is time to find Him. Yours days are numbered. Then it's too late to get God.

God's loving hand is reaching out for a taker. He's available for you to get your life in order before you run out of time.

Today is the day of salvation. Now is the time to accept Jesus Christ as your personal Savior and become Lord of your life. Another day or minute may be too late.

Time is of the essence. Take time right now to make that vital decision. Don't postpone. There's no time.

Dear Lord, please come into my heart and save me from
my sin. I need You now and for all time. Amen.

Time Does Matter

We all get the same 24/7. Time is brief.

—1 Corinthians 7:29

Time allotted to us
Time with its purpose
  Cultivate the why
  Through time's minutes
     Don't assume there's plenty
     Don't overlook its limits
     Time passes quickly
     When gone, there's no return
       Open your heart and hand
       Provide assistance
       Take time for people
         Count their value
         Measure resources
         Spend them wisely
           Look for time
           Schedule it in
           Plan for its use
             Has time been bribed?
             Undo its wrong
             Demand proper use
               Find the time
               Before it's late
               Count its worth
                 Remember time's history
                 Repent of its loss
                 We'll give account for it
                   Be thankful for time
                   For it's temporary

Time is now
To find Jesus
And salvation
   Don't forget time.
   Don't ignore time.
   Don't waste time
      Running out of time
        Is a big matter.
          Eternity runs forever,
             Where there is no more time.

Dear Lord, may I not take time for granted.
Each moment is vital. Amen.

Things?

Do not love…the things of this world.

—I John 2:15

Old things were yesterday.
New things will come today.
Grand things may come someday.
Or
Yesterday things now gone.
New things come with the dawn
Grand things bring a new song.
Or
Things:
We had them
We called them
We want them
We lost them.

However it's rhymed, things come and go. We strategize and work hard to achieve things. Then we get sick or old and the things are sold off, given away, and not available to us anymore.

Their time was brief though counted in years. Yet in the value of life, things barely exist. We, too, were in that yesterday. We have right now. Tomorrow we desire, wish, hope for grandness, but it may not come our way.

Did all our plans of things cause us to forget to plan for the time beyond these earthly things?

Yesterday we can't, yet today we can prepare for our eternal tomorrow.

But if tomorrow becomes our privilege, what will we do with it? More things? Or living with an eternal value?

Now is the time to give it serious thought.

Things were there yesterday.
Things possible today.
Things may bring much sorrow
In our unknown tomorrow.

Cast aside all those things.
Seek the Lord, king of kings.
He secures our tomorrow
From which we cannot borrow.
Do it today. Don't delay. Tomorrow may not come our way.

Dear Lord, take my things. I want more of
You today, tomorrow, always. Amen.

That's Piecemeal Stride

Trust God at all times…people… God is our refuge.
—Psalm 62:8

We all have a *that* which needs a solution. But the process is taking so long, nudging that *that's* painstaking degrees. One fraction or two advances *that* is section by section.

This process does seem to fit *that's* conclusion. But why must *that* move so slow? *That* doesn't give any hint of what's to come in the days ahead. Who knows what *that* is about to do?

On *that* we place some person (or situation's) name. *That* seems to move inch by inch according to some individual(s) discretion.

We're forced to rely on God. Then we ask ourselves, "Why did we not go to Him first? Nothing maneuvers in or around us without His permission."

Within each stage of *that's* progress, God is there. He's leading us through each of those maddening little steps. He wants us to pursue Him, trusting Him to lead us in those piecemeal steps.

God leaves just enough light for our progress. He stays with us. If the trip gets too tough, He'll carry us on to the next step. Nothing gets overlooked. God holds all of *that's* pieces in His hands while taking us to the completion of His perfect plan for us. Each of *that's* puzzle will then fit into place.

Dear Lord, I'm confused and frustrated. I do trust You to walk me through that's *piecemeal steps of my trip. Amen.*

Anointed

Do not touch my anointed or cause them harm.
—Psalm 105:15

(Numbers 12)

Moses had been called of God. He was comfortable in God's presence. Their communication was face-to-face. Moses was God's blessed servant.

Moses's siblings knew this. Yet Aaron and Miriam chose to speak against him. For some reason, they didn't like his wife. They complained to each other about her.

The reason for that disapproval, we can only surmise. Whatever the excuse, they forgot Moses had been chosen by God.

The punishment God gave to these siblings was severe. Moses pleaded with God on their behalf. Thus He reduced the sentence.

Anyone who is a believer in Jesus Christ as their Savior is a Christian. This individual of any age, personality, descent, upbringing, denomination, ability, income, or outlook can be anointed by God.

If this person reveals he or she has been called, we'll know they're anointed. But if calling has not been mentioned, we still treat each Christian as if they have been. We don't speak, act, or react with any disrespectful or know-it-all attitude, or some catastrophe could come upon us.

Instead, we give God thanks for our Christian brothers and sisters. If we have a disagreement of any size, take it before the Lord and discuss it with Him.

Let's give each other love, honor, encouragement, gratefulness, and prayer. They are unique in their own way, just as you and I are. We know we are special, and so are they.

Dear Lord, when that someone bugs me, I will bring him or her to You. You can deal with them after you have dealt with me. Amen.

Onesimus

Because of this I will continue to thank God.
—1 Thessalonians 2:13

Onesimus was thankful. He had been owned by Philemon. For some reason, slave Onesimus fled from his master.

He might have been guilty of being evil and misbehaving. Scripture does not tell the reason for his running away from Philemon. We do know Onesimus was guilty of escaping from his servitude to Philemon.

How long it was between that made-a-break-from-his-slave-owner and the date Paul met him, we have no idea. It was obvious there must have been a fair space of time between that hour and the time of Paul's writing to Philemon.

Onesimus had become a Christian and was a valuable friend and helper to Paul.

Onesimus's bent to sin was cancelled because of Jesus's love on his behalf.

His freedom from Philemon's ownership of him happened because Paul was the middleman pleading in Onesimus's interest.

Double set free, this young man was filled with gratitude. How relieved he was from having been set free from all that had entangled his life.

We, too, can be ensnared by something or someone that holds us captive. The only freedom from the slavery of sin is with a repentant heart crying out to Jesus and a turned-around life because of Jesus's intervention in our situation via our prayers.

Dear Lord, I thank You for using necessary individual(s) to set me free from any and all concerns that may beguile me and trip me up. Thanks for looking after me. Amen.

Psalm 139

You're hands designed and made me, may I
understand and learn your commandments.

—Psalm 119:73

1. Lord, You've checked me out and know me well.
2. You're aware of me when I sit, stand, and my faraway thoughts.
3. You know what's ahead of me and will help me rest.
4. You already know what I'm going to say.
5. You're both in front and behind me. Your hand is upon me.
6. This is far too super to believe.
7. Wherever I go, Your Spirit is there. I can never leave Your presence.
8. If I go to outer space or if I go to the ocean bottom, You're there.
9. If I could float on the morning breezes or ride them to the distant parts of the seas,
10. Even there You'll lead me and hold me with Your right hand.
11. If darkness tries to hide me, that nighttime shines light around me.
12. Darkness cannot hide me from You. It becomes as light. Day and night are the same to You.
13. You grew all my delicate parts together, covering me with skin and flesh.
14. I praise You for making me so intricate. I know what You've done is extraordinary.
15. You saw me when I was conceived in private.
16. Your eyes saw my unformed person even before conception. In Your book, my future was catalogued before I was.
17. How priceless to know You're always thinking about me.

18. If I could count Your thoughts about me, they're more than can be numbered. When I awake, You're still thinking about me.
19. Yes, Lord, You'll destroy the wicked people away from me.
20. The depraved speak against You and profane Your name.
21. Shouldn't I, O Lord, abhor those that hate You? And be saddened with those who oppose You?
22. I'll despise and consider them as my enemies too.
23. Search my heart, O Lord. Test me and know my thoughts.
24. Show me all the sinful ways in me. Direct me to everlasting life.

Dear Lord, I'm special because You wanted me to be here now. May I use my years to bring You glory. Amen.

Give Thanks

In all things give God thanks for this is His will…regarding You.
—1 Thessalonians 5:18

Thank You, God, for turkey roasted golden brown
And for the fixings that graciously abound.
Thank You for the smiles and hugs of those around.
It's fun when loved ones come to town.
We love to sing and dance and make a lot of sound.
Then games we play until a winner's found.
Far too soon the day is spent and coats are brought on down.
Then, hand in hand, we speak a sentence prayer around,
Thanking God for blessings abundantly abound.

Dear Lord, may I always be grateful for family and friends. Help me to appreciate each one and the time we are able to be together. I am truly blessed. Amen.

Seek God First

No sparrow can fall…that God doesn't see.

—Matthew 10:29

Seek God first.

—Matthew 6:33

This was Friday morning past Thanksgiving, the date set for our family's get-together. It was scheduled to be at one son's house.

Our dog was let outdoors. When he came back in, he could barely walk. Then vomit spued forth. His vision seemed impaired. What happened to our dog Cuddles?

My husband and another son left for our family Thanksgiving. I stayed home and, on the floor, arms over Cuddles, I was crying and praying for his life. He couldn't hold his head up and had no interest in food.

As the day progressed, he didn't improve or get worse. I remained with him the rest of the day, praying and praying. The only hope for our dog was the Lord. He cares about whatever concerns me.

The weekend was long. Finally, it was Monday. We were able to get to a veterinarian. At this appointment, Cuddles was treated for dehydration and given some medicine. All blood work showed he was fine. It was presumed, because of his age of nearly fifteen, he had geriatric vestibular syndrome.

Within a few hours, Cuddles was doing okay. Today his health and activity are excellent. Whatever might have been underway in our much-loved dog didn't happen. God intervened because of continuous, fervent, and tear-filled prayers.

If God hears and answers prayers for a dog, how much more will He hear and answer the heart's cry prayers for people, even during a holiday weekend?

Dear Lord, Thanksgiving reminds me that You do care and are there for me whatever my problem may be. Amen.

Then What?

Get ready to meet thy God.

—Amos 4:12

Tragedies happen. Destruction of property or loss of things take a back seat to injuries and fatalities of people. Some of these calamities are caused by natural disasters, accidents, physical disorders, an abrupt heart stoppage, or preplanned by an individual.

No one can be sure when such a catastrophe will occur. We don't know the time, place, or effect that casualty will cause.

Of course, I reason this type of thing happens to others, not to me. But what if I am not exempt and death does come my way? What lies on the other side of my last breath, beyond this life's climax?

I remember hearing some preacher read from the Bible. He said there is an appointed time for me to die and a judgment follows.* Ouch!

But that preacher man also said, "We people are all sinners." Our sin made it necessary for Jesus to die for us.* Now if we admit we are sinners and accept Jesus into our hearts, we are saved.* Then whenever that unforeseen time arrives and I die, I will be ready and prepared for that supreme court case in the sky.

Dear Lord, now I know the answer to that "Then what?" I have made preparations to meet God when death does come my way. Amen.*

---

* Hebrews 9:27; Romans 5:8; 1 John 1:9.

Heaven? Be Certain!

Unless people are born again, they can't
go to heaven and be with God.

—John 3:3

When someone dies
We often say they're gone
Where did they go?
Why is it so?
What choice was made for that decision?
      Was the deceased informed
      To take Jesus as their Savior
      The only way to heaven?
      Ignoring Him
      Opens the door to hell
            That now expired body
            Is cold and lifeless
            Empty of he or she
            They're gone, you see
                  Their breath took leave of them
                  Were they ready and prepared
                  To go to heaven or not?

To be sure

Let us do today
Let us not delay
For this may be the day
We'll be on our way
      Save me, Jesus
      Before my soul departs
      Come into my heart

That I may live with Thee
Where I'll never be apart
When I am dead
My choice will have been
Jesus as my Savior
To live forever with Him
For I've been born again

Dear Lord, come into my heart and save me from sin. I want to be with You when my last breath does leave me. Amen.

The Rapture

The Lord Himself will call true Christians up to
Heaven with a shout...and with the trumpet of
God...for them to meet Him in the air.
—1 Thessalonians 4:16

It will happen
In the twinkling of an eye
Jesus will call us home
Then true Christians will fly.

Transported up high
In clouds we've been told
Higher than the price
Any ticket could be sold.

We will be right here
Or maybe over there
Doing daily routine
Working out this life's fare.

When the trumpet gets blown
Only believers will hear
Instantly all are gone
Not one will be left here.

It shall happen very soon
When all ready Christians
Disappear like a popped balloon
No others will hear that tune.

They'll get stuck here
Let that not be you
Completely stumped
Not knowing what to do.

Yes, Jesus will come
As a twinkle of the eye
Leaving many behind
With an eternal bye-bye.

Dear Lord, I am waiting for You to come for me. Help me tell my loved ones, neighbors, friends, and even enemies of Your salvation so they, too, will be ready to go to heaven when You call for us. Amen.

Eating Too Much

Have you found food? Eat only what your body needs,
otherwise you may become ill and vomit it.
—Proverbs 25:16

Beginning the Christmas season is fun. I plan and prepare for two large parties. Each menu contains a quantity of the normal Christmas fare of candy, cakes, cookies, breads, brownies, trifle, and much more.

I enjoy presenting my guests with an attractive and large variety spread for their pleasure. Their appetites are always pleased. I am blessed. Leftovers are abundant.

The rest of December, I snack on those many sweets. Then I find myself sitting, stuffed, moaning, and feeling sick.

Gently, the Lord reminds me of Philippians 4:5: "Let people observe your moderation." Moderation is the same as self-control. I do need to tell myself no. That's tough! However, through this very scripture, the Lord encourages me. The verse concludes with "The Lord is accessible." In other words, He will help me in the struggle.

I am now planning for the upcoming Christmastime to be handled with me being disciplined in all the munching. This determination will bring for me an enjoyable season with no regrets, making all festivities special.

*Dear Lord, thank You for helping me get my eating
under control. May I celebrate this Christmas holiday
with more in joy and less in food. Amen.*

Food Poor

When you sit down to eat...think about...what is
before thee. For...the glutton will attain poverty.
—Proverbs 23:2, 21

The above references should influence us to have a wholesome dietary regimen. True, we must eat to keep ourselves up and moving. It's essential. God has provided a large variety of fruits, vegetables, grains, and even meats for our use. We research and learn tasty methods to prepare and serve or eat out to partake of God's abundant supply of food.

Too many of us go beyond the need of a sound diet to a craving desire for more breakfast, lunch, dinner, and plenty of snacks before, after, and even during those meals.

At that moment, the need of nourishment leaves and gluttony takes over. Then we gotta have more and more and still more of the munches and beyond.

After continued indulging in our eating appetite, poverty kicks in—poverty of health and finances. This affects our grocery shopping, restaurant eating, home cuisine making, or dessert baking.

Then the bathroom scales report the truth, mirrors display it, and doctor's appointments confirm what we've done to ourselves.

Relishing food and gusto eating steals health from our bodies, blood, bones, and joints. Our vitality wanes, strength diminishes, sleep lessens, and medical expenses grow. Saying nothing about the possibility of losing or not getting a job.

This all leads to poverty (damage) to our once-in-a-lifetime body from which we get no second helpings.

Dear Lord, help me to say no to extra foods that are unnecessary to keep me alive and well. I want to be a healthy Christian. Amen.

Names of Jesus

God...gave Him a name higher and
greater than any other name.

—Philippians 2:9

For many years, my husband and I have made our Christmas cards. One particular year, the names of Jesus were chosen as the topic.

The Bible speaks of many names given describing Who Jesus is. It's certain He is the Messiah, the only Begotten Son, the bread of life, rock of our salvation and lamb of God. Plus, He is the king of the Jews, light of the world, Mighty God, everlasting Father, Son of God, and prince of peace.

In writing these names, it became clear they are not as important as what Jesus is to us personally, eternally. We need to "believe on the name of the Lord Jesus Christ to be saved" (Acts 16:31). He then becomes our Savior.

It's extremely vital Jesus becomes Lord of our lives and we allow Him to guide us through our earthly living and witness.

The completion of the introductory verse used at the beginning of this devotional is "that at the very name of Jesus every one of us will someday bow." When this time arrives, we want Jesus to be our redeemer and not our judge.

Until then, we get to enjoy today, rejoicing with great joy in the Holy God Who gives us many blessings, Christmases, and beyond.

*Dear Lord, the names of Jesus only begin to
describe what You are to me. Amen.*

The Birthdays

Today a Savior is born, Christ the Lord.

—Luke 2:11

Little Tommy's mom planned for an entertaining birthday. When birthday time came, guests arrived. They all enjoyed the merry-making and food. Mom gave small gifts to all the guests, and they also exchanged gifts with each other. Although it was his birthday, Little Tommy received no gifts. Worse yet, he was ignored. Did Little Tommy cry?

Do we do the same on December 25? We say it's Jesus's birthday. We say, "Let's celebrate." So we plan, party, and eat. We wait for that special day. Then we exchange presents with festivities. Jesus receives nothing. Jesus gets ignored. Does Jesus cry?

Hey, Little Tommy's mom, you're wrong for treating his birthday so. After all, it was Little Tommy's birthday. The celebration belonged to him.

When Jesus's birthday comes along, gifts belong to Him. What gifts can we give to Jesus? It's simple. It's you. It's me. It's our hearts yielded to Him. No other gift does Jesus want. That is why Jesus came—for you and me.

No, Little Tommy did not cry. Mom changed her party plans. Neither will Jesus be sad. We will give Him a gift. We will give Him *us*.

Dear Lord, Tommy's story is an allegory. It reveals too much truth of what I do at Christmas. Forgive me for overlooking You, the real reason for Christmas. This year's plans will be centered around You. Amen.

Thumbs and Big Toes

…captured him and amputated his thumbs and big toes.
—Judges 1:6–7

We wash our hands to keep them clean and free from germs. This process holds colds and other potential sickness at bay. We also wash our feet.

When we cleanse our hands and feet, do we take special notice of our thumbs and big toes? Of what specific value are these digits? I had not noticed until I read the report of Judah and Simeon's action toward the captured leaders of Israel's enemies. These men proceeded to have the king's thumbs and big toes removed. Why?

It would be tough to walk or write without those phalanges we call toes and fingers. Our great toes provide balance for walking, and our thumbs secure control when using pencils, cups, tools, keyboards, even brushing our teeth.

Often, thumbs and big toes are ignored or overlooked. We simply take them for granted, expecting they'll always be there.

Many people go unrecognized for their value. It's expected they'll always be around. After all, they're only a big toe or a thumb. But no family, church, or business can operate without these vital people. They remain unswerving by any attitude toward them.

Dependable were the big toes and thumbs of the captured leaders. Removing them kept the kings from being used in directing harm toward Israel.

Dear Lord, my big toes and thumbs remind me of the faithfulness of people, regardless what position they hold. May I be thankful for them and their never-ending faithfulness. Amen.

Reflection

Let your light so shine before everybody so they will see
what you are, thus give your heavenly Father glory.
—Matthew 5:16

At breakfast, I noticed, through sliding glass doors, a reflection of red hanging in the spacious outside. Curious. There was nothing red around me.

A few days later, while in the dining room, my attention was drawn to red Christmas candles on the table. They were aglow from the sun's glistening rays.

"Hmm. Could these red candles be the answer to the reflection I saw the other day?" I went back to the kitchen and looked out those glass doors. Sure enough, that red reflection was suspended in midair.

The dining room is not that near the kitchen. It's angled a distance away. Yet the sun took the candle's red color through the room's window and displayed it in a totally different area.

This was a great reminder that the truth in all hearts will be shown (and known) for its reality at some point somewhere, unplanned and out of our control.

Lord, what I will be reflected in places and to people at times and locations unexpected and unknown to me. May that reflection be a clear image of You, especially in this Holy season called Christmas. Amen.

The Holy Spirit

He will teach all things.

—John 14:26

We cannot command or control or save any soul.
That's the responsibility of the Holy Spirit.
He has not made us His junior.
He does His job right the first time around.

It's our job to love, care, and
discipline young in the Lord with Christlike joy.
This might be tough, inconvenient, or time-consuming,
but it is our assignment as Christians.

Remind ourselves what it was like
when we became new believers.
We were excited and desirous to know more about our Savior.
How were we treated?
What response would we have preferred?

Truthfulness displays.
Honesty spills
Thoughts and words
That Christian living works.

Let's relay and portray the very fact
God is real, God is true.
His Word will always come through
When we live and teach what we know
Because the Holy Spirit has told us so.

He'll do the convicting,
We'll do the witnessing.
He'll do the drawing,
We'll do the showing.
He'll do the nudging,
We'll do no fudging.

People need the Lord. The Holy Spirit will do
the telling. We are to do the living.

*Dear Lord, I will be as I should be and let the Holy Spirit do His work:
convicting, teaching, comforting, and being there for all peoples. Amen.*

Christmas for *Those* People?

We are more than conquerors through Him that loved us.
—Romans 8:37

Look at those people. They're awful, dumb, uncouth, thoughtless, irresponsible, and dirty. We wouldn't give them the time of the day. Yet they're there and breathe our air.

God sees everyone and loves all without exception. It's tough to believe He sent Jesus for the likes of those. Yet He arrived as a normal, wrinkled, and crying newborn that Christmas morn.

Thus, December 25 has been set aside to remember Jesus's birthday. It's been calendared in so we'll give celebration that He came. Can you believe He came for those that are thumbs down distasteful to us?

Today, let's see those with a different perspective. Those are also qualified to receive God's love at Christmastime. He placed us here to give, do, and share with those very people. This allows us the privilege to provide presents, time, food, or a fun-filled party for them.

The surprise will then become ours to learn those very people are more than okay. They're unique, agreeable, special, and needed our sharing the joy and message of Christ's birth.

Those people will be pleased to have had a good time at our home or as we went to theirs. They were glad. We were blessed. Those ones we discovered gave us the best of celebrations.

Jesus came and gave. So did we. Merry Christmas.

Dear Lord, I didn't think I could deal with those
people. Afterward, I was grateful. They are okay. I like
them and will consider them friends. Amen.

Think on These Things

Brothers and sisters, think about things that are
truthful, just, clean, lovely, good report,
virtuous, and worthy of praise.
—Philippians 4:8

To what measure
To reach pleasure
Worthwhile treasure?
　Does it supply
　Or apply
　For us satisfy?
　　Let's be sure
　　Truly for sure
　　Cravings pure,
　　　Heart's desire
　　　Efforts to acquire
　　　Thus to aspire
　　　All we require.
　　　　Do we embrace,
　　　　Or do an about-face
　　　　Or work to replace
　　　　For none to me trace
　　　　Yet want God's grace?
　　　　　So
　　　　　　What will
　　　　　　　we do
　　　　　　　　with the
　　　　　　　　　time
　　　　　　　　　　given
　　　　　　　　　　　to us?

Dear Lord, these questions are puzzling. May I give each serious thought as I reread the list, filling my mind with answers to bring You glory and Christlikeness in me. Amen.

Pompous

Don't come near me for I'm holier than you.

—Isaiah 65:5

Would you believe anyone would wear such self-importance to say our presence would defile them? Can you imagine such a highfalutin attitude and overbearing pride would speak forth such arrogance? They are convinced they are holier than the rest of us.

This type of individual invokes many people to stay clear of them. If this superior-than-you Christian, from any status of life, carries this behavior, the humble and unsaved would walk on the other side of the street to keep their distance.

Our Lord, having come from the royalty of heaven, welcomed everyone. He held children, touched the leper, forgave the adulteress, restored sight to a blind beggar, raised the dead, and specifically chose his apostles from a non-grandiose lifestyle.

Paul wrote in Galatians 3:28 that all nationalities, financial status, males and females are equal in Christ Jesus.

The Lord God gave Moses instruction that there would be no respect of persons in judgment (Deuteronomy 1:17).

People are all created in the image of God (Genesis 1:26). No exceptions.

Allow no professing Christian carrying a pretentious tone to distract you. (They have their own problem.) We are precious in God's sight, specialized by His personal attention, and all receive the same amount of love, barring no one. Don't forget it.

Dear Lord, may I never wear an inflated attitude. I am me, and You love me just as I am. Amen.

Obey and Pray

I...mention you in my prayers.

—Philippians 1:4

It's easy to bring family and dear friends' names before the Lord. We ask for His blessing upon each one. Our prayers get answered. Those specific ones are progressing fine and doing well.

What about the others? They may be as a pebble in our shoe, an embarrassment to us, ugly, have a questionable personality, not smell so good, or are a brief acquaintance or stranger. Do we pray for them?

Occasionally, one of those individual's name, face, or behavior crosses our mind. Admittedly, that man or woman could be repugnant to us. (We might have a valid reason to keep a distance.) Yet our daily schedule requires us to be near that one person on the job, at church, or neighborhood. We cannot get away from them. We have no choice but to be around that individual.

They make life difficult just to know them. God still says to pray. So we do. Our simple and unseen obedience amends and transforms their lives.

We can't change their character. God can. We simply mention that unpleasant person in conversation with God during our regular devotions or at that very moment they need us to pray. In so doing, we begin to understand the whys in the lives we have disliked.

Things happen because we choose to pray.

Dear Lord, You know those I love and the ones that irritate me. Please work in lives as You know is needed. Amen.

You Have Prayed

I have heard your prayer.

—2 Chronicles 7:12

We pray our request to the Lord. The concern may be urgent or some daily obligation. Whatever the burden may be, we pray, cry, and hope for results. The inescapable atmosphere surrounds us, pressing in its weight.

We have asked, checked, and researched any possible way we can to bring about our answer. Still, the issue continues to glare our direction.

The responsibility seems to single in hard. There is evidence others know but offer no assistance. We are at a loss. We do not see any way possible that an answer could arrive in time.

This trouble grows heavier by the day, almost by the hour. Continuously, we talked to the Lord about solving the ongoing concern. It remains and increases.

We hear the news, read the paper, see the events arising, and hold no solution for the problem in our hour of need.

Then the Lord reminds us of His promise to Solomon that the Lord Himself has and always will hear our prayers. They have not landed on deaf ears. God does listen and will respond.

So we back off, repeat the scripture verse as often as needed, and believe.

Dear Lord, what a promise is ours knowing our prayers
have been heard. Yes, You have been listening. Amen.

Believe It

If you can believe…all things will be possible.
—Mark 9:23

Can we believe the answer for our request will be fulfilled? Do we believe our petition is too large or too complicated for an answer? Maybe it's too expensive to face off the cost. If not, then where will funds come from? When will they arrive? Will it be in time? How can we be sure and give correct reply to the collector?

Believe? We sure want to believe. We know we need to believe, but we can't see any way positive results will happen this time. Our understanding cannot conceive how any serious answer is at all obtainable.

Think about it.

God brings the sun up every day and sets the bright moon in the night's sky.

Seasons blow in their variations of weather.

Birds survive fine without a paycheck or grocery store.

Fish of the sea and land turtles eat just fine, reproduce, and grow older, all without a worry.

On a hot summer day, cool breezes provide refreshment to us overwhelmed and underpaid humankind.

The same God that cares for this planet and all that's going on in the universe is the very same God simply saying, "Believe in Me."

If we know God is awesome and trustworthy, we can believe He will take care of us through any of our personal conditions. Yesterday's unmet needs, today's expected response, tomorrow's fearful unknowns, God will see us through them all. Believe it.

Dear Lord, it's possible. I believe You see, know,
and will take care of me. Amen.

Convinced?

Let every person be convinced in his or her own mind.
—Romans 14:5

I can't change because this is who I am. Who am I, and of what am I convinced? We learn the world is round, snow is white, the sun gives off warmth, fruits and vegetables start from seeds, and when falling in the mud, we will get dirty.

But what of these are we convinced? With education, are these things worth being convinced? Absolutely?

We do need oxygen to breathe. Are we convinced we must breathe so we can live and then someday that breath will stop?

Is this information certain enough to convince ourselves and tell others? Are we convinced we should realize we all have one last breath coming?

Are we convinced the only means of rescue from hell is salvation through Jesus? That His death on the cross and all His blood was spilled on our behalf? The purpose of that crucifixion was to pay for our sin? This was God's living sacrifice as the only means for our eternal life in heaven, as opposed to damnation in hell?

How convinced are we for ourselves and then to convince others, or maybe we're not convinced at all? Whatever it might be, Christ left His action of love's choice up to us.

Not only can we change and get convinced, but we can begin to do the convincing so those others can change too.

Dear Lord, I am convinced for me and will
tell try to convince others. Amen.

Obeyed That Nudge

…care for each other.
—II Corinthians 12:25b

Shopping today
For there's no other way
For me to acquire
What I desire
To find that gift
That'll give a lift.
So that every one
May have fun
Raising their chin
Helping them to win
Over discouragement
Gaining encouragement.

That'll be fun
To know I had won
With gift in hand
Love in heart
From greetings start
I was so-o pleased
Their spirit was raised.

Fulfillment.
Contentment
Released peace
Because
My care
Was shared
And
Brining
A Yipper-do
Smile right on through

Do join me in caring,
And sharing
With blessings
Both of us receiving
Hey, it's fun
Job's done
All have won
'Cause I listened
To God's nudge.

Dear Lord, Christmas this person won't miss. Glad I obeyed that nudge bringing blessings to me and the receiver. Loved it. Thank You, Lord. Amen.

Wish

Working with his hands to do that which is good.
—Ephesians 4:28

Work with one's own effort.
—1 Thessalonians 4:11

You want it? You must work for it. Paying the dues won't get it for you. Those funds provide opportunity for you to achieve your wish. You can walk through the doors, wear a smile, and have complimentary words, but that doesn't bring the desired solution.

Hard work opens the way to attain the wish. That degree or simply losing weight will not materialize with just a wish from payment of entrance.

No one of any heritage, location, or age can have what is wanted by stopping at the door. Move on in, get serious, and do what must be done to attain the yearned for wish.

Any elementary wish can be acquired with little difficulty. But to get that good-paying job, receive a college education, or win at a physical competition, one must put in hard work.

The ability to do surgery, write a book, or walk a mile goes beyond the first step. Determination encouraged with action by taking the next step and continue pursuing the very call that began it all.

Nothing gets done when money is paid and no work is applied. Get up, get busy, and go for your desired wish. After all, God placed it there.

Dear Lord, You know my wish. Help me to become as prepared as possible to receive the wish I desire. Amen.

The Wow Present

For what does it profit a person, if he or she gains the
whole world, but ends up losing their own soul.
—Mark 8:36

We are born, grow up, and receive education from childhood to adulthood. Jobs are found, families arrive, and stuffed are acquired.

We push to prove ourselves and attain our goals so we can live well. We work hard, buy real estate, lose sleep, acquire money, and even compromise family life. For what? Things? Recognition? Retirement?

All too soon, we've matured. Throughout those past years, we did our career, traveled, had pleasure, leisure, attained profit from financial or self-fulfilling achievements, and all too soon costly health issues make their unwanted appearances. Change happens!

We may need a new address and all those sought and bought worldly things must be sold, given away, or taken from us. Those accumulated belongs or rank become but a memory.

Have we made arrangements for what follows and did our presumed goals? When life has its finality, which it will, what preparations have been made to face that destiny? Today is the very day to do so.

Let's be ready to face our after-the-last-breath future. Eternity is for certain. Its time slot will last well beyond what our sought-and-bought efforts have produced.

Christmas season is the perfect time to accept the gift of Jesus. Now that's the wow present.

Dear Lord, I give You my heart and life. There's no better
present for my life that Your presence in my life. Amen.

Second Birth

Unless a person is born again they
cannot see the kingdom of God.

—John 3:3

The last phrase in verse 3 of the Christmas carol "Hark the Angels Sing" is "born to give them second birth."

I had sung this carol for more than half a century before I noticed these words—"born to give them [sons of earth/humankind] a second birth." My first birth was not enough to carry me through this earthly life and into an eternal heaven.

Jesus willingly left the royalties of heaven to come to earth as a baby and grow up among all types of people. At times, they loved and followed Him. Then they turned on Him, seeming to cause His crucifixion. This was not so. Jesus's death was preplanned (that's why He came to earth) so we, all humanity, could be saved and have that second birth.

If we choose to accept His sacrifice for us and take Him as our Savior, we will have a second birthday.

This is the very reason Jesus coming as a baby was written in this Christmas carol. It reminds us of our need for a second birthday. Have we had it?

*Dear Lord Jesus, today I accept You as my Savior.
Now I have that second birth. Amen.*

Giving

Don't give gifts to be seen of people, or you'll lose
your heavenly reward. Keep that gift secret, so
only God will see and thus reward you.
—Matthew 6:1, 4

Giving is associated with Christmas. It's often said "to do so is the
Christmas spirit." Yet people need help those other days of the
year. Needs are all around, maybe in our own neighborhood.

The need to give is everywhere for all ages. We can't help everyone, but we can help someone.

Be alert to what's happening around by observing family, neighbors, and strangers. People hurt especially this time of the year. May
we notice.

There are many Christian ministries whose sole purpose is to
assist people. They can be in our own neighborhood, through our
church, or another location with no specific denomination. Yet they
are giving to people local and elsewhere.

These ministries need material things and certainly finances.
Opportunities to give are everywhere. Ask the Lord what He would
have you do right where you are with the abilities you have.

I give as often as possible. I prefer to do it in secret. Then I can
sit back and enjoy hearing and sometimes seeing how the blessings
flowed to the receiver. The joy of having done so gives back pleasure
beyond words. It's fun to give any day of the year.

Try it. You'll like it.

*Dear Lord, show me what person or ministry I can
give to and what that gift should be. Amen.*

Profit Value

What' value has it been to profit and lose my own soul?
—Mark 8:36–37

Things this world has to offer are attractive and pleasant. We can enjoy many of the opportunities made available. Trips and travels, snacks and buffets, cars and trucks, campers and motor homes, one or two houses, shopping for more possessions or the best Christmas gift, paychecks with interest to acquire a larger salary to fit the position matching our desired image.

Yet when our days are through and there's no time left to do, have, or be anymore, all that remains to us is our soul. What happens to it? Where does it go when all we've done is finished? At the moment it's all gone, we learn the true value of this our life.

> Importance of value
> That is our soul
> Jesus went to the cross
> To make us whole
> For eternal benefit
> To save our soul.

> Things and power will pass away
> But there remains is our soul
> It alone reigns of most value
> Than any present offered today.

> It's Jesus the soul Maker
> It's Jesus the soul Giver
> It's Jesus the soul Taker
> It's Jesus the soul Placer,

It's Jesus with Whom we must secure our soul's final
destination—the Arranger.
For Jesus has given far beyond the value of
any ribbon-tied package.

*Dear Lord, when all I have left is my soul, the greatest value of all, I've
prepared it to go to heaven when my life from here is called. Amen.*

December 21

It's only for a season.
—2 Corinthians 7:8

Today marks winter's start. Br-r flows from each person facing its chill. Daylight hours have shrunk. Darkness grows.

Discouragement talks as high caloric meals are consumed while noting rising utility cost, extra clothing needed, and much snow for shoveling.

True. But then there are many indoor and outdoor games designed for this very weather. They're available for our pleasure and merrymaking.

Warm fires, close comfort, and bright colors cheer the spirit, plus all those stored quilts, comforters, and snugly throws are now put to use. And those yummy pastas and tasty desserts do fill the air with luscious fragrances, tantalizing the appetite.

Winter can bring hardship on people because of health, circumstances, family issues, finances, loss of a loved one, or whatever is difficult and trying in life. Dark and blustery sadness may fill this one with a dreary existence. Whatever may be the strain, lift the chin and give God praise for sending Jesus, and Jesus that He came. Be certain God will give you the needed and individualized gift of strength to make it through each moment of the day.

Winter will become how one chooses to consider it. One may determine to be pessimistic or have an attitude change, and accept God's presence in this nippy white season.

Relax and enjoy a cup of hot chocolate.

Dear Lord, I will top off that hot chocolate with a few
mini marshmallows and realize all seasons do come
to an end. With You, this one I can do. Amen.

The Miracle of Jesus

To the virgin named Mary the angel Gabriel said she would
have a Son and name Him Jesus, He would save the world
from their sin, the women at Jesus's tomb found it empty.
This angel present said, "He is not here, He is risen. Through
this God showed His love because we are all sinners. There
is no other name possible by which we can be saved.
—Luke 1:27, 30–31, 24:3; Matthew 1:21; Mark
16:5–6; Romans 5:8; Acts 4:12; 1 John 5:4

He came to us by a virgin womb.
He conquered death by the empty tomb.
The years in between
Brought change to be seen
For those people back then
And us here today when
God's Word we heed
As we believe and read.

Jesus loved.
He came.
He did.
He died
Then came alive.

We sin.
We need.
We sought.
He supplied
Salvation free (for you and me).

Our life to win
To save us from sin
So we could enter in
And live with Him
In heaven above
Because of God's love
Through Jesus Christ
Who came to earth humbly
But left it victoriously.

Dear Lord, the promise of Your birth brought to me forever salvation. This promise will take me through my earthly life's travels and on into eternity. Because of the victory You did for me, I get to enjoy this colorful, blessed, and fun-filled Christmas season. Amen.

God's Timing—Doubted

When he saw the angel, he was troubled.

—Luke 1:12

(Luke 1:5–20)

According to tradition, the elderly Zacharias stood burning incense in the temple.

Soon after this sacred process began, the angel Gabriel gave him a visit. He brought an answer to Zacharias's prayer. He and his wife, Elizabeth, would have a son, and they would name him John

Maybe Zacharias thought, *This can't be so. We've waited so long. It's too late.*

"We've prayed and accepted our wish for a child wasn't God's will. Now all these years later? Come on. We're too old and accustomed being childless. No, this couldn't be for us."

After Gabriel delivered God's exciting message for Mr. and Mrs. Zacharias, Zacharias gave excuses why this could not be possible.

Zacharias knew God and had served Him with gladness. He did his job well. But this message didn't arrive in his expected timing or manner. Zacharias doubted.

Consequently, Gabriel struck Zacharias with muteness. He became speechless, mum, totally quiet from that moment until God's promise was fulfilled and John was eight days old.

We, too, have requests we present to God. He does hear and will answer. Let's not set a time limit for our gift of an answer nor expect it to arrive in the manner we presume.

Dear Lord, You know me best. You know all that my life entails and the time slot Your answer will arrive. I will continue to trust. Amen.

The Law—Obeyed

Everyone went to…their own city.

—Luke 2:3

(Luke 2:1–5)

The Roman emperor Caesar Augustus wanted to know how many people were in his district. Maybe he was thinking of future money via taxes. Counting the people would be essential for such an accounting.

Everyone must return to the location of their family's origin and resister. The law said all must go. No one was exempt.

Mary and Joseph had been married only a few months when this law was written. She was very pregnant with Jesus. They had to make that long trip from Nazareth to Bethlehem.

There was no car for this couple to travel those approximate seventy miles. Scripture doesn't tell us how they made that trip. Biblical movies relating to the birth of Jesus shows Joseph walking the whole trek and a very pregnant Mary riding a donkey. Walking or riding, it was a long journey. They had no choice but to make it.

I'm sure they often cried out for God's strength. With His help, they made it all the way.

The law is the law. Rules, mandatory requirements, essential directives or commands expected from us are a "ya gotta do it."

At times, we have no choice. Difficult or not, we're obedient.

Mary and Joseph's trip wasn't easy. It was hard. But they did it one step at a time.

We can as well.

The blessing of their pushing on was worth it. Our Savior Jesus was born.

Dear Lord, thank You for coming to earth for me. Because of Your love, I get the greatest gift of all—Jesus as my Savior forever. Amen.

Christmas—Eons Ago, God Asked Jesus Answered

God sent Jesus…that we might live through Him.

—1 John 4:9

Eons ago, God knew people yet to be created would need a Savior. These mortals would sin—a little, a lot, too often.

So the question was placed in heaven, "Who will go and be a sacrificial lamb for people?"

Jesus said, "I will go."

He came two thousand plus years ago as a baby. Can you believe God's Son came to earth to be our Savior, arriving as an infant?

It was so. Today, we call it Christmas. Back then, it was simply Jesus's earthly birthday.

Angels announced it to overnight sitters of sheep. These men were called shepherds. They proceeded to go and see if this could be as the angels reported.

Jesus was found wrapped in strips of cloth. Now these shepherds knew this was the way an unmarred newborn lamb, meant to be sacrificed, was treated at birth. Instantly, they understood this baby born in an ordinary manner was destined for sacrifice. Surely, this was the prophesied Messiah to be the Savior of the world.

Returning to the fields, these men informed everyone along their way that Jesus had been born. No parties. No presents. No bright lights or fancy wrappings but joy in the hearts and praise from their lips. Jesus is here.

The now toddler Jesus's family received gifts from certain star-following wise men. These items were not toys for the child Jesus to play with, but they helped and answered to the purpose of His arrival.

Jesus grew healthy and strong, perfect in all His ways, loved by some, hated by others, yet visible and instructive to all who would listen.

God's question and Jesus's response culminated on Calvary's cross. He was sacrificed so we, you, me, all peoples could be rescued, saved from our sin.

Jesus became our Savior. The response we must have is, will we accept Him who was sacrificed for us?

What will we do this Christmas? Take Jesus or set Him aside and have festivities where all the presents are given to each other for our temporary pleasure?

God asked. Jesus answered. God sent. Jesus came. The rest is up to me and you. What will we do?

Dear Lord, thank You. We can be filled with
the wonder of Jesus's love. Amen.

Moment's Breath

Now is the...time...for salvation.
—2 Corinthians 6:2

This moment God gave.
This moment is mine.
This breath God provided.
This breath is mine.

Someday I'll lose them both.
They will be my last.
I'll have no more moments.
That breath will have passed.

Then where will I be?
Is it Jesus I will see
Or absent would He be
For all eternity?

Where thick lonely darkness
Will cover and surround me
And there I'll reside
For that eternity?

Use this moment
Use this breath
To make that decision
In Jesus to rest.

Another moment
Another breath
May not be mine
To answer this test.

Dear Lord, today I take Jesus as my Savior. Now I am saved to have Jesus with me throughout all eternity. Amen.

Getting Older

Don't forget me now that I am older with less strength.

—Psalm 71:9

Aging happens to everyone fortunate to survive previous years. The body slows down, physical strength lessens, skin displays wrinkles, topped off with gray hair, white hair, or no hair.

The body deteriorates in its years, but God's given abilities and gifts do not. They've become first rate.

What was learned in the youth, practiced through the years, and by the time old age comes around, those talents and understanding have smoothed out to a precise technique. *Lovely, excellent*, and *superb* are some adjectives used to describe what God has done in and through us.

It's our maturity in knowing the Lord and His Word, living and sharing His truths, combined with our practical knowledge that can now be used further for the Lord.

Some may think white hair means spent out and used up. Not so. Older years contain valuable experience.

We may feel our white hair and many wrinkles set us outside with only memories. Not today. It's in this now we step out and step up to the plate in God's strength, wisdom, and our own learning to teach, help, and bless this generation.

For God taught us in our youth. Today I declare His wonderful works.

Now that I have white hair, God will not forsake me as I tell today's generation, if they will listen, of the great things God has done for me, available for them too. (Ps. 71:17–19)

Dear Lord, You've done it in me. I ask that You will do it for them and that their hearts will be receptive. Amen.

Promptings

Your ears…hear a voice…saying…this is the time.
—Isaiah 30:21

Gentle promptings aren't easy to ignore. This evening, my husband and I received them.

Our day had given us thirty degrees with a bright sun and blue sky. We were able to take our walk. It was a cold trek. We were grateful to have completed the walk and back to the warmth of our home. Off we went to finish the day's afternoon, on to supper and a relaxed evening.

Then it snowed, a little then a lot. We saw it but didn't take it seriously. We were comfortable to stay put.

The snowplow drove by. I checked our two driveways. Sure enough, snow had been piled at their entrances.

There was a slight but persistent prompting to us: "Go out and shovel." Reluctantly, we got up and donned our winter gear.

It was 9:00 p.m. The snow had stopped. It was fluffy, and up to four inches of deep removal began. Ten degrees of bitter temperature bit our fingers and toes. Shoveling continued until the snow's accumulation was gone.

This well-done job took forty-five minutes. Br-r-r. It was one cold late night's job completed.

When morning came around, the temperature had dropped. The wind increased. All shoveled areas looked good. Everything was open.

Now we didn't need to go outdoors in the icy winter air and shovel any snow. We had obeyed God's gentle prompting and were the better for it.

Whatever the prompting may arrive to you, go with it. You'll be thankful you did.

*Dear Lord, what a lesson this day has taught because
we followed Your gentle prompting. Amen*

Over the Years and into the New

Give God thanks, He's good; He remembered me when I was weak
and inadequate; He fed me; helped me when I was in trouble;
nothing good did He keep back from me, because I am upright.
                                    —Psalm 46:1; 84:11; 136:1, 23, 24

From the moment of my beginning to these passing, fleeting minutes, God's been there. He's seen my body forming and guided each cell with His plan for my existence. He watched the very start, when the beating of my heart triggered that my life should be.

God knows the frailty of my frame and stays with me all the same. When days of my life go wrong, He never leaves. He walks beside me and at time carries me along.

He's heard my groans and my laughter, allowing them to calm my fears. As I grow older, how reassuring to know God's still with me. He knows I'm but dust, and my days are few from the early sun to end of my days.

He heals my hurts, giving strength to face each hour, and is merciful when I fail too many times. Not once has He failed me.

He's never too busy, never too bothered with the petty, medium, large, and oversized requests I roll onto Him at all times of the day or night.

Through the blood of Jesus, my sins are forgiven, ensuring me a place in heaven. So what more is left to say, but God is there, faithful and true, has and does take me through whatever I must do.

Dear Lord, You've been with me over the years. I give You praise. Amen.

New Year before Us

The night is over, the new is at hand.
—Romans 13:12

Wind it down, close it up, lock it shut. This year is done. All its days are completed. Nothing more possible. It's over.

So then how did we live? Did we live for our careers, reputation, family, or ourselves? Or did we set them on the back burner and be a soul winner?

Have those young, old, and all ages in between that heard us, saw us, know about us, or read what we have written see Christ in our lives?

We got up, worked through each day, then fell into bed, exhausted from all that came our way. What did they include? Did each hour have sixty minutes of meaningful Christian value? Did our presence benefit those we encountered?

What about circumstances? How were they handled? Was God involved?

Were our lives lived as if we would always be here, or knowing that Jesus could come at any moment?

In every avenue of this past year, we had choices. How were they chosen? Were they moral or as an "oh well," or followed the crowd's worldly culture, or Christlike?

How did we express Jesus in us in our daily lives? Did we remember even if we didn't notice Him, He saw us?

So many questions await our answer. Whatever they may be resides personally in us and can be applied toward the new year now before us. What will that be?

Dear Lord, I plan, with Your help, to live the new year's moments, reflecting Jesus at every turn offered to me. Amen.

Completion

That we shall remain...complete in...the will of God.
—Colossians 4:12

The year has come to an end.
What has been done?
Where have we been?
The words we have said
Were placed in some heart
Expressed what was fed
From this year's very start.

December 31 is the goodbye day for its previous 364 (or maybe 365). The final weeks of our American calendar sets opportunities for parties, feasting, overspending, and overdoing in many ways, celebrating the end-of-the-year days.

We all know the exact split second each scheduled year is completed. But none of us know the moment that ends our life on earth. When will be our last split second?

At that instant, what would we have wanted to leave our loved ones? Money? Houses? Real estate? Material things? Good memories? Work effort? Legal will? Jesus?

Of all that is left behind, what or Who has the most worth? Earthly profit? Afterlife value?

The accomplishment of our 366 days reigns at its completion.
The time of our years, days, split seconds reflects its accomplishment.

Where will we be
or give to our family
at life's finality?

Dear Lord, I pray the life I lived this past year displayed
Your truth and eternal benefits to others. Amen.

The author is an ordinary gal living an ordinary life from birth to this very current day and hour. Her family was raised ordinary. Ordinary was their daily routine. Ordinary is simple and basic. Ordinary remains comfortable.

She and her husband, Lew, have five children, nine grandchildren, and to this date, eleven great-grandchildren. For certain, in time, there'll be additions to that total. All are beautiful, precious, and ordinary. For certain, their quiver is full (Ps. 127:3–5). They are blessed.

CPSIA information can be obtained
at www.ICGtesting.com
Printed in the USA
JSHW032325310722
28698JS00001B/8